Reassessing the Park Chung Hee Era, 1961–1979: Development, Political Thought, Democracy, and Cultural Influence

HYUNG-A KIM

and CLARK W. SORENSEN, Editors

Center for Korea Studies Publications

The Northern Region of Korea: History, Identity, and Culture
Edited by Sun Joo Kim

The Center for Korea Studies Publication Series published by the University of Washington Press is supported by the Center for Korea Studies and the Academy of Korean Studies.

The Center for Korea Studies Publication Series is dedicated to providing excellent academic resources and conference volumes related to the history, culture, and politics of the Korean peninsula.

Clark W. Sorensen | Director & General Editor
| Center for Korea Studies

Reassessing the Park Chung Hee Era, 1961–1979

Development, Political
Thought, Democracy,
& Cultural Influence

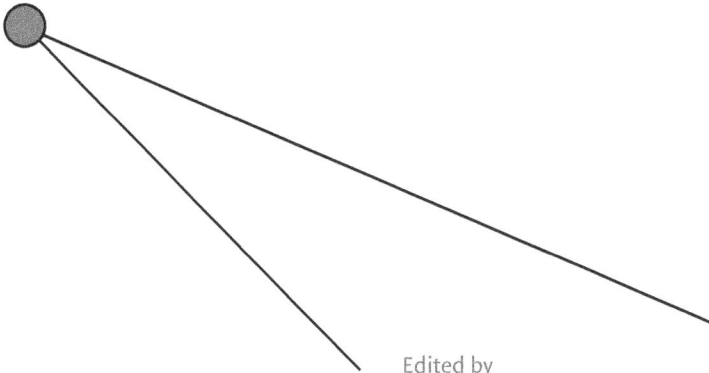

Edited by

HYUNG-A KIM and
CLARK W. SORENSEN

A CENTER FOR KOREA STUDIES PUBLICATION

UNIVERSITY OF WASHINGTON PRESS | SEATTLE & LONDON

This book is published by the Center for Korea Studies at the University of Washington with the assistance of a grant from the Academy of Korean Studies.

© 2011 by the Center for Korea Studies, University of Washington
Printed in the United States of America
17 16 15 14 13 12 11   1 2 3 4 5

CENTER FOR KOREA STUDIES
Henry M. Jackson School of International Studies
University of Washington
Box 353650, Seattle, WA 98195-3650
http://jsis.washington.edu/Korea

UNIVERSITY OF WASHINGTON PRESS
P.O. Box 50096, Seattle, WA 98145 U.S.A.
www.washington.edu/uwpress

LIBRARY OF CONGRESS CATALOGING-IN-PUBLICATION DATA
Reassessing the Park Chung Hee era, 1961–1979 : development, political thought, democracy & cultural influence / edited by Hyung-A Kim and Clark W. Sorensen.
    p. cm. — (A Center for Korea Studies publication)
  Includes bibliographical references and index.
  ISBN 978-0-295-99140-5 (pbk. : alk. paper)
  1. Korea (South)—Politics and government—1960–1988. 2. Park, Chung Hee, 1917–1979. I. Kim, Hyung-A, 1948– II. Sorensen, Clark W., 1948–
  DS922.35.R43 2011
  951.9504'3092—dc23   2011025231

Contents

Preface

This book grew out of the International Korean Studies Conference (IKSC) held at the University of Wollongong, Australia in November 2004 under the theme "The Park Era: A Reassessment After Twenty-Five Years," which examined some of the key questions surrounding the Park era, especially how it affected Korea's development into what it is today. The conference was sponsored by POSCO, BHP, Rio Tinto, and the Australia-Korea Foundation, Department of Foreign Affairs and Trade, Australia. The IKSC attracted many distinguished participants, including twenty-six prominent figures and scholars from Australia, Korea, Japan, and the Unites States.

As the organizers of the IKSC, we strove to ensure that the presenters would deliver diverse viewpoints with a sharp focus on Korea's modern experience under Park's rule, while including a broader perspective beyond the hitherto prevailing dichotomies of industrialization versus democratization.

Reassessing the Park Chung Hee Era, 1961–1979, is distinctive in the sense that several authors with ideological differences, that is conservatives and progressives, are engaged in a face-to-face discussion on the Park era. In this respect, we are particularly pleased to secure a special chapter from Professor Paik Nak Chung (Paek Nakch'ŏng), a prominent literary critic and editor of the leading quarterly journal, *Ch'angbi* who was also one of the two keynote speakers at the IKSC and has generously revised his original keynote paper for this book.

Paik's chapter, entitled "How to Think About the Park Era," reflects on one of the key questions to which many Koreans try to find answers in the public debate on the Park era. With his understanding of such on-going public interest, whether positively or negatively, Paik examines Park's version of development which, he argues, was fundamentally unsustainable because it was built on a "militarist ethos" which brought about Korea's environmental destruction. Paik also views Park's version of development as unsustainable because, according to Paik it was rooted in the shallow developmental philosophy of "Let's live well" (*Chal sara pose*) which he dismisses as "beggar philosophy."

This is not to say that Paik denies due acknowledgement to the extraordinary economic achievements of the Park era and to Park's choice of an export-led development model which Paik assesses as "a more realistic appraisal of the possibilities actually offered . . . by the capitalist world-system and Korea's standing within it."

Paik's interpretation is not necessarily shared by all Koreans and thus the topic he raises remains open to further research and questioning.

In the course of preparing this manuscript, which took much longer than initially anticipated, I have received generous support from the Department of Political and Social Change at the Australian National University. Also, the Center for Korea Studies at the University of Washington partly supported my 2006 business visit there.

My sincere thanks go to all of the contributors of chapters to this book as well as to those who participated in the IKSC. From the Korean side, I would like to thank Kang Sam-Soo and Yu Han-Sik, chairman and president of EM Korea Co. Ltd, as well as Messrs Lew Byung-Hyun, Lee Hun-Kwŏn, and Jhee Kyung-Jun, whose joint support for this project was vital in enabling me to complete this long-awaited project.

Lastly, I would like to express my special thanks to Professor James B. Palais, who passed away in August 2006. His analysis of Korea's democracy stimulated much debate and discussion at the IKSC. His original essay, published as chapter six of this book, is therefore one of his last research-based commentaries, which will be treasured by many students of Korean studies for years to come.

Hyung-A Kim
Canberra
June 2011

List of Illustrations

Reassessing the Park Chung Hee Era, 1961–1979

Development, Political Thought, Democracy,
and Cultural Influence

Introduction

HYUNG-A KIM and CLARK W. SORENSEN

In the second half of the twentieth century, the Republic of Korea (ROK) achieved a double revolution. In a few short years, South Korea shifted from an underdeveloped agricultural economy to an industrialized, high-income economy with highly developed heavy industry and information technology. During the same time South Korea shifted from military authoritarian regimes to civic democracy. These historical changes began under President Park Chung Hee (Pak Chŏnghŭi) (1961–79) who seized power through a military coup on May 16, 1961, and then ruled the country for almost eighteen years until his regime collapsed after his assassination on October 26, 1979. It has been widely observed that the state played a dominant role in East Asian industrialization,[1] and in this regard the ROK has been particularly notable for its rigid centralization, combined with a competent technocracy, among other driving factors.[2]

During the Park era, the growth rate of South Korea's Gross National Product (GNP) averaged 8.5 percent per annum.[3] Exports, which had stood at a mere $100 million in 1964, when the Park state launched export-led industrialization, amounted to $10 billion in 1978, the year before Park's assassination. In 2008, South Korea reached an estimated $432 billion in exports.[4]

The top-down industrialization through the Park state's guided economy became known as the "Miracle on the Han River," (Hangang ŭi kyŏk) and was admired by many political leaders in the region, including Deng Xiao Ping in China and Mahathir in Malaysia, who both adopted the Korean model of development for their own countries. International recognition of the ROK's

Table 1 Average Annual GDP Growth Rates in Four Year Increments 1955–2004

Year	GDP Growth Rate
1955–1959	4.2
1960–1965	6
1966–1970	10.6
1971–1975	7.4
1976–1980	7.2
1981–1985	7.8
1986–1990	9.8
1991–1995	6
1996–2000	4.4
2001–2004	4.75

successful economic development, however, did little to mollify Park's domestic critics. Over the last thirty years, especially since South Korea's democratization in 1987, many Koreans continue to question the extent to which the socio-cultural and institutional legacies of the Park era may have created the continuing imbalances in South Korean society. In the meantime, the ROK's economic miracle has baulked twice, initially in the 1997–8 financial crisis and again in the global economic crisis brought on largely by the U.S. in 2008, which reduced the ranking of the South Korean economy from the thirteenth largest in the world to the fifteenth.

Yet, the ROK's recovery from these economic crises has in both instances been swift, although at a high price, paid particularly by ordinary working people. Following the 1997–8 crisis, many ordinary Koreans suffered layoffs or became irregular workers as a result of neo-liberal economic restructuring and subsequent reforms since the liberal government of Kim Dae-jung (Kim Taejung, 1998–2003). In 2009, South Korea, the fourth largest economy in Asia, is reported to have recorded the sixth fastest increase in economic growth in the April–June period among the group of twenty economies, with a 2.5 percent increase.[5] The Republic of Korea's democratic consolidation is no less impressive. According to the Freedom House survey published in 2006, South Korea received a rating of one for political rights (with one indicating the most free and seven least free), and a two for civil liberties.[6] In regard to freedom of the press, South Korea ranked higher than Australia,

France, Italy, Japan, and the United States.[7] In 2010, Korea ranked twenty-sixth among 127 of the most democratic nations in the world. Although the success of the ROK's economy and democracy must, in its final analysis, be considered as a collective outcome of the efforts of all Koreans, the South Korean case serves as a prototype for the Asian developmental model, with the defining feature of detailed intervention in manpower planning, particularly in the state's implementation of the Heavy and Chemical Industrialization Plan launched in January 1973. A brief review of the Park era (1961–79) is useful and sheds some light on the extraordinary changes in South Korean society over the past three decades since Park's assassination.

HISTORICAL REVIEW

In 1961, when Major General Park Chung Hee and his young army colonels staged a military coup and overthrew the Chang Myŏn administration of the Second Republic (1960–61), South Korea ranked as one of the poorest countries in the world with a per capita income of only $87. Under martial law, the Supreme Council for National Reconstruction (SCNR)—formerly known as the Military Revolutionary Committee—appointed a special military tribunal to purge the military, the government, and society itself of people regarded as corrupt or undesirable. The military junta also dissolved the National Assembly. At the same time, Lieutenant Colonel Kim Chongp'il, Park's nephew-in-law, established the Korea Central Intelligence Agency (KCIA) in June 1961,[8] which concentrated primarily on suppressing domestic political opposition.

From the beginning of his military junta, Park promoted an "economy first policy" together with anti-Communism as a prerequisite for "restoring" democracy. He insisted on applying what he termed, "administrative democracy" or "Koreanized democracy," a radically centralized measure, which according to the military junta was the key to fostering "National Reconstruction." After nationalizing four major banks and creating a super-ministry called the Economic Planning Board (EPB), Park subsequently launched South Korea's First Five-Year Economic Development Plan. The military junta's problem was that they had neither the financial nor administrative resources to carry out their plan and thus the First Five-Year Plan had to be radically revised in mid-1964. In September 1963, for example,

South Korea was on the verge of national bankruptcy with National Treasury holdings of U.S. currency amounting to just $93,298,000.[9]

Although Park struggled with American pressure and his Communist past, which had become a hot issue just five days before the election, Park won the presidential election by a narrow margin of 1.5 percent on October 15, 1963. Thus in May 1964, when Park adopted an export-led industrialization (EOI) policy for his new government, he and his newly appointed economic ministers knew all too well that they needed to generate exports at any price in order to save the country from bankruptcy. The EOI policy rapidly shifted the focus of manufacturing in South Korea from import substitution to exports, particularly the export of light industrial products such as textiles, clothing, footwear, and human hair wigs. As a strategic adjunct to this policy, Park also adopted a clear set of export earnings targets of $100 million, $300 million, and $1 billion for 1964, 1967, and 1970 respectively.

The Third Republic (1963–71) turned out to be a political paradox for Park. While his regime successfully induced rapid industrialization and urbanization, the workers who streamed into the cities did not automatically support Park politically. In fact, rapid urbanization led to an equally rapid erosion of Park's political support, especially among workers (see Chapter 7). Furthermore, as the United States became mired in Vietnam, the international environment became increasingly more unpredictable, especially when President Richard Nixon announced his plan to visit China. This announcement took place in March 1971, a little more than three months after the U.S. had withdrawn one-third of its 62,000 troops stationed in South Korea. Faced with this major change, Park declared a state of emergency in December that year and then under martial law declared the Yusin (Restoration) Reform on October 17, 1972. Ten years after his military coup, Park again suspended the National Assembly and dissolved all political parties. Under the new Yusin Constitution (promulgated in December), Park emerged as a president with supreme power, a leader indirectly elected by the National Council for Reunification. The new constitution stipulated that one third of the National Assembly (and all administrative offices down to the county head) be appointed by the president himself.[10] Moreover, Park equipped himself with supreme power dubbed "Presidential Guidance" (taet'ongnyŏng chisi), which in practice represented the law itself, particularly when it came to implementing the state's HCI Plan as the top priority of Park's Yusin State (1972–9).

Not surprisingly, the state's HCI policy triggered a burst of anti-Park and anti-government protests. In fact, the state's suppression of workers' rights under the HCI policy sparked the Pusan-Masan uprising of 1979 that ultimately led to Park's assassination. The extraordinary twist following Park's assassination, however, was that army Major General Chun Doo-whan (Chŏn Tuhwan) seized power through a highly orchestrated coup on May 17, 1980, with the Ronald Reagan administration's blessing coming in June.[11] The public protest against this military coup quickly turned into the heroic May democratic struggle in Kwangju which marked a turning-point for the South Korean people's democratization movement. It also opened the new era of the South Korean minjung (working people)[12] culture movement of the 1980s. This movement combined heated debate among radical student activists, later known as undongkwŏn, and progressive dissident-intellectuals known as chaeya in the Korean social formation discourse (Han'guk sahoe kusŏngch'e): debate that discussed in detail the question of what sort of character and identity South Korean society should have in terms of structure and practice.[13] According to minjung theorists, the minjung are the driving force of Korean society and they alone are the subjects (chuch'e) of Korean history. Needless to say, the concept of minjung was built on historical teleology with the perceived social contradiction between the people (minjung) and wealthy business entrepreneurs or chaebŏl; the former being historically portrayed as economically, politically, and culturally exploited by the latter.[14] By the early 1990s, however, the minjung movement and the debate on South Korea's social formation had virtually died out, or more accurately, been replaced with the new phenomena of civil society and the proliferation of NGO movements, which ultimately shaped the character of South Korea's citizen-led "miraculous democracy,"[15] particularly notable since the Roh Moo-hyun administration (2003–8).

The Park Syndrome: Myth and Reality

In the wake of the 1997–8 financial crisis, the public demanded an answer to how such a disaster had erupted. Some speculated that the economic failure of the late nineties was the result of "crony capitalism,"[16] despite voluminous evidence to the contrary.[17] Ordinary Korean people, meanwhile, reacted to the crisis with an overwhelming sense of national humiliation. The public reaction, especially against rampant political-economic corruption coupled with mismanagement of the national economy, ironically popularized the so-called Park Chung Hee Syndrome, with many looking to Park's strong leadership that had brought about the economic miracle in South Korea. The Park Syndrome, in other words, was and remains a simplistic but enduring expression of many South Koreans' disappointment and anger towards their country's increasingly weary economic performance marred with continuing corruption among the leaders of the political, economic, and bureaucratic community, even under democratically elected governments.

It is fair to note, however, that Korea is not the only country in Asia where its people increasingly entertain themselves with authoritarian nostalgia. According to a recent survey, many countries in Asia that have adopted "third-wave" democracies such as Taiwan, the Philippines and Mongolia, for example, show symptoms of authoritarian nostalgia, and even the Japanese are not exceptions from such longing.[18] Curiously enough, public perception in South Korean society of President Park changed dramatically within one generation. Park went from being the most loathed president to the most admired president in contemporary Korean history, with an almost cult-like status among many, both young and old. In this respect, the unrivaled popularity of Park Guen-hye, Park's daughter and former chairwoman of the ruling Grand National Party, who is expected to run for presidency in the 2012 presidential election, perhaps reflects Park's enduring legacy. Not surprisingly, therefore, public debate on the Park era and his authoritarian leadership over South Korea's rapid industrialization has been highly charged with emotion, whether for or against. Some argue that Park did not seize power in a vacuum, but built on the educational successes and other achievements of the Syngman Rhee (Yi Sŭngman) administration. They argue that much of the personnel necessary for economic planning had already been assembled by the end of the Rhee administration, and significant economic planning had already begun.[19] In fact, in his memoirs published in 1999, Yi Kihong, former director-general of planning for the Ministry of Reconstruction (1960–61) explains in detail how he had drawn up the Republic of Korea's First Five-Year Economic Development Plan under the Rhee and Chang Myŏn governments.[20]

In his ambitious initial attempt to draw up the ROK's First Five-Year Economic Plan, the then Major General Park Chung Hee, as chairman of the Supreme Council for National Reconstruction (Kukka Chaegŏn Ch'oego

Hoeŭi), certainly adopted a range of political and economic policies from the Rhee administration. However, many observers seem to ignore or underestimate the poor state of South Korea's administrative capacity at that time, especially the capacity to draw up a long-term economic plan and implement it. One of the key reasons for the military junta's radical administrative reform under Prime Minister General Song Yoch'an (July 1961–March 1962) was to lift the standard of the civil service, in order to secure American support for the First Five-Year Economic Development Plan on which Park and his military clique staked their own political survival.[21] A U.S. Embassy telegram dated August 12, 1961, reveals the following insight:

> Prime Minister Song (who is far more capable as a manager than as a policy maker) is working his ministries 18-hour days to drive through programs and decisions. He has commented to me several times that he simply cannot understand how govt [sic] ever functioned heretofore. He said civil service simply has no idea of how to work up a staff paper or effect interministry [sic] coordination and he has instituted methods used by [the] military, i.e., staff studies defining the problem, discussing the issues, and coming up with alternate recommendations for top level decision. He has established task forces and date deadlines for completion. He has started two, three, and four weeks training seminars for senior and junior executive grades with compulsory attendance one hour daily to learn how to do their jobs. . . . Offenders are being disciplined and even fired.[22]

PUBLIC DEBATE ON THE PARK ERA TODAY

Almost three decades after the end of the Park era, public debate on this era and Park's role in contemporary South Korean history continues to rage between two camps—those who approve of Park-style modernization and now promote the "advancement" (sŏnjinhwa) of South Korea,[23] and others who insist that Park-style "compressed" economic development inherently delayed South Korea's democratization and now promote social justice and economic equality. The rivalry between these two camps is also seen in the ideological divide between the older and younger generations: the older generation showing more conservative and the younger generation more progressive tendencies. The popular movements of the so-called New Right and New

Left are two examples, although the former claims to promote "rational conservatism" instead of old, extreme, rightwing principles, and the latter a "sustainable progressiveness" with the aim of creating a new, ideological paradigm different from the traditional leftwing philosophy. The rivalry between these camps boils down to an argument over how people should understand the Park era and contemporary history.

The older generation, at large, tends to agree more with the necessity for strong authoritarian leadership than the younger generation who, in general, demands more radical change in South Korean society and rejects the legacies of Park-style modernization built on the three pillars of statism, growth-firstism, and authoritarianism.[24] Few dispute the need for a serious assessment of the Park era, not only to understand South Korean modernity, but also to pave the country's future direction, especially by reconciling the national past. In this regard, the establishment of the Truth and Reconciliation Commission by the Roh Moo-hyun administration in December 2005 was notable not only because it attracted about 11,000 cases of alleged state crime and abuse submitted by individuals and organizations since its establishment, but also because it opened a new door for national reconciliation, however imperfect and controversial.[25]

One of the aims behind the Committee to Clarify the True Facts of Anti-National Pro-Japanese Acts (Ch'inil Panminjok Haengwi Chinsang Kyumyŏng Wiwŏnhoe) was to reassess many Koreans' suspicions that wealthy families, who had benefited from state-led industrialization, were the same families who had previously been co-opted by Japanese colonial authorities.[26] Similarly, the presidential committee to clarify "questionable" military history sought to reveal the truth behind civilian massacres during the Korean War and human rights abuses during the military authoritarian period. In addition to this and other government-led investigations, several new studies on the Park Chung Hee era, including *inter alia* on Park's policies and leadership,[27] coincided largely with the twentieth anniversary of the ROK's democratization in 1987 and sparked yet another round of public debate on Park and his policies. The *Tonga ilbo* pointed out that these new studies opened a new dimension to public debate and broadened the hitherto prevalent dichotomous approaches noted above.[28]

The aim of this volume is to offer a selected collection of new interpretations by leading experts on the topics of both Park Chung Hee and the Park era. The contributors to this book address some key questions including: What is the link between South Korea's economic miracle and political oppression during the Park era? How have the legacies of this era affected South Korean society today? And what impact has the Park era's industrialization had on to today's South Korean democracy? Of course, the authors represent a variety of points of view that do not, as a whole, provide a unified narrative of the Park period. The common characteristic of these authors, however, is that they share a view that any historical evaluation of the Park era, whether of the events or the individual, cannot be definitive, but needs to be intentionally tentative and provide an honest assessment that could lead to answers to the fundamental questions raised above.

National Development and Democracy

When we look at Park and the Park era historically, we note a number of critical turning points that demand explanation: the move from military junta to an elected civilian president in 1963; the policy switch from import substitution to export-led industrialization (EOI) in mid-1964; the declaration of the authoritarian Yusin reform in October 1972, followed by the state-led HCI Plan in 1973; and finally, the demise of the Park regime. Hyung-A Kim shows how Park, with his extremely nationalistic, anti-Communist strategy, institutionalized state-led industrialization, especially through the HCI Plan. She argues that the implementation of HCI was primarily aimed at building South Korea's homeland security posture, especially as a counter to North Korea's security threats, which, Kim contends, became one of the most defining legacies of the Park era. By focusing on the state's national security policy behind the HCI program, this interpretation challenges the structuralist approach to economic development.

Tadashi Kimiya, by contrast, sees Park's adoption of the EOI policy in the early 1960s as a "virtue made out of necessity," and the search for political and economic autonomy as a defining feature of Park's leadership. He emphasizes the heavyweight politics of the cold war, particularly the political process by which the Park regime garnered its "strategic position as a frontline state directly facing a communist rival" to achieve economic growth.

In this respect, Seok-Man Yoon's chapter on POSCO, formerly Pohang Iron and Steel, reveals details of ROK-owned industry and focuses specifically on the leadership of Pak T'aejun, founder and president of POSCO for twenty-three years, from 1968 to 1992.[29]

Yoon explains that state-led industrialization offered benefits as well as obstacles. His essay is perhaps most persuasive when he stresses that "strong leadership" is the key prerequisite for building a successful institution and a company's own brand of "spirit," or what Yoon characterizes as the official representation of "institutional culture" such as the "POSCO Spirit" cherished by POSCO today.

Democracy

In *Development as Freedom*, a study into the types of freedom that are fundamental to the quality of life, Amartya Sen, winner of the 1998 Nobel prize for economics, asks: "What should come first—removing poverty and misery, or guaranteeing political liberty and civil rights, for which poor people have little use anyway?"[30] Contrary to Sen's salient message that the "intensity of economic needs adds to—rather than subtracts from—the urgency of political freedom," South Korea's rapid development, as Sen himself noted, took off precisely under Park's authoritarianism. In 1972, Park declared the authoritarian Yusin reform as a pretext for his final plan to revolutionize South Korea's industries by prioritizing the building of its national military defense capability. The political oppression during the Yusin State, in other words, was the opposite side of South Korea's industrial revolution through HCI implementation. This is what makes the Park era so controversial and Park's ideas of "democracy" so confined, especially in terms of valuing the state's rights before an individual's rights. From the beginning of his leadership, Park adopted an emergency measure which he termed "administrative democracy" or "Koreanized democracy" as a prerequisite for national reconstruction, especially for an "independent economy" and "independent national defense." Park dismissed liberal democracy such as Western/American-style democracy, with his personal belief that such a democracy was "meaningless to the people suffering from starvation and despair."[31]

Park regarded economic deprivation and poverty as threats to national security on the basis that South Korea, like many underdeveloped countries in Asia where Communism was the biggest national security threat, could not fight Communism while the people were struggling with starvation.[32] Park's reason for rejecting Western/American-style democracy was not rooted in Confucian attitudes and custom-led "Asian values" or the "Lee-thesis" formulated by Lee Kuan Yew, the former prime minister of Singapore, but rather on the harsh reality of the cold war. Hence, Park insisted that the South Korean people distinguish the values of political freedom, between that of big freedom (k'ŭn chayu) or the survival of the state (kukka) and that of small freedom (chagŭn chayu) or the protection of individuals' rights.

Retracing Park's governing ideas, especially the concept of these "small" and "big" freedoms, Young Jak Kim questions whether liberal democracy should be the "only basis or the supreme criterion" for evaluating political leadership. James Palais, on the other hand, criticizes much of the discussion about the expansion of civil society and democracy for leaving out the issue of the South Korean people's struggle. Viewing "struggle" as a necessary condition for the establishment of democracy, Palais contrasts the superficiality of Japanese democracy imposed by the American Occupation to the robustness of the current South Korean democracy attained through sustained struggle over more than forty years.

This, for Palais, is precisely the dialectic legacy of the Park era. Hagen Koo's essay suggests that the structural characteristics of internal consistency of labor policies and relations were the chief merits of the Park era. Viewing Park's approach to labor as "productionist and instrumental," Koo points out the instrumental approach of Park's economic planners, who rarely noted the "human side of labor" other than seeing labor as a potential source of disruption to the nation's productivity. Koo contends that the labor policies of the Park era were not sustainable in the long-run because "strong mistrust among labor, capital, and the state" were the product of those policies.

Cultural Influence and Civil Society

The assessments by Clark Sorensen and Myung-koo Kang deal with the cultural influence of Park's rapid industrialization policy on South Korean society, especially on the perceived national character of the Korean people. While, Sorensen reflects on what he terms, "peasant mentalité" of the earlier phase of the Park era, Kang examines the "developmentalist mentalité" of the South Korean people today and links its roots to the Park era. The two portrayals of images of the South Korean people's national character, according

to these two authors, are largely the product of Park's modernization policies. Retracing the historical roots of rural development policies of the Park
era to the colonial era, Sorensen raises skepticism about the originality and
effectiveness of rural development under Park and argues that Park, like
many leading figures in the colonial era, accused the rural peasantry of being
an "impediment to development" because of their "traditional peasant
consciousness."

Such an elitist "colonial" view, Sorensen asserts, was the basis of Park's
rural development program, the Saemaŭl (New Village) movement during the
1970s,which focused on cultivating a "New Village Spirit (Saemaŭl chŏngsin),"
or simply "Can-Do" spirit. The thinking of liberal intellectuals in the 1970s
and thereafter, however, changed more radically, especially in their struggle
against the state's forced-draft rapid development at the cost of the human
rights of workers.

In this light, Myung-koo Kang argues that South Korean society today is
in a critical mess because "civil virtues and morals of solidarity and tolerance
have been replaced with avaricious desire for material possession and indiscriminate competitive survival mentalities." Kang labels this peculiar mentality of the Korean people today as "developmentalist mentalité" which,
according to him, was formed during the Park Chung Hee era.

The final chapter in this volume by Gavan McCormack takes us to the
emergence of "people power" during the Park era. He notes that apologists
for national security claim that the domestic opposition movement, and the
international forces that supported it, were guilty at best of blindness to the
reality of North Korean repression, and at worst of submission to
P'yŏngyang's orchestration and direction. However, he argues that in the end
the anti-fascist and anti-dictatorship movement in South Korea in the 1970s
and 1980s was victorious. He essentially argues that the history of the Park
era should not neglect the dimension of the international civil society network
that evolved in and around the struggles of that time.

NOTES

1. See Chalmers Johnson, *MITI and the Japanese Miracle: The Growth of Industrial Policy, 1925–1975*; Alice Amsden, *Asia's Next Giant*; Robert Wade, *Governing the Market*; Ezra F. Vogel, *The Four Little Dragons*; World Bank, *The East Asian Miracle*.

2. See Hyung-A Kim, *Korea's Development under Park Chung Hee*.

3. Kwan S. Kim, "The Korean Miracle (1962–1980) Revisited."

4. CIA World Fact Book.

5. "Gov't report: S Korea's Economic Recovery Sixth Fastest among G20 Economies."

6. This rating reflects global events from December 1, 2005 through to December 31, 2006. In 2004, South Korea ranked a two for political freedom. The Freedom House Website, http://www.freedomhouse.org/uploads/press_release/fiw07charts. pdf.

7. *The Canberra Times*, May 11, 2007. South Korea ranked thirty-first, Australia and France tied with the rank of thirty-fifth, Spain forty-first, Japan fifty-first, and the United States fifty-third.

8. The Korea Central Intelligence Agency (KCIA) changed its name to the Agency for National Security Planning in 1981.

9. Han'guk Ŭnhaeng Chosabu, *Kyŏngje t'onggye yŏnbo*, 204.

10. These changes in the constitution were passed by a national referendum held on November 21, 1972.

11. For detailed background on Chun's rise to power and the American blessing, see Hyung-A Kim, "Behind the Carter-Park Standoff."

12. For the debates on the question of who exactly the *minjung* were, see Kenneth M. Wells, *South Korea's Minjung Movement*. During the Park and Chun regime, most writers were careful to avoid defining the *minjung* as a class in the full Marxist sense because, under the National Security Law, one could easily have been arrested.

13. Pak Hyŏnch'ae and Cho Hŭiyŏn, *Han'guk sahoe kusŏngch'e nonjaeng*.

14. See Pak Hyŏnch'ae, *Minjok kyŏngje wa minjung undong*; Han Wansang, *Minjung sahoehak*.

15. Chaibong Hahm, *South Korea's Miraculous Democracy*, 128–9.

16. See David C. Kang, *Crony Capitalism*.

17. See Hajun Chang, Hongjae Park, and Gyue-Yoo Chul, "Interpreting the Korean Crisis; Jim Crotty and Gary Dymski, "The Korean Struggle: Can the East Asian Model Survive?"

18. Chang Yu-tzung, Chu Yun-han, and Park Chong-min, "Authoritarian Nostalgia in Asia," 66–80.

19. David H Satterwhite, "The Politics of Economic Development."

20. Yi Kihong interviewed by Hyung-A Kim in September 2004. For details of Yi's

explanation on the background of the ROK's First Five-Year Economic Development Plan see, Yi Kihong, *Kyŏngje kŭndaehwa ŭi sumŭn iyagi*, 263–77.

21. For a critical analysis of the military junta's administrative reforms, see Hyung-A Kim, "State Building."

22. U.S. Embassy telegram 293, August 12, 1961. Cited in Hyung-A Kim, "State Building."

23. This term was initially articulated by Pak Se-il, Professor of Law, Seoul National University. Pak Se-il, *Taehan Min'guk*.

24. Kang Wŏnt'aek, "Sedae, inyŏm kwa No Muhyŏn hyŏnsang"; Song Hogŭn, *Hanguk, musŭn il i irŏnago inna*, 79–107.

25. Since the publication of its latest report in late 2009, the Commission has been winding down mainly because its four-year mandate will expire at the end of March 2010 and President Lee Myung-bak has publicly made it clear that the mandate will not be renewed.

26. For a well-known study of one such "co-opted nationalist" see Carter Eckert, *Offspring of Empire*.

27. Studies include: Hyung-A Kim, *Korea's Development Under Park Chung Hee*; Hyung-A Kim, *Pak Chŏnghŭi ŭi yangnal ŭi sŏnt'aek*; Cho Hŭiyŏn, *Pak Chŏnghŭi wa kaebal tokchae sidae*. The Academia Coreana of Myongji University, for example, began its range of academic activities on issues concerning the Park era in December 2005 when it hosted a seminar entitled, "Park Chung Hee Era in Korean Modern History." Its regular forum on the Park era and issues related to Park's policy still continues in 2011.

28. "Taehan Min'guk, 21-segi sin inyŏm chihyŏng: Yanggŭk esŏ tagŭk ŭiro [Republic of Korea, the landscape of the twenty-first century ideology: From the dichotomous approach to a multidimensional approach]," *Tonga ilbo*.

29. Since 2001, Pak T'aejun remains Honorary Chairman of POSCO.

30. Sen, Amartya, *Development as Freedom*.

31. Park Chung Hee, *Our Nation's Path*, 196.

32. Ibid., 197.

PART ONE—Development

1

Heavy and Chemical Industrialization, 1973–1979: South Korea's Homeland Security Measures

HYUNG-A KIM

The goals of developing an "independent economy" (*charip kyŏngje*) in the 1960s and an "independent defense" (*chaju kukpang*) in the 1970s were at the core of the political economy of the Park Chung Hee (Pak Chŏnghŭi) era. These two phases of South Korea's development are explained predominantly in terms of the impact of the cold war, particularly the change in U.S. foreign policy in the Northeast Asian region that led to the historic East-West détente when U.S. President Richard Nixon visited China in February 1972. What is not fully explained is South Korea's response under President Park to national security as a countermeasure to North Korea's intensified armed attacks on the South on the one hand, and U.S. reduction of troops in South Korea on the other.[1]

In the aftermath of the North Korean commando attempt to assassinate Park in January 1968,[2] an unequivocal act of terrorism in today's terms, Park sought to build weapons factories in order to arm a reserve force of 2.5 million, which he founded as the Homeland Guard (*Hyangt'o Yebigun*) on April 1, 1968. Park's plan to build a defense industry in fact turned into the South Korean government's Military Modernization Program when the United States initiated the normalization of relations with China. By then, Park's confidence in the U.S. security commitment to the Korean peninsula had reduced to the extent that he became determined to build South Korea's own defense posture by producing military weapons in response to North Korean armed aggression.

Park's top development priority, in other words, was national security, especially through the implementation of the Heavy and Chemical Industrialization (HCI) Plan, officially declared on January 12, 1973. To carry out this forced-draft industrial revolution, Park had already introduced the controversial Yusin (Restoration) political reforms on October 17, 1972. A narrow core of power, a triumvirate of Park himself and two of his secretaries in the Blue House, Senior Economic Secretary O Wŏnch'ŏl (1971–79) and Chief of Staff Kim Chŏngnyŏm (1969–78), subsequently implemented the HCI Plan. In this context, the South Korean model of rapid industrialization, or what was dubbed "compressed modernization," (apch'uk chŏk kundae-hwa) during the Park era consisted of Park's own ideas and plan for industrialization rather than some U.S.-inspired economic theory. Similarly, South Korea's HCI Plan was inseparable from Park's authoritarian Yusin reforms because the HCI Policy itself was designed and implemented within the Yusin system, like a double-edged sword.

With the power of the Yusin Constitution, Park imposed almost monolithic control over all governmental and non-governmental institutions: the army, private big business (chaebŏl), unions, workers, students, and the young and old without exception. Thus political oppression became the norm under the Yusin system (1972–80) while South Korea's top-down military modernization through the HCI Program was in full gear, even at the risk of breaking up relations with the United States. Park's pursuit of his "independent defense" policy, however, did not mean that South Korea found its own line of national security outside the ROK-U.S. alliance. To the contrary, Park and his key advisors, especially his two HCI triumvirs, had no illusions about the importance of the ROK-U.S. alliance to South Korea's security. In this regard, their attitude toward the United States was cunningly realistic in the sense that they were eager to secure a U.S. security commitment to South Korea without compromising the ROK's own national interest, particularly political and economic independence. Nevertheless, ROK-U.S. relations deteriorated to their worst when in December 1976 the U.S. learned about South Korea's clandestine nuclear weapons and missile development program, officially unveiled as the Korean Nuclear Fuels Development Corporation (Han'guk Haegyŏllyo Kaebal Kongdan, KNFDC).[3] This clandestine program, guarded especially against U.S. interference, was an important cause of the deterioration of relations with the United States.

Ironically, President Jimmy Carter's plan to withdraw U.S. troops from South Korea further drove Park's determination to build South Korea's own solution for national security. In this light, the aspect of military modernization within the framework of HCI has not been sufficiently analyzed despite its profound impact on South Korea's national defense capability building, not to mention economic modernization.

This chapter examines how South Korea's defense industry development stood at the core of the HCI Program, and how that program provided the fundamental infrastructure for South Korea's homeland security. I will first trace the connection between Park's pursuit of defense industry construction and the HCI Program in South Korea, and then analyze Park's Military Modernization Program, with particular attention to how Park and his technocrat advisers sought to overcome U.S. policymakers' unilateralism and to exploit inconsistencies in the American policy of troop withdrawal from South Korea. With the view that national security essentially means the security of the state, especially within the "division system" of the Korean peninsula,[4] this chapter argues that HCI was Park's second phase of industrial revolution to build South Korea's security posture and, as such, it became one of the most visible legacies of the Park era, defining the character of today's South Korea as an industrialized nation.

PARK'S PLAN FOR A DEFENSE INDUSTRY

Park's pursuit of constructing South Korea's defense industry began in 1968 after he established the ROK Homeland Guard, following the North Korean attempt to assassinate Park at the Blue House presidential residence on January 21. A total of twenty-three South Korean soldiers were killed and fifty-two injured in this attack, while twenty-seven North Korean commandos were killed and one North Korean officer, Kim Sinjo, was captured. Park called for immediate retaliation and demanded U.S. support, which was flatly refused.[5] The tension between the United States and South Korea over this incident quickly escalated when, on January 23, the North Koreans captured the U.S. military spy ship, Pueblo, and the U.S. decided not to retaliate against North Korea but instead unilaterally negotiated with North Korea for the eighty-one captured American crewmates. Park launched a raft of protests against the American containment policy towards North Korean terrorism, while simultaneously criticizing the United States for unilateralism in their negotiations with North Korea on the *Pueblo* incident.

President Lyndon B. Johnson's personal envoy, Cyrus B. Vance, flew to Seoul on February 12, 1968, to offer appeasement to Park, including financial support for the construction of a munitions factory to manufacture M-16 rifles, plus an extra $100 million in military aid. In spite of this offering, which South Korea accepted, Park's doubts about the U.S. commitment to the defense of South Korea increased. In fact, just four days before Vance's arrival in Seoul, Park publicly announced that he would create the South Korean Homeland Guard consisting of 2.5 million reserves. By then, the friendly alliance between the Johnson administration and the Park government had effectively ended as Park had cancelled his commitment to deploy South Korea's Third "Light Division" to Vietnam,[6] to which he had previously agreed with President Johnson in late December 1967 while visiting Canberra, Australia.[7] This cancellation was far too expensive for Park to have taken lightly because in return for South Korea's additional deployment, President Johnson, in a personal letter to Park, had promised hefty rewards, which included a mixture of military hardware, a special program to strengthen the ROK national police, and assistance in the construction of a modern highway between Seoul and Pusan, among other gifts.[8]

Park seemed to have already made up his mind that the United States had become less reliable in ensuring ROK's security against North Korean armed attacks. By this time Park had, in fact, already anticipated the U.S. intention to withdraw its forces from Vietnam, following his meeting with President Johnson in Honolulu in April 1968.[9] Not only did Park publicly declare a zero-tolerance policy against the North by declaring that "there is a limit to [our] patience and self-restraint,"[10] but he also campaigned to build ROK's "self-reliant" defense posture, especially by mobilizing the South Korean Homeland Guard. Park saw that the future of South Korea's economic prosperity and security depended on the strength of its national security posture, and thus he was determined to arm every member of the Homeland Guard with "Korean-made" weapons, which they could use to guard their own homes, villages, towns, and cities. Park's approach to national security, however, ironically resembled that of Kim Il Sung, the "Great Leader" of North Korea, who commanded a North Korean National Guard of almost 1.2 million workers and peasants, including the Red Young Guards with 700,000 members.

Just as Kim called his National Guard a "flawless defense system," Park defined the South Korean Homeland Guard as "the soldiers of homeland security who would work while fighting and also fight while working."[11]

Park's skepticism about the U.S. containment policy on the Korean peninsula, as well as in Asia, turned out to be well founded. In July 1969, President Richard Nixon (1969–74) not only declared the new U.S. foreign policy, the Nixon Doctrine on Far East Asia, but also officially announced in July the same year the withdrawal of the Seventh Infantry Division's 20,000 troops.[12] The U.S. made these decisions less than a month after North Korea had abducted a South Korean navy patrol boat on the west coast of the peninsula, which was followed by further North Korean terrorism—detonating a bomb at the main gate of the National Cemetery in an attempt to assassinate government members and officials, including President Park, who had been scheduled to attend the twentieth anniversary of the Korean War on June 25, 1970.

This string of North Korean provocations drove Park to order Kim Hangyŏl, deputy prime minister and minister of the Economic Planning Board (EPB, Kyŏngje Kihoegwŏn), to build what was initially known as the "Four Great Core Factories" (sa taehaek kongjang), comprised of cast iron, steel, heavy machinery, and shipbuilding plants.[13] Needless to say, Park's aim was to build the basic material factories necessary for producing weapons with which to arm the Homeland Guard of 2.5 million reserve soldiers. He also created the Agency for Defense Development (ADD, Kukpang Kwahak Yŏn'guso) in August the same year, which soon became the leading agency governing the production of Korean-made weapons. Park's attempt to build the Four Great Core Factories, however, became bogged down with a lack of funds. Despite more than fifteen months of desperate searching for foreign loans from Japan and several European countries, Kim Hangyŏl's EPB utterly failed to raise the necessary funds because the United States, with its suspicions about Park's intent behind the construction of these four key factories, prevented South Korea from obtaining loans from these countries. When the EPB reported to Park about its failure to raise the funds at the cabinet meeting on November 10, 1971, he is known to have become exceedingly frustrated, demanding that Chief of Staff Kim Chŏngnyŏm find a solution. This desperate situation ironically led to a most extraordinary development when O Wŏnch'ŏl, then assistant vice minister in the Ministry of Commerce and

Industry (MCI) and member of the ROK defense industry's "Four-Member Committee,"[14] suggested to Kim Chŏngnyŏm his idea for solving this problem.[15] Kim was so impressed with O's idea that he, with O, instantly met with Park in Park's study.

O's idea was that South Korea could immediately manufacture weapons without spending extra funds by mobilizing South Korea's existing resources and technological capability, available particularly among big business, the chaebŏl. O suggested that South Korea should develop independent defense industries by restructuring South Korea's industries within the framework of heavy and chemical industrial development. O's idea, which convinced both Park and Kim, was based on the engineering principle that, "all weapons can be disassembled into parts, and these parts can be separately produced, as long as they are manufactured in accordance with a plan and within strict specifications."[16] At this meeting, Park approved a five-point directive, which outlined the framework for the development of South Korea's defense industry based on the existing production system of private chaebŏl. The building of Korean-made weapons factories to arm 2.5 million reserve soldiers was, of course, just one of many projects that were decided at this extraordinary meeting between Park, Kim, and O on that day.

Another extraordinary development that came out of this meeting was the appointment of O on the following day, November 11, 1971, as head of the newly created Second Economic Secretariat (SES; *Kyŏngje Che-2 Pisŏsil*) at the Blue House (Ch'ŏngwadae). O's key responsibility of being in charge of defense industry development, however, was deliberately undisclosed for security reasons. Instead, his responsibility was officially stated to be the development of heavy and chemical industries. This development was the beginning of what was to become President Park's HCI triumvirate consisting of himself, O Wŏnchŏl, and Kim Chŏngnyŏm.

Park and his HCI Triumvirs

Born to an impoverished tenant farming family in North Kyŏngsang Province on November 14, 1917, Park Chung Hee began his career as a primary school teacher before he miraculously transformed himself into an officer in the 8th Corps of the Japanese Kwantung Army after graduation at the Manchukuo Military Academy (1942) and the Japanese Military Academy in Tokyo (1944).

When Japan surrendered unconditionally on August 15, 1945, Park, at the age of twenty-nine, became a second lieutenant in the South Korean army, but in February 1949 he was sentenced to life imprisonment for his communist activities that implicated him in the Yŏsu Rebellion. The outbreak of the Korean War in June 1950 brought Park a second chance by his being reinstated in the ROK army, and his army career from then on continued relatively smoothly until he rose to the rank of major general. Nevertheless, Park was rarely content with his career in the army, and he ultimately led the military coup on the dawn of May 16, 1961.

As leader of the military junta (1961–3), Park relentlessly promoted anti-communist "guided capitalism" through the first Five-Year Economic Development Plan which, in June 1964, took off under its export-oriented industrialization strategy. The first half of the Third Republic, from 1963 to 1967, was epoch making, not only in terms of Park's leadership over South Korea's rapid economic growth, but also in terms of South Korea securing American support as a reward for Park's foreign policies, including Japan-ROK normalization (ratified in August, 1965), and troop deployment to Vietnam. Park's alliance with the United States, however, became abruptly strained in January 1968 when, as I explained above, the United States showed indifference toward the North Korean commando attempt to assassinate Park.

Just as the establishment of the Homeland Guard with a 2.5 million reserve force demonstrated Park's fury over U.S. containment strategy toward North Korea, the creation of the HCI triumvirate showed Park's centralized approach to power, which he saw as necessary in order to carry out the restructuring of the government and industries as the means to achieving South Korea's all-out industrial revolution.

In contrast to Park's turbulent personal past, blotted with pro-Japanese collaboration and communist activities, O Wŏnch'ŏl was born into a wealthy landlord family in North Korea on October 2, 1928. In his final year in chemical engineering at Seoul National University, O entered the Korean Air Force when the Korean War broke out and served until August 1957 as a major. In May 1961, as an aspiring young engineer at the age of thirty-three, O was drafted by the Military Revolutionary Committee, which appointed him to the Ministry of Commerce and Industry (MCI).

O's subsequent career in public service was entirely within the MCI. Understanding O's role in South Korea's rapid development is important because, as the chief architect of the Heavy and Chemical Industrialization Program, he not only implemented the HCI Program, but also managed the ROK's Military Modernization Program—later known as the Yulgok Operation—together with President Park's clandestine nuclear weapons and missile capability development. It could be said that O's role epitomized the character of the South Korean model of industrial revolution, especially the modus operandi of the HCI triumvirate: President Park's strong leadership, O's industrial and engineering skills, and Kim's financial-economic expertise.[17]

The third member of the HCI triumvirate, Kim Chŏngnyŏm, responsible for economic management, especially for raising funds for the HCI Program, was born on January 3, 1924. Kim began his career in 1943 at the Bank of Chosŏn (the Bank of Korea after liberation) after graduating from the Oita College of Commerce in Kyushu, Japan. Kim obtained his fiscal planning expertise and reputation after he drew up a draft plan for South Korea's first currency reform (carried out in February 1953). With an MA degree in economics from Clark University in America, obtained in 1959, Kim was appointed director-general of the finance bureau in the Ministry of Finance, which was later known among South Korean economic bureaucrats as the "Republic of Finance" (ijae konghwaguk) for the key role it played in ROK's fiscal management. Like O Wonch'ŏl, Kim was also recruited by the military junta in 1961, and by June 1962 he rose to the rank of vice minister in both the Ministry of Finance and the Ministry of Commerce and Industry (MCI) before being promoted to minister of the MCI in October 1967. Kim's role in managing the Park government's rapid economic development increased dramatically from October 1969 when he was appointed chief of staff at the Blue House, which he swiftly transformed into President Park's famously centralized power machine, especially for overseeing the HCI "Big Push." Entrusted by Park as his "economic manager," Kim in fact managed what can be termed the golden era of the South Korean economy for over nine years until December 1978. Overall, the combined role of the HCI triumvirate should be understood in the context of a deliberately concentrated control system under Park himself and his two economic czars, O Wŏnchŏl and Kim Chŏngnyŏm.

KOREAN-MADE WEAPONS PRODUCTION

On April 3, 1972, less than five months after O had received Park's emergency command to carry out weapons development to arm twenty divisions of reserve forces, eight light-weapon prototypes—including MI carbines, MI9s, A4 machine guns, and 60mm trench mortars—were manufactured and ready for preview by Park, government officials, military personnel, and the media. Under the code name "Lightning Operation" (*pŏn'gae saŏp*), the newly created Agency for Defense Development (ADD) produced these weapons through a twenty-four-seven operation. In many respects, the way this operation was carried out demonstrated Park's supreme control over his government even well before he introduced his authoritarian Yusin Reforms (in October 1972) and the Yusin Constitution (in December the same year).

The significance of the development of these light-weapons, albeit prototypes, was that it enabled Park and his policy advisers finally to persuade the United States to assist South Korean production of weapons by providing both technological advisers and technical plans. Until then, the South Korean military had been abjectly dependent on the U.S. for the supply of light weapons. For Park and his advisers, therefore, this was a new beginning in their all-out race to build South Korea's defense capability, which Park defined as self-sustainable national defense.

All-Out HCI Program

On January 12, 1973, the ROK defense industry development program took a giant leap forward when Park declared the government's "Heavy and Chemical Industrialization Policy" as the top priority of Yusin Reforms. This declaration of the HCI Policy[18] was Park's official guarantee to technocrats to go ahead with the state-planned HCI Program. Park's declaration also pledged managerial autonomy from any political intervention or repercussion.[19] The HCI Program was designed to achieve $10 billion in export earnings and a per capita GNP of $1,000 by the early 1980s. This is not to say, however, that the Park state was ready for implementing the HCI Program. As already explained, Park decided to go ahead with a heavy and chemical industrial sector mainly through the mobilization of the chaebŏl-owned manufacturing companies as South Korea's industrial engine. In May 1973, a team led by Deputy Prime

Minister T'ae Wansŏn travelled to the United States in an attempt to raise $5.8 billion, half of the approximately $10 billion needed for the HCI Plan, which had been first unveiled to key cabinet ministers and other senior officials in the Blue House basement shelter on January 31, 1973.

Through his extremely secretive and intimidating methods,[20] Park militantly pushed for the development of the ROK's defense industry, and by late 1979 a total of eighty-four manufacturers had become engaged in the construction of six industrial complexes, each focused on a target industry: heavy machinery at Ch'angwŏn, steel at P'ohang, shipbuilding at Okp'o, electronics at Kumi, petrochemicals at Yŏch'ŏn, and nonferrous metals at Onsan. Ch'angwŏn, South Korea's largest heavy machinery complex, located near the Masan harbor, boasted a military, fortress-like city plan and was designed to house 104 factories with a holding capacity of over 100,000 workers.

The population of Ch'angwŏn was originally about 10,000, with 1,700 households occupying about 13,900 hectares of farmland. This massive transformation from what were basically small agricultural holdings to one of the largest industrial complexes in the world reflected Park Chung Hee's political will and strategy to build a newly industrialized modern Korea. To achieve top-down industrialization, the government planned to invest 22.1 percent of the total national investment between 1973 and 1981, amounting to 2.98 trillion *wŏn* (approximately $9.8 billion at 1970 prices), or 63.9 percent of the total investment in the manufacturing sector.

Park also conducted a comprehensive restructuring of governmental ministries and other institutions, while also introducing many dictatorial measures and related legislation to minimize any interruption that might hinder the progress of the HCI Program. The state's promulgation of the Industrial Parks Development Promotion Law on December 24, 1973, was particularly effective in opening efficient operational channels for the implementation of HCI. Considering the fact that the ROK's per capita GNP at that time (in 1972) was merely $319, it is not difficult to understand why Park risked almost everything on carrying out the second phase of his industrial revolution even at the cost of his own demise less than six years later.

As noted earlier, this line of Park's thinking was nowhere more obvious than in the managerial structure of the HCI triumvirate. The nation-wide expansion of the Saemaŭl Community Movement after 1973 was another control mechanism,[21] especially through the Saemaŭl policy training of the masses. The Factory Saemaŭl Movement, as Hagen Koo notes in Chapter 8, was a most effective device for controlling the working people, and thus it was inescapable for Park to be increasingly confronted with nation-wide anti-state protests, especially against the authoritarian Yusin system. Yet, Park's push for carrying out the HCI Program rapidly turned into an all-out operation for South Korea's military modernization.

The Yulgok Military Modernization Program

In March 1974, Park approved a top-secret defense project under the code name "Yulgok Operation," to purchase advanced military equipment and to modernize the military. This operation was an emergency measure, which Park initiated immediately after the North Korean navy attack on Paengnyŏng Island.[22] Outraged by this attack, Park immediately launched his own campaign by sending a personal message to the islanders that if North Korean troops were to invade the island, they should "fight to the last [and] hold out just for a week" for the ROK military to recapture the island.[23] Designating himself as a war president, Park obviously took on what could be described in today's terms as a "war on terrorism" against North Korea.

The state raised a total of 16.13 billion wŏn (approximately $32 million) between 1974 and 1975 through the media campaign known as the National Defense Fund, and then in July 1975 a compulsory National Defense Tax was introduced as the new revenue base for the Yulgok Operation. Between 1975 and 1976, South Korea spent 6 percent of the national GNP on the Yulgok Operation, and by 1980 the state had collected a total of 2,600 trillion wŏn, or about 5.158 billion U.S. dollars.[24] At the beginning the Yulgok Operation was managed by a "Five-Member Committee"[25] within the Ministry of Defense (MOD) led by a deputy minister and four other representatives, including O Wŏnch'ŏl, Park's senior economic secretary as well as chief of the HCI Planning Corps. O was placed on this MOD committee under Park's orders, and in so doing, Park strictly controlled the Yulgok Operation in all its stages, from the selection of military weapons and equipment, to their purchase. As a means to ensuring appropriate checks-and-balances, Park introduced his own brand of watchdog system with a three-tiered system of committees to oversee the Yulgok Operation. This three-tiered watchdog system was comprised of the MOD's Five-Member Committee, the Blue

House Five-Member Committee made up of Park's special aides and senior secretaries, and a "no-name" committee of the five top-ranking officials: Park himself, Chief of Staff Kim Chŏngnyŏm, O Wŏnch'ŏl, the minister of defense, and the chief of the Agency for Defense Development.[26] In addition, Park introduced several extra measures, including "Special Measures for Military Supplies" (in 1973) and the "Measures for Weapons Supply with Foreign Loans" (in May 1975). Under these measures, every purchase under the Yulgok Operation was to be made directly with the manufacturer, which also would guarantee the exclusion of any commission, brokerage, or other intermediary fees under contracts.[27]

To be sure that his watchdog system in this highly complex and secretive military operation ran effectively, Park relied on his multi-layered intelligence agencies to tap every official involved in the purchase of military hardware and advanced technology under the Yulgok Operation. From a strategic and management viewpoint, therefore, the Yulgok Operation was effective for Park in exploiting to the utmost North Korea's provocation of the South as a wake-up call, highlighting the need to speed up Korea's long-awaited military modernization. For the procurement of advanced technology and military hardware, in particular, Park and his close advisers strategically exploited the inconsistency of U.S. arms control policy with the idea that the U.S. often made concessions or altered policy only when the South Koreans showed their own ability to complete things.

In late December 1971, for example, Park ordered O Wŏnch'ŏl to develop a missile capability program, which led to South Korea's emergency purchase of French anti-ship Exocet missiles in spite of strong U.S. opposition. This purchase also led to South Korea's unexpected procurement of two American–made Harpoon anti-ship missiles, which South Korea had been trying to purchase for several years without success. Until then, U.S. officials had offered only outdated missiles. It was this purchase experience that encouraged Park and his key advisers to exploit the inconsistency of U.S. policy to the edge, especially in South Korea's pursuit of technologically advanced weapons development.

By late 1974, Park openly questioned American policy, especially its policy of troop withdrawal from Korea. In his visit to Seoul in November 1974, President Gerald Ford assured Park that "we have no intention of withdrawing U.S. personnel from Korea."[28] Park, however, did not trust Ford's personal pledge to him. Following the fall of Saigon in April 1975, Park was convinced that the United States would abandon South Korea, just as it had abandoned Vietnam. He essentially feared the worst-case scenario, a North Korean surprise attack on Seoul, which the South might have to face alone because the U.S., as in Vietnam, might pull its troops off the Korean peninsula due to public pressure.

The ultimate irony of the fall of Saigon, especially in terms of Park's pursuit of military modernization at almost any cost, was that North Korean leader Kim Il Sung visited China at this time—the first time since April 1961—as if to proclaim new pressures against the South. Kim's sudden visit to Beijing not only stirred Park to tighten national security through his draconian Yusin rule but also gave rise to open speculation in South Korea that the U.S. was considering changing its East Asian defense perimeter and subsequently might sell out on South Korea. In this regard, U.S. Ambassador Sneider's report to the secretary of state dated, April 1975, illuminated Park's all-out push for South Korea's independent defense and armament policy:

[U.S.] Congressional attitudes and fear that in conflict situation Congress (and American public) may—as in the case of Vietnam—deny funds and use of U.S. forces needed to defend Korea and even force U.S. troop withdrawals before then. . . . Korea's only alternative is to achieve a degree of self-reliance that will cushion possible loss of U.S. support before or during conflict.[29]

Park's Clandestine Nuclear Weapons and Missile Capability Program

In July 1975, Park took bold action by concluding an agreement with France for a loan for the construction of nuclear reprocessing facilities and two nuclear power plants. This was just seven months after South Korea had signed a contract to purchase propellant plant manufacturing facilities and advanced missile technology from the American Lockheed Corporation, despite the U.S. State Department's strong opposition.[30] The difference in the ROK approach between the earlier purchase from Lockheed and the latter from France was significant. Whereas South Korea ostensibly made efforts to consult with the U.S. regarding the Lockheed deal, Park and his key advisers took an entirely independent path in negotiating with France in regard to ROK programs of nuclear reprocessing facilities and missile development.

With drastically reduced confidence in the U.S. security commitment in Northeast Asia, especially after witnessing the U.S. withdrawal from Vietnam in April 1975, Park was determined to secure a firm U.S. security treaty commitment even by alarming U.S. policy makers. From the outset, Park may appear to have overreacted to the rapidly changing international situation, especially towards U.S. policy in Northeast Asia. But, when one considers the intensified North Korean armed attacks on the South at that time—especially the repeated assassination attempts on Park, one of which, allegedly linked to North Korea, resulted in the death of First Lady Yuk Yŏngsu on August 15, 1974—his fear of a second Korean War should not be dismissed as merely a self-serving excuse or anti-communist paranoia. The assassination of the First Lady was the third of four North Korea-linked assassination attempts on South Korean presidents during the fifteen-year period from 1968 to 1983.[31]

In June 1975, Park warned the United States that South Korea had the capacity to produce nuclear weapons and that the ROK would have to develop nuclear weapons if the U.S. nuclear umbrella were to be removed from Korea.[32] By then, Park had already warned Sneider that he had directed Sim Munt'aek, the chief of the Agency of Defense Development, to develop in-country missile capability.[33] This led to U.S. Secretary of Defense James Schlesinger's visit to Seoul two months later in August, during which he promised decisive U.S. support in the event of a North Korean attack. Schlesinger, however, made this promise without authorization from Washington.[34] Yet, by making this promise, he obtained Park's agreement not to develop nuclear weapons.[35]

This is not to say, however, that either the United States or South Korea honored their promises to each other. Just as officials in Washington did their best to stalemate Park's secret nuclear weapons program, Park and his key advisers sought to carry out their own plans with no less vigor. In this regard, no case is more telling than the episode behind the French government's cancellation of the sale of their reprocessing plant to South Korea in early 1976.[36] The United States conducted this cancellation through personal negotiations between President Jimmy Carter and President Valéry Giscard d'Estaing of France.[37] At the same time, the U.S. Congress deliberately withheld South Korea's loan application for an import-export bank loan of $132 million and an additional $117 million of credit guarantees for the construction of the light water reactor, Kori No. 2, approved in 1974.[38] In spite of obvious financial difficulties, however, South Korea swiftly purchased CANDU, a Canadian reactor, in January 1975.[39] The more severe the pressure from the United States, the more determined Park became, especially when it came to tightening security against U.S. intelligence agencies.[40] Similarly, U.S. intelligence kept a close watch on many high-level Korean officials, especially O Wŏnch'ŏl during his weapons purchase visits to Europe and Israel in 1974.[41] In short, Park's nuclear weapons and missile program was a most heavily guarded secret operation.

In the case of constructing the Korean Nuclear Fuels Development Corporation, known under the pseudonym, Taejŏn Machinery Depot (Taejŏn Kigyech'ang) with the code name "Sacred Farm" (sinsŏng nongjang), for example, this plant's security was so tight that even the police commissioner in that province (South Ch'ungch'ŏng) was denied entry. Similarly, the city of Ch'angwŏn, the home of the largest heavy machinery industrial complex, was another security-tight zone originally planned and built as a military fortress.[42] In his brief talk with the author in December 2003, retired Colonel Kang Yŏngt'aek, who was the first Director of Ch'angwŏn Industrial Complex, recalled his mission as that of maintaining the security of the Complex: "It was completely a military operation with absolute security."[43]

On December 2, 1976, KNFDC was officially unveiled with the aim of building Korean-made nuclear facilities for strategic reasons because, despite the low profitability of operating a heavy water fuel rod plant, President Park was determined to keep it as a countermeasure against a change in U.S. policy towards South Korea in the future.[44] In order to avoid U.S. surveillance, especially on his nuclear missile capability program, therefore, Park managed his nuclear program in total secrecy.

Given this extremely tense situation, President Jimmy Carter's widely publicized dislike of Park, from 1977 until Park's assassination in 1979, must be considered with caution. Carter was known to have loathed Park for his abuse of human rights. Undoubtedly this was the initial reason for Carter's attitude, for in his moralistic presidential campaign he had promised the withdrawal of U.S. troops from South Korea as one of his key policies. Beneath Carter's fury over Park, however, sat a much more serious cause for the ROK-U.S. conflict, namely, Park's secret nuclear weapons and missile program. As early as September 1976, and thus less than a month after the notorious Axe Murder Incident at Panmunjŏm in the DMZ,[45] U.S. Ambassador Sneider

expressed concern about what he coined "the longer term" of "Park's emo-
tionally-charged drive to seek self-sufficiency and self-reliance through a program of nuclear weapons and missile development."[46]

In spite of their watchful observance, however, U.S. officials did not have
clear information on just how advanced the ROK was in developing high-
technology weapons until South Korea revealed its plan to launch a guided
missile. In fact, the missile named NH-K was launched in September 1978,
and South Korea claimed to have become the seventh nation in the world with
its own domestically developed missile. This new development stirred up a
stormy panic in Washington. From early November 1978 to June 1979, until
President Carter's visit to Seoul on his way back from the G-7 summit meeting in Tokyo, there continued a chain of so-called "inspection tours" initially
begun by Secretary of Defense Harold Brown, including a seventeen-member
group of high-ranking officials from the National Security Council, the U.S.
State Department, and the Pentagon.[47]

PARK-CARTER STANDOFF

By then, ROK-U.S. relations had become so hostile that when Carter met Park
in Seoul, neither party paid attention to diplomatic protocols toward each
other. The summit meeting between the two allied countries' presidents
quickly turned into a quarrel to the extent that U.S. Ambassador Gleysteen
later recalled, "Never before in numerous summit meetings I had attended in
the past had I seen leaders mangle the process of communication the way
these two men did that morning."[48] Their quarrel boiled down to two counter
arguments: Carter's demand that South Korea reduce the military disparity
between the North and the South, and Park's insistence that Carter assure
that the U.S. would not proceed with further withdrawals of U.S. ground
forces from South Korea. Park insisted that the ROK needed more time.

In spite of their unshakable differences, the two presidents finally came to
accede to each other's demands. Park subsequently announced the release of
180 South Korean political prisoners and, on July 20, Carter suspended U.S.
withdrawal plans from the ROK until 1981. One may ponder how such a compromise could have been reached, especially in light of the U.S. habit of
unilateral foreign policy formulation. One reason was that, even with his
iron-willed resolve and the power of the presidency, Carter, as Oberdorfer

pointed out, could not "decouple the United States from the high-stakes military standoff on the Korean peninsula."[49] Another reason, and perhaps more politically relevant, was that almost every policy adviser, including those among his own presidential staff, was against the withdrawal plan. Many military advisers regarded Carter's policy to be unworkable to the extent that they engaged in a full-scale rebellion against him. The counter activities of two U.S. army generals, who at that time were at the frontline on the Korean peninsula, were particularly noteworthy. One was chief of staff of the U.S. forces in Korea, Major-General John Singlaub, who publicly warned in his interview with the *Washington Post* that "if U.S. ground troops are withdrawn on the schedule suggested, it will lead to war."[50] Because of this head-on challenge, Singlaub was quickly removed from Korea to serve at a domestic post.

The other was General John Vessey, the U.S. military commander in Korea, who advised President Park to formulate counter tactics to Carter's withdrawal plan by demanding a hefty compensation package which the U.S. government would not be able to pay as it would tie Congress up in debate on its cost vis-à-vis withdrawal.[51] Subsequently, Carter apparently approved $1.9 billion in military aid as a compensation package, but "not a single senator or representative spoke up in support of the withdrawal."[52] In addition to this near mutinous challenge, Vessey threatened to resign if the withdrawal of troops were to proceed without the compensation package. Carter's withdrawal policy was a strategic disaster overall, exacerbated by the already strained U.S.-ROK relations. In fact ROK-U.S. relations throughout the Park era had been anything but harmonious, except for the period of the Vietnam War under the Lyndon B. Johnson administration. From June 1963, when U.S. Assistant Secretary of State Averill Harriman began planning troop withdrawals in the same year,[53] U.S. troop reduction plans in Korea remained under consideration, and in 1971 President Nixon pulled out 20,000 troops from Korea. Thus Carter's suspension of his troop withdrawal plan until 1981, from Park's perspective, hardly changed anything at all, especially in terms of his military modernization policy with the focus on the construction of an independent national defense system.

Despite the many outstanding contributions it made to South Korea's development, especially after the Korean War (1950–53), the United States failed to provide even the basic necessities for South Korea to guard against

North Korean provocations. As late as August 1975, South Korea repeatedly begged the United States for what the South Korean government termed "appropriate aid," such as "fire power, including [a third of a line is whited out] air, and logistics support."[54] This is not to say, however, that the United States was ignorant about the urgency of South Korea's need for military modernization. The U.S. promise to modernize the South Korean armed forces had initially been outlined in the "Brown Memorandum" in March 1966[55] and again in mid-January 1971, with an extra $1.5 billion as compensation for the U.S. withdrawal of troops from Korea. However, the U.S. deliberately delayed the release of its military assistance to South Korea, largely because Washington officials did not trust Park who, they suspected, might strike the North if the South were equipped with adequate supplies of weapons. In short, the U.S. strategically restrained the South from any sort of military confrontation with the North by strictly limiting military supplies. In addition, the U.S. Congress was cautious about being seen as supporting Park's repressive regime. And in this regard nothing was more blatant than Secretary of State Henry Kissinger's drastic modification of the 1977 Five-Year Military Assistance Program from $47.3 million to $8.3 million. Kissinger came up with this reduction proposal in December 1975 while the famous Koreagate bribery scandal rocked the U.S. Congress after over ninety congressmen and other officials were found to have been involved.[56]

Over twenty years later, in his memoirs, U.S. Ambassador Gleysteen described the U.S. attitude towards Park as "indiscriminate" in its criticism, focusing especially on Park's human rights abuses.[57] Nevertheless, Carter's withdrawal policy ironically strengthened Park's all-out drive to give effect to his authoritarian Yusin Reform agenda: the construction of South Korea's independent defense and armament capability as the top priority of the HCI Plan. To achieve this highly risky but intrinsically nationalistic ambition for South Korea's economic-military modernization, Park ruthlessly employed his draconian methods and tyrannical repression over his opponents—including workers, students, and dissident intellectuals—and ultimately was shot dead by Kim Chaegyu, director of the Korea Central Intelligence Agency, on October 26, 1979.

SOUTH KOREA: LOOKING BACK THIRTY YEARS LATER

So, what was the overall result of Park's all-out heavy and chemical industrialization revolution? Did South Korea, as a result, achieve the construction of a national defense capability strong enough to guard against external aggression, especially from North Korea? It unquestionably did. In fact, the idea of heavy and chemical industrialization was primarily conceived as South Korea's core national homeland security measure and, by and large, was very effective, to the extent that it ultimately changed the face of South Korea into an industrialized middle power in the region, with the fifteenth largest economy in the world and a political democracy that is arguably the most vibrant in Asia.

My aim here, however, is not to downplay the destructive nature of Park's forced-draft rapid industrialization or the unsustainable flaws and contradictions in the HCI Program itself. As discussed in this chapter, Park's extremely centralized HCI Policy, especially as the top priority of the Yusin Reforms, was so oppressive that not only did many Koreans fall victim to its developmentalist power structure but also Park himself fell victim to his own success. In this respect, Park's demise at the hands of his own chief of intelligence essentially illustrated the fundamental volatility of the HCI Policy, particularly in terms of concentrated decision-making power, which paradoxically exposed inherent governance problems in response to changing circumstances. It is no surprise therefore that South Korean society even three decades after Park's death is still divided between those who approve of the Park-style rapid industrialization and those who fundamentally reject the Park-style dictatorship. Despite the fierce conflict between these two forces, the influence of Park over today's South Korean politics, economy, and society remains strong, although the debate over the nature of his influence is as heated as ever. Most tellingly, the dramatic change in Park's public image within one generation from having been widely regarded as the most reviled dictator to now the most admired president in contemporary Korean history came about primarily because of his leadership in driving South Korea's economic modernization through heavy and chemical industrialization.

Of course, the long-term merits of South Korea achieving national homeland security through HCI, especially against North Korean aggression, may not be known for some time, at least until the two Koreas finally reunite and harmoniously live together as one united nation. Koreans, in the meantime, could more fully appreciate the transformation of their country through both industrial and democratic revolution, which is itself a great achievement and has made a substantial contribution to the building of prosperity, peace, and openness in the region and world politics. In this respect, Koreans could also appreciate the historical legacies of HCI-led homeland security posture building during the Park era.

NOTES

1. On March 27, 1971, just a month before South Korea's seventh presidential election, the U.S. completed its withdrawal of about 20,000 American soldiers stationed in Korea.

2. The most recently available documents regarding this armed attack, known widely as the "Blue House Incident," and other security conflicts between North and South Korea, including the USS *Pueblo* Incident, were released by the Nautilus Institute, which obtained them under the U.S. Freedom of Information Act. See the Nautilus website: http://www.nautilus.org/foia/foiachrons/c%20sixtyeight.pdf (accessed April 11, 2006).

3. For detailed discussion on the Korean Nuclear Fuels Development Corporation see Hyung-A Kim, *Korea's Development under Park*, 193–99.

4. For an analysis of Korea's "division system," see Paek Nakch'ŏng, *Hŭndŭllinŭn pundan ch'eje*.

5. U.S. Ambassador, William J. Porter reportedly told Park that he should "Do it alone." Yi Sangu, "Pak Chŏnghŭi nŭn yongin ŭi chŏnjae yŏnna?" 88–89.

6. "Rostow to LBJ," Memo, December 7, 1967, NSF, Country, Box 91, Lyndon B. Johnson Library.

7. Both Park and Johnson were in Canberra to attend the funeral of the Australian Prime Minister Harold Holt, who had disappeared while swimming.

8. State Department Telegram 3104 (Seoul), December 23, 1967, NSF, Country, Box 91, Lyndon B. Johnson Library.

9. Yugyŏng Chaedan, *Pak Kŭnhye int'ŏbyujip*, 298.

10. Chŏng Chaegyŏng, *Pak Chŏnghŭi sasang sŏsŏl*, 253.

11. Taet'ongnyŏng Pisŏsil, *Pak Chŏnghŭi taet'ongnyŏng*, vol. 5 (1969): 141.

12. Foreign Minister Ch'oe Kyuha received formal notice of the withdrawal of U.S. Seventh Division in Korea on July 5, 1970, but by then the withdrawal had already been

under way for at least six months and the Park government had not even been officially informed. For a detailed discussion on this issue, see Robert Boettcher and Gordon L. Freedman, *Gifts of Deceit*, 95.

13. Initially it was five not four core factories; including a copper factory.

14. The "Four-Member Committee" was established to carry out the construction of the defense industry as Park had directed. The three other members were: Hwang Pyŏngt'ae, assistant minister in charge of management, EPB; Sin Wŏnsik, Ministry of Defense assistant minister in charge of war supply loans; and Sim Munt'aek, deputy chief, KIST.

15. However, in contrast to O's account, Kim stated that O had called Kim and requested a meeting, which took place as noted above. See Kim Chŏngnyŏm, *Hoegorok: Han'guk kyŏngje chŏngch'aek 30-nyŏnsa*, 322.

16. O Wŏnch'ol, interview by Hyung-A Kim in May 1995 and January 2000. For full details of the points, see O Wŏnch'ol, *Han'gukhyŏng kyŏngje kŏnsŏl*, vol. 5, 24–25 and vol. 7, 388–89.

17. See Hyung-A Kim, *Korea's Development under Park*.

18. Park declared this policy in his New Year press conference. For details of Park's press conference see, *Pak Chŏnghŭi taet'ongnyŏng yŏnsŏl munjip*,10:58–59.

19. O Wŏnch'ol, interview by Hyung-A Kim, October 1996.

20. To ensure the unanimous approval to spend $10 billion on HCI, Park held the meeting of the defense industry at the Blue House basement shelter which had been converted into a temporary weapons showroom with newly produced Korean-made weapons presented all around in a warlike atmosphere. Seven key cabinet ministers, the prime minister, and other senior officials plus Park's senior secretaries had been ordered to attend the meeting.

21. Please note that Saemaŭl Undong (New Village movement) was initially introduced in April 1970 as a nationwide campaign for rural development. Here the English term, Saemaŭl Community movement, however, implicitly distinguishes the changed character of the Saemaŭl movement after 1973 when Park officially declared the Saemaŭl movement as a training ground for mass education in "Korean democracy" in both the rural and urban areas. In 1979, a collection of Park's speeches on the Saemaŭl movement was published in an English translation with the title, *Saemaŭl: Korea's New Community Movement*.

22. Between October 1972 and the time of this attack, North Koreans reportedly intruded the waters surrounding this island and four other neighboring islands over eleven times.

23. "Kungmin ton, han p'un to pujŏng ŭn andwae," [No corruption of the national fund, not even a single a cent, is tolerated], *Sin tonga* April, 1995, 415.

24. Ibid., 480.

25. This committee later changed its membership twice: to a "Six-Member Committee" in July 1975 and again, in January 1978, to a "Ten-Member Committee." In November 1978, it was renamed "Promotional Committee for Reinforcing War Capability."

26. Two ministers, Sŏ Chongch'ŏl and No Chaehyŏn, represented the Ministry of National Defense (MOND) from December 1973 to December 1977, and from December 1977 to December 1979.

27. The "Measures for Weapons Supply with Foreign Loans" also included eight separate terms and conditions for security purposes. For details, see O Wŏnch'ol, *Han'gukhyŏng kyŏngje kŏnsŏl*, 7: 242; and Kim Chŏngnyŏm, A, *Pak Chŏnghŭi*, 296–97.

28. Cited in "Comments on Secretary Schlesinger's Discussions in Seoul" in the issue entitled: "U.S. Reaction in Event of North Korean Aggression," undated attachment of a memorandum sent to Carl Albert, speaker of the House of Representatives, from the Office of the Deputy Assistant Secretary (security assistance), OASD/ISA, Documents concerning relations between the USA and the ROK between the fall of Saigon (April 1975) and the Tree Incident in the DMZ (August 18, 1976), Washington, DC, Gerald Ford Library.

29. Embassy telegram to SECSTATE (Secretary of State), Subject: "ROK Views of U.S. Security Commitment," April 1, 1975, Box 11, File: Korea, Gerald Ford Library.

30. It seems that the ROK purchased materials from the Lockheed Corp. mainly because the U.S. had failed to coordinate its arms control policy between the U.S. Department of State and the U.S. Department of Defense when dealing with South Korea. See, George S. Springsteen, executive secretary of the Department of State, to Lieutenant General Brent Scowcroft, February 4, 1975. Country File: Korea (3), National Security Adviser: Presidential Country Files for East Asia and the Pacific, Gerald Ford Library.

31. The first attack on the Blue House occurred in January 1968. On June 22, 1969 a team of three North Korean commandos attempted to set off a bomb in the National Cemetery, and on October 9, 1983, an attack at Rangoon's Martyrs' Mausoleum led to the death of seventeen Korean and four Burmese high-ranking government officials.

32. Park originally made this statement in his interview with U.S. columnist Robert Novak in early June 1975.

33. Ibid.

34. Memorandum for General Scowcroft from Thomas J. Barnes, "Subject: Secretary Schlesinger's Discussions in Seoul," September 29, 1975, NSF. Country File: Korea Box 9, Gerald Ford Library.

35. No Chaehyŏn, *Chŏngwadae pisŏsil*, 80.

36. The cancellation was formally signed on January 23, 1976. For details in Korean, see No Chaehyŏn, *Chŏngwadae pisŏsil*, 82–83.

37. Oberdorfer recorded 1978 as the year that Washington blocked South Korea's discussions with the French, but evidence from the President Gerald Ford Library as well as Korean sources suggest otherwise. For details, see Don Oberdorfer, *The Two Koreas*, 193–95.

38. Memorandum to the Assistant to the President for National Security Affairs, written by Acting Secretary of State Robert S. Ingersoll, July 2, 975, Box 2, file no. 9, Gerald Ford Library.

39. Reports and Recommendations of Jan M. Lodal and Dave Elliott, NSC, to Secretary [Henry] Kissinger. July 11, 1975 (Declassified on May 27, 1997), Country. Box 2, file no. 9; also Seoul Embassy Telegram to Secretary of State, Washington DC, American Embassy, Ottawa July 1975. (Declassified January 29, 1998), NSF. Country. Box 9, Gerald Ford Library.

40. See Korea-State Department Telegrams to SECSTATE-NODIS, No. 14, April 1976 (Declassified on June 8, 2001), NSF. Box 9, Gerald Ford Library.

41. O Wŏnch'ŏl, "Yudot'an kaebal," 388–411.

42. Interview by Hyung-A Kim with several senior executives of heavy machinery weapons companies in the Ch'angwŏn Industrial Complex in December 2003. For a detailed discussion on the rigidity of security checks on personnel at the Ch'angwŏn Complex, including during its construction period, see Hyung-A Kim, *Korea's Development*, Chapter 8.

43. In addition the author also interviewed several former senior executives of heavy machinery weapons companies at the Ch'angwŏn Industrial Complex. For a detailed discussion on the rigidity of security checks on each member of personnel at the Ch'angwŏn Complex, even during its construction period, see Hyung-A Kim, *Korea's Development*, especially Chapter 8. Colonel Kang was initially second to O Wŏnch'ŏl's Second Economic Secretariat in the Blue House.

44. O Wŏnch'ŏl, "Nuclear Development in Korea in the 1970s," 11–18.

45. For the background of this incident, see Don Oberdorfer, "Murder in the Demilitarized Zone," *The Two Koreas*, 74–83.

46. Brent Scowcroft, Ambassador Richard Sneider, and William Gleysteen, Memorandum of conversation, Subject: "August 18 Incident at Panmunjŏm: U.S.-Korean Relations," Box 10, File: Korea no. 20, Gerald Ford Library.

47. Hyung-A Kim, *Korea's Development*, Chapter 9.

48. William H. Gleysteen Jr., *Massive Entanglement, Marginal Indulgence*, 47.

49. Don Oberdorfer, "End of the Carter Withdrawal," *The Two Koreas*, 108.

50. *Washington Post*, May 19, 1977.

51. Yi Tongbok, "Bessi saryŏnggwan," 260–87.

52. Don Oberdorfer, *The Two Koreas*, 91.

53. Memorandum of Conversation, Kennedy and ROK Ambassador Kim, June 17,

1963, NSF, Country, Box 127, John F. Kennedy Library.

54. See National Security Decision Memorandum (NSCM) 282 and 309, National Security Study Memoranda and Decision Memoranda, 1974–1977, Box 2, Gerald Ford Library.

55. This fourteen-point memorandum was announced by U.S. Ambassador Brown on March 7, 1966. It became one of the main sources for many critics to characterize the South Korean troops in the Vietnam War as "mercenary." See Frank Baldwin, Diane Jones, and Michael Jones, *America's Rented Troops*, 7–14.

56. Don Oberdofer, *The Two Koreas*, 92–93; Robert Boettcher and Gordon L. Freedman, *Gifts of Deceit*.

57. William H. Gleysteen Jr., *Massive Entanglement, Marginal Influence*, 61.

2

POSCO: Building an Institution

SEOK-MAN YOON

INTRODUCTION

Having been a key driving force behind the Republic of Korea's (ROK) rapid industrialization, Pohang Iron & Steel Co. Ltd. (POSCO) is now the fifth largest steel company in the world, with an annual production capacity of 30 million tons of steel. POSCO has been widely recognized for its accomplishments, particularly as an international leader in productivity and efficiency; its global status stands on its record of achievement. In terms of return on investment, for example, the South Korean government initially spent a total of 220 billion wŏn ($863 million 1968) on the construction of POSCO. In October 2000, after POSCO was privatized, it had accumulated a total capital value of 3.9 trillion wŏn ($3.4 billion).

By the end of 2004, POSCO had contributed nearly 4.8 trillion wŏn (approximately $4 billion) in taxes. Given the fact that POSCO was founded in 1968, during the early phase of the Park Chung Hee (Pak Chŏnghŭi) era less than four decades ago, POSCO's phenomenal development represents a model case of South Korea's rapid industrialization. It sheds light on ROK-style development, which on one hand brought about an economic miracle within the decade of the 1970s and on the other suppressed the South Korean people's push for democracy by rigidly guiding economic development under the state's authoritarian Yusin system (1972–80). Park decided to build POSCO as a strategic necessity and initiated POSCO's institution building strategy. He insisted on this even though the ROK, in that economic context, did not display a significant domestic demand for iron or have a supply of natural resources such as iron ore or coal, not to mention capital, technology, or skilled manpower. In Park's vision, the Republic of Korea needed a key pulling force for South Korea's economic development—an integrated steelworks industry. For many developing countries under similar circumstances, where state-led industrialization strategies are almost inevitable and necessary, the study of the POSCO experience provides a rare opportunity to learn about South Korea's industrial know-how. South Korean political will, government policies for nurturing corporations, and how the management strategies of the POSCO leadership created an effective institution building strategy are especially helpful. In addition, the managerial paradigm of the corporation and how it was altered according to each phase of the institution building process provides immeasurable information. By the term "institution building strategy" I mean a strategy which developing countries may choose in order to build and nurture an organization that can, by mobilizing total available resources and capacity, fulfill a specific national task.[1]

The purpose of this chapter is to explore POSCO's institution building strategy, especially through the construction of Pohang Iron and Steel, as the basis for constructing other key industries in the Republic of Korea. This chapter focuses on POSCO's leadership development, especially in its early stages, from April 1968, when Pohang Iron and Steel was founded, until February 1981, fifteen months after the assassination of President Park Chung Hee. This chapter attempts to answer three main questions: (1) What was the relationship between the President Park administration and POSCO in the implementation of the basic tasks of this institution building strategy? (2) How did the POSCO leadership cultivate the key principle of autonomy while adhering to the government's "guidance" over the company? (3) How was POSCO affected by political change in South Korea?

First, this chapter will briefly trace the historical background of the South Korean steel industry. It will review the relationship between the President Park Chung Hee government and Pak T'aejun, founder of POSCO, while examining the latter's leadership during the first thirteen years from 1968 to 1981.[2] The chapter will then analyze the characteristics of the early phase of POSCO, especially with regard to the effectiveness of its primary role, required type of leadership, and management paradigm. In conclusion, the chapter will briefly discuss the benefits and costs of a government-driven institution building strategy with respect to the POSCO case.

CONSTRUCTING POSCO: HISTORICAL BACKGROUND

South Korea's modern steel industry emerged as part of the Japanese munitions industry under Japanese colonialism. By the time Korea regained independence from Japan in 1945, however, the steel industry, like the rest of the
peninsula, had been largely destroyed. Private capital did not exist and most
of the engineers were Japanese. Most of the peninsula's steel production
facilities had been concentrated in North Korea, and the few remaining steel
facilities in South Korea were decimated during the Korean War. In 1958,
under the Syngman Rhee administration (1948–60), the South Korean government realized the importance of the steel industry and set up a plan to construct its first integrated steelwork industry. However, the plan to build a
plant with an annual pig iron production capacity of 200,000 tons failed due
to insufficient capital, lack of cooperation between government ministries,
and the difficulty of finding a person to lead the project. When Major General
Park Chung Hee took office as chairman of the revolutionary Supreme
Council for National Reconstruction in 1961, a plan to build a steel industry
again began to take shape. Park's military-led administration pursued strong
economic development policies under the First Five-Year Economic
Development Plan (1962–6) and aimed to achieve, what the Park state termed,
"economic independence" or a "self-sustaining economy."

With rapid economic growth the Republic of Korea quickly generated a
rapidly increasing demand for steel, the basic material for many industries.
However, South Korea's crude steel industry was producing far below demand
at that time. In pursuit of overcoming economic underdevelopment, while
promoting balanced economic development in the private sector, the Park
state developed the comprehensive First Five-Year Economic Development Plan
(1962–6), which included the construction of the steel and petrochemical
industries in addition to the Seoul-Pusan expressway. The difficulty the Park
state faced, however, was that it lacked the knowledge and expertise required
to construct a modern, integrated steel industry. Hence South Korea failed to
attract foreign capital, and the construction of a steel industry again fell
through. There were other attempts, including a project to build a steel working plant with an annual production capacity of 370,000 tons, a concept promoted by a private investment consortium involving the West Germany based
companies: Demag Cranes & Components, Krupp, and Gutehoffnungshütte

Gruppe[3] in April 1962. Korea Steel and an American investment consortium led another project for a steel plant with an annual production capacity of 310,000 tons; both projects faced the same difficulties in raising capital and ultimately succumbed to failure.

Despite these circumstances, however, President Park actively promoted the construction of a steel industry as a key project of his administration during the Second Five-Year Economic Development Plan (1967–71). For example, Park, in order to emphasize the Republic of Korea's need for development loans and technical assistance, met in May 1965, with U.S. President Lyndon B. Johnson and Fred Foy, chairman of Koppers, a U.S.-based company that specialized in steel construction technology. In January 1966, Park again met with Foy and asked him to form an international consortium. The South Korean integrated steel project showed its first concrete sign of progress when, in December 1966, the Korea International Steel Associates (KISA) established an office in Pittsburgh, Pennsylvania. The South Korean government decided to set up, in two construction phases, a steel plant with an annual production capacity of one million tons and used KISA to attract foreign capital for the project. Seven companies from the United States, Britain, West Germany, and Italy participated. A French company joined the consortium later in August 1967.

Despite chronic financial difficulties, especially having very little private capital, President Park single-mindedly pursued economic development and focused his attention on the construction of a heavy and chemical industry. This meant, in practice, fostering a state-planned strategy for capital-intensive basic industries. What was notable about Park's state-planned strategy was that he placed priority on the building of the Pohang integrated steel mill as the driving force for South Korea's economic and industrial development. Park's aim in constructing the Pohang integrated steel mill, in other words, was to utilize it as the basis for South Korean development. Park was convinced that building a steel industry was essential to developing other industries, such as the automotive, shipbuilding, and machinery industries. In fact, Park publicly declared, "Steel is national power." (Ch'ŏlgang ŭn kungnyŏk)[4]

The Founding of POSCO

The Park state officially launched Pohang Iron & Steel Co. Ltd. on April 1, 1968 with thirty-nine founding members. Pak T'aejun, former president of Korea Tungsten (Taehan Chungsŏk) and lead appointee of the Steelworks Project Promotion Committee, became the first president of POSCO. The Ministry of Finance and Korea Tungsten were the initial investors, with an initial authorized capital of 800 million *wŏn* (equivalent to $2.91 million).[5] The initial paid-in capital of 400 million *wŏn* (equivalent to $1.46 million) came from the Ministry of Finance and Korea Tungsten, each paying 300 million *wŏn* and 100 million *wŏn* respectively.[6]

Pohang Iron & Steel Co. Ltd. started off as an incorporated company under the Commercial Act. This decision has been attributed to the fact that a state-owned company supported by a special act would sit under the strict supervision and control of the government and the ROK National Assembly. Although there were many benefits to being a public enterprise, such as financial support, reduced taxes, and freedom from union action, there also was, inter alia, the added risk of insufficient incentive to enhance competitiveness. In addition, as a public enterprise, POSCO had limited its capacity to obtain the necessary freedom of managerial autonomy, which restrained the company's international competitiveness. Pak T'aejun personally believed that the only way to succeed would be to allow POSCO to have full responsibility for its own management, and thus he insisted that POSCO be incorporated.

In the meantime, KISA initially planned to borrow funds from the International Bank for Reconstruction and Development (IBRD) and the Export-Import Bank of the United States (EXIM) for steelwork construction. However the IBRD, which had originally been supportive of the plan, changed its mind and opposed it. In the IBRD's critical report on the state of the ROK economy released in March 1969, the IBRD argued that it was too early for South Korea to construct a steel mill, given that the Republic of Korea had a pre-modern industrial structure and an especially poor ability to repay its foreign debts. Consequently, the Park state's plan to attract investment funds through KISA failed once again.[7]

Seed Funds

In a situation where fundraising through KISA had become seemingly impossible due to IBRD's negative evaluation of its steelworks project, the only available alternative to raising seed money for POSCO was to secure a portion of Japan's post war reparations, which had been designated for primary industries such as agriculture and fisheries. Japanese reparations amounted to $500 million, including $300 million in interest-free commercial credit and $200 million in public loans. However, South Korean policymakers, especially Pak T'aejun, lobbied frantically for the adoption of a new strategy to redirect $119.48 million, or 23.9 percent of total reparations, including $30.8 million from the claims fund and $88.68 million in loans, to the steelworks construction project. This was no small sum for the Republic of Korea at that time, considering that, by September 1963, South Korea had been on the verge of bankruptcy, as its foreign reserve holdings in U.S. currency amounted to a mere $93,298,000[8] and all exports in 1964 amounted to a mere $100 million. South Korea's per capita GNP was just $169 in 1968, the year POSCO was formed. Thus the construction of POSCO itself was a bold and risky venture upon which President Park staked not only his own political leadership, but also the future of the South Korean people.

Nevertheless, the Japanese government maintained a passive attitude toward the ROK's steel plan, largely because Japan remained extremely cautious regarding reparation issues that may entail further demand for war compensation from other countries, including the Philippines. Japan was also cautious about over committing to a financial burden if it were required to pay the remainder of the reparations all at once. Understanding the complexity of these issues, the ROK actively lobbied to change the policy with the Japanese government by dispatching high-ranking officials from the Economic Planning Board (EPB) to Japan. At the same time, President Park Chung Hee played an important role in attaining public consensus, as well as agreement from the National Assembly. Behind the scenes, Pak T'aejun, chairman of POSCO, played an equally active role by visiting Japan's top three steel companies: Yawata Steel, Fuji Steel, and Nippon Kokon to seek economic and technical support. Pak also lobbied Japanese government officials and other influential people to seek their support. These efforts finally paid off when in August 1969, Japan decided to cooperate with the construction of

South Korea's steel plant. It had been eight years since President Park first sought to build an integrated steel mill in 1961, and a total of five trial and error attempts since Korea's liberation from Japanese colonization. In December the same year (1969), Japan and South Korea agreed to construct POSCO. Under this agreement, the role of fundraising for the construction shifted from KISA to Japan.

SYSTEM DEVELOPMENT STRATEGIES

Relations with President Park and the Government

In the founding phase, while funds and resources needed to be raised and mobilized, POSCO received a wide range of special assistance and privileges through President Park and his government. As a political leader with a strong commitment to economic development, Park single-handedly provided both political and administrative support, as well as his own personal confidence, in the founding of POSCO. Park's keen interest in POSCO's construction was evident in his frequent visits to POSCO, a total of thirteen visits over an eleven-year period, from November 1968 when he first visited the construction site, to October 1979 just before his assassination. In addition, Park acted as a "shield," blocking POSCO from unwarranted political pressure while simultaneously refraining from interfering with POSCO's management affairs.

Park was particularly committed to introducing special measures as a means to help POSCO build its steelworks within the shortest possible time, as well as facilitating POSCO's managerial efficiency. In so doing, Park strictly prevented politicians and their connections from seeking political campaign funds or employment from POSCO. In regard to the former, Park's action to block his party from raising presidential campaign funds from POSCO in April 1971 was the most concrete evidence of this intervention, especially as Park's popularity at that time had hit rock-bottom following the constitutional amendment enabling a third term election. In regards to using political connections to gain employment in POSCO, Park apparently issued a written memo, widely known as the "Paper Horse Warrant" (*chongi map'ae*),[9] to Pak T'aejun stating that Pak T'aejun alone had authority concerning POSCO's management. Most notably, Park demonstrated extreme confidence in Pak T'aejun by approving Pak's authority to tap into the finances made available through Japanese postwar reparations. President Park also gave Pak a free hand in choosing facility suppliers and provided a government guarantee on POSCO's behalf, which, in turn, helped POSCO win contracts without competition. At the same time, conflict amongst government agencies and policymakers in the course of policy execution during the early stage of POSCO's construction did not affect POSCO because of President Park's iron-willed leadership backed by the authoritarian enforcement of legal systems and the administrative apparatus. In this context, the founding phase of POSCO could be viewed as a state agency or a "state within the state,"[10] rather than an industry operating according to market principles.

Under his banner, "Steel is National Power," President Park declared the Steel Industry Promotion Act (SIPA; ch'ŏlgang kongŏp yuksŏngbŏp) in 1970.[11] Although Pak T'aejun appears to have had personal reservations in regard to this act, particularly concerning its legal grounds for bureaucratic intervention into POSCO's management,[12] the ROK government nevertheless designed the act to give full support to the construction of an integrated steel mill. It stipulated that eligible steel companies may receive special privileges, such as long-term foreign loans with low interest rates, support for raw material purchases, equipment supplies, discounts on utility charges, as well as the use of infrastructure, including harbors, water, electricity, roads, and railways. The benefits provided by SIPA allowed POSCO to purchase required equipment at a lower cost and reduce construction expenses.

The Heavy and Chemical Industry Promotion Act (HCIPA) in 1973 was another law specifically designed to promote and foster the heavy machinery, shipbuilding, and petrochemical industries by controlling businesses' entry into the industries covered by the act. The HCIPA essentially controlled entry to the heavy and chemical industry in accordance with the state's Heavy and Chemical Industrialization Policy (HCIP) officially declared in January 1973.[13] What we can appreciate here is the political will to build South Korea's domestic steel industry as part of a comprehensive heavy and chemical industrialization process. Between 1972 and 1973, for example, the government introduced more than a dozen special laws and decrees, including the Tax Deduction Control Act (1965), the Public Investment Fund Act (1973), and the Introduction of Foreign Capital Law (declared in 1966 and revised in March 1973), as means to effectively implement the HCIP. This legal framework became a fundamental base upon which POSCO was founded from scratch, and readied it for successful operation. This distinctively Park-style development of POSCO reflected not only the rigidity of South Korea's developmentalism, but also the vast scale of the Heavy and Chemical Industrialization program, which in effect had begun several years earlier when Park publicly promoted the Republic of Korea's own policy of "independent defense" (chaju kukpang) after the North Korean attack on the Blue House in January 1968. In fact, Park founded the ROK National Homeland Guard, a force of 2.5 million reservists, in April that year, and afterwards relentlessly sought foreign capital in order to construct the "four key factories" to assemble South Korea's own defense industry. The construction of South Korea's own iron and steel mill—POSCO—sparked the idea of building the four key factories.[14] Deputy Prime Minister Kim Hangnyŏl's interview, in Tokyo in August 1969, clearly reflected the South Korean perspective of national security at that time, especially President Park's determination to build POSCO:

> Frankly speaking, if [we] cannot agree on the issue of building POSCO, I will leave [Tokyo] without announcing a joint communiqué. . . . Demand for iron and steel in [South] Korea is increasing because of economic development . . . thus [South] Korea independently began to construct an integrated iron and steel mill. . . . [South] Korea approaches economic development while defending against the North Korean [armed] threat. Aren't the 600,000 armed forces in [South] Korea the strongest in Asia? It's imperative for the peace and prosperity of the Asia-Pacific region to co-operate between [South] Korea with a strong army, and Japan with strong economic power.[15]

Thus the efficient construction of POSCO within the quickest possible time frame was more important to President Park than any other project at that time. With such support from the president, POSCO's construction, in practice, operated like a military institution. Securing a site for the construction of POSCO was one clear example of this Park-style, quasi-military operation.

For example, the governor of Yŏngil County directly managed the site procurement of about 2,800 acres. The governor also took care of relocating 1,250 households and 2,700 graves from the site, as well as compensating the owners of hundreds of building structures to be demolished. This task was not an easy one to accomplish within a short period when there was strong resistance among residents who were forced to move. Yet the provincial government of North Kyŏngsang established the Pohang Industrial Park construction site headquarters, and the governor as its director actively engaged himself in overseeing the painstaking negotiations with residents. Despite the difficulty of estimating land prices, which had risen rapidly following the announcement of the POSCO construction site, the provincial government launched an unusual campaign under the slogan, "Local Patriotism Movement" (aehyangsim undong) and encouraged residents to sell their land at the price that had been set prior to the announcement of the construction site. Five financial agents in Pohang took joint responsibility for land appraisal.

The essential infrastructure that needed to be constructed for an integrated steel mill included a port, industrial water supply, urban engineering works, and railways. Relevant key ministries, including the Economic Planning Board, the Ministry of Finance, the Ministry of Construction, and the Ministry of Transportation carried out this work in accordance with government policy. With an investment of 715 million wŏn (approx. $2.8 million), the construction of a railway to the steel mill site was completed first. This in turn enabled the smooth transportation of the huge amount of building material required for the first phase of construction. In regard to the building of harbor facilities, which was the next most urgent project, the Ministry of Construction announced the establishment of a waterway 200 meters (656 feet) wide for the construction of inner breakwaters, a bank wall, and an embankment. The Ministry of Construction built a reservoir with a total capacity of 7.65 million cubic meters nearly three kilometers west of the water intake station to hold the 100,000 tons of industrial water the steel mill would require each day.

The Economic Planning Board (EPB) supervised POSCO instead of the Ministry of Commerce and Industry (MCI), which by law was responsible for supervising the steel industry, including POSCO. President Park established this unusual arrangement and thus reduced MCI's role in the founding stage of POSCO to that of "cooperation," meaning in effect that the MCI must follow orders from the EPB. It should be noted that this was the period when the EPB, as a "super-ministry"[16] empowered by President Park, controlled the Republic of Korea's economic development with substantial autonomy, and its minister, Kim Hangyŏl (1969–72), dominated the ministers of all agencies related to the economy and directly reported to and was instructed by the president, without reporting to the prime minister, on matters related to the economy.[17]

With the president's total trust, Kim Hangyŏl's EPB provided economic and technical rationality and bureaucratic professionalism, with very little interference from political parties, interest groups, or military factions. This unusual circumstance spurred the formation of a non-political elite group to ensure that important economic and political decision-making processes were protected and isolated from political pressure. Any possible conflict arising from ministries concerning POSCO's construction was either skillfully negotiated beforehand or dealt with through the intervention of the EPB. As a result POSCO rarely confronted bureaucratic battles in its efforts to produce a speedy construction timeline. This is not to say, however, that POSCO was unconditionally immune from challenges and competitors. To the contrary, whenever POSCO confronted challenges and competitors, including disputes with policymakers, Pak Taejun balked at almost nothing to fight for POSCO's interests.[18]

In 1978, for example, when POSCO's third phase of expansion was near completion, the government's long awaited plan to construct the "second steel mill" (che-2 chech'ŏl) in addition to POSCO led to intense disputes between government policymakers and private big business (chaebŏl), including Hyundai. Needless to say, POSCO's Pak T'aejun fiercely campaigned for the right to construct the second steel mill. A team of influential policymakers led by President Park's Senior Economic Secretary O Wŏnch'ŏl, the chief of the Heavy and Chemical Industry Promotion Committee Planning Corps (HCI Planning Corps; Chunghwahak Ch'ujin Wiwŏnhoe Kyehwoektan) opposed Pak's campaign. As architect of South Korea's Heavy and Chemical Industrialization Policy, O insisted that Hyundai should construct the second steel mill on the basis that Hyundai had submitted a written proposal to finance the entire construction of the second steel mill, thus reducing the government's financial burden while simultaneously activating private business.[19]

O's argument essentially reflected HCI policy, which stated: "The early phase of an induced industry must be formed in a private-public cooperative system, and those industries with international competitiveness must be led by the private sector."[20] In October 1978, the final decision was made in a meeting involving Pak T'aejun and President Park's three most senior staff, Chief of Staff Kim Chŏngnyŏm, Senior Economic Secretary O Wŏnchŏl, and First Senior Economic Secretary Yi Hŭiil; all agreed that the second steel mill would be constructed by Hyundai. Several days later, however, Pak sought President Park's intervention directly, in a private meeting with him, and successfully persuaded the president to change the earlier decision, such that POSCO received the assignment to construct the Second Steel Mill.[21] This was how POSCO came to build the second, larger steel mill in Kwangyang Bay in South Chŏlla Province (in 1987).

In summary, the buildup of POSCO as the basis for the Republic of Korea's rapid industrialization under President Park cannot be fully explained without considering the extraordinary roles of President Park and Pak T'aejun who, as Park's handpicked confidant, led the POSCO development just as Park Chung Hee had envisioned. The extraordinary relationship between these two key figures in the founding stages of POSCO construction reflected the core character of President Park's leadership style. On the one hand Park demanded and received unbridled loyalty from his agents such as Pak T'aejun. On the other, Park communicated through action rather than words. In this context, Pak T'aejun's loyalty towards President Park could be seen as the driving factor behind his widely known "performance-oriented style of leadership." Like President Park, Pak T'aejun also equated the importance of steelmaking with national power. In fact, his management strategy for POSCO was built entirely on his personal belief in what he termed, "Make steel, serve the nation" (chech'ŏl poguk).[22]

As J. Schumpeter noted, the innovative leadership of the founder is critical in the initial stage of building an institution, especially in terms of the leadership's impact on the national economy. In the course of managing the connection between an institution and its environment, the founder of an institution must be able to identify this connection accurately and deal with it immediately even without the benefit of any previous examples. The founder must also activate the internal organization by linking environmental elements with the internal relations of the organization. In this context, Pak T'aejun showed model leadership in building the POSCO institution. Often referred to as the "King of Steel" (Ch'ŏl ŭi Wang), Pak's leadership was critical to the development of what became known as the "POSCO Spirit"; the official representation of POSCO's institutional culture built on Pak's four personal principles. To understand POSCO growth, especially in its founding stages, therefore, it is important to consider the personal background of Pak as well as his four principles.

LEADERSHIP: PAK T'AEJUN AND
HIS FOUR ADMINISTRATION PRINCIPLES

Pak T'aejun was born in late September 1929 in Imnang-ni, a coastal village in Tongnae County in South Kyŏngsang Province, at a time when Japanese colonial rule in Korea was at its peak.[23] He was the eldest of six children. Like many Korean villagers at that time, Pak's family, as a result of economic hardship, abandoned their hometown and left for Japan where young Pak entered Iyama Secondary School located in Nagano Prefecture in 1940. From a very early stage, Pak is known to have shown academic excellence, especially in algebra and mathematics, which led him to enter Waseda University in 1945 as a student of the Department of Science and Engineering. Following Korean liberation from Japan in August 1945, Pak returned to Korea and in 1948 was admitted as a cadet to the sixth class of the Korean Constabulary Officers' Training School (which later became the Korean Military Academy). It was here where, for the first time, Pak met Captain Park Chung Hee who, as cadet commander, taught ballistics. Pak was then twenty-one years old. In 1960 at the age of thirty-three, Pak again met the then Major General Park Chung Hee as Park's newly appointed chief of staff at the Army Logistics Base Command in Pusan.

However, despite their close relationship, or perhaps because of it, Park Chung Hee deliberately omitted Pak T'aejun from his list of military coup plotters until the morning of the coup on May 16, 1961. From that morning on, however, Pak played a key role in a variety of capacities, including chief of staff to Major General Park Chung Hee, who was then the chairman of the Supreme Council for National Reconstruction (SCNR). In August 1963, when Park Chung Hee officially declared his intention to retire from the military to run for the presidency, Pak T'aejun, who opposed Park's entry into politics, resigned from his position as member of the SCNR's Committee of Commerce and Industry, as well from his position as major general in the army. Contrary to his plans to study at Washington University in the US, however, Pak was assigned in early 1964 to a special mission to support the normalization talks between the Republic of Korea and Japan, through personal contact with Japanese political and economic elites. Pak's role in President Park's plans rapidly increased when, in December the same year, he was appointed president of Korea Tungsten, one of the key industries in

South Korea, accounting for about 30 percent of the ROK's total exports. Korea Tungsten, however, just like most government-owned companies at that time, had been suffering chronic losses.

In September 1967, while he was in London to negotiate the sale of Korea Tungsten, Pak received a telegram from Deputy Prime Minister Chang Kiyǒng, who was also the minister of the Economic Planning Board, stating that Pak should immediately return because Korea Tungsten had been chosen to lead the construction of South Korea's integrated steel mill. This was about two months before Pak's unofficial appointment as chairman of the Integrated Steel Mill Construction Committee. Seven months later on April 1, 1968 Pak, in his inauguration speech at the POSCO opening ceremony, publicly pledged his "steel-making mission" with a handpicked founding staff of thirty-eight.[24] Pak was just forty years old, with a burning ambition and commitment to achieve his "mission" to construct a world-class, high capacity steel mill at minimum cost.

The Four Principles

Steel-Making Patriotism

Pak T'aejun established his management strategies on his confidence in "Make steel, serve the nation" (chech'ǒl poguk). He recognized steel as the "rice of industry" as it provides the most basic resource for all industry, just like rice is a fundamental source of life and sustenance. For him, as for President Park, this phrase referred to the mass production of quality iron and steel at a lower cost for the South Korean industry, especially the defense industry, and for economic development as a means to strengthen national capacity against North Korean threats. Steel-making patriotism imbibed the long cherished goal of the South Korean government and its people to achieve modernization. Pak emphasized the value of every employee's personal contribution and devotion to the company. He actively encouraged employees on the basis of their loyalty and commitment to the company to perform to the best of their ability by exerting themselves with a sense of mission, or what he termed "spirit of turning to the right" (uhyang ǔi chǒngsin). This meant that if the construction of POSCO were to fail everyone should turn to the East Sea, namely Yǒngil Bay, located to the east of the construction site, and drown themselves to redeem their historical sin for such a failure. In openly promoting patriotism as the core of POSCO's code of conduct and institutional culture, Pak also drew attention to the history of Japanese postwar reparation in the form of blood money, which had financed the construction of POSCO.

Underpinning Pak's message was nationalistic imagery that the sacrifice and suffering of his own and other Korean people's ancestors under Japanese colonial rule symbolized the construction of POSCO itself. Thus every member of POSCO owed it to the nation to serve the nation to the extent of their own lives. This extraordinarily nationalistic approach unquestionably led to the shaping of a military-like self-discipline, an exceptional *esprit de corps*, and a spirit of solidarity among POSCO employees. In October 1970, for example, when the first phase construction project—a hot-rolling plant with an annual production capacity of 1.03 million tons, costing three times the cost (120.4 billion *wŏn* or approx. $742 million) of building the Seoul-Pusan highway[25]— was delayed, Pak declared a state of emergency.

Pak mobilized all employees, including executives and office workers, for an extraordinary work-marathon termed *tolgwan kongsa* in an all-out effort to complete the construction on time. Referred to as the "hot-rolling emergency," this project was three months behind schedule and suppliers deliberately attempted to further extend the terms of supply by exploiting POSCO's inexperience in construction.

Consequently, insufficient material and labor aggravated an already difficult situation. Despite this mix of problems—lack of experience, materials, and engineers—POSCO successfully reclaimed the completion date by completing the concrete pour in two months instead of five, as had been initially planned. This "do-or-die" approach ultimately led to the completion of the first phase of construction within thirty-nine months, one month earlier than scheduled. Given the fact that Japan took forty-two months to construct a similar scale steelworks plant, and Italy completed a steel mill with a production capacity of 2.6 million tons within forty-nine months, it is not difficult to appreciate the intense focus and capability of POSCO's workforce led by Pak T'aejun. Shortening the construction period was significant in that it reduced not only the interest paid to creditors, but also the cost of raw material inventories which enabled the company to start product sales earlier than expected and eventually generate earlier cash flows. Equally significant, if not more so, was the psychological effect that the successful, early completion had on morale and the individual psyche of every employee.

Responsibility and Perfectionism

Pak based his management strategies on radial responsibility. Despite the estimation of many prominent experts and advanced international steelmakers that the construction of POSCO had been set to begin too early and was unrealistic, Pak was totally driven by the construction of the steel plant. He knew full well that, if he failed, history would consider him the "culprit." He emphasized that POSCO was an epochal event in South Korea's history and that the creation of something from nothing could change the fate of the nation. He therefore believed that his undertaking of this responsibility and opportunity had to be treated with personal honor. Pak insisted that all managers be scrupulous in managing the company, more so than they were with their own private assets, and that company employees would be fully accountable for the consequences of their own actions should discrepancies arise.

Pak placed great importance on the social responsibility of the enterprise; entrepreneurs were required to change their management principle from one based on rapid growth and profit, to one that placed priority on the public good. He encouraged everyone to cultivate a strong sense of social justice in their management of POSCO in order to realize the corporate ethic that placed priority on public service. POSCO should be developed, Pak insisted, as an enterprise made by the public and trusted by the public, while at the same time it should cultivate a strong sense of loyalty to and love of the company in order to achieve a level of professionalism akin to one's own personal faith.

In regards to decision making, Pak made decisions based on his own judgment. Like many charismatic leaders in Korea's modern history, including President Park, Pak T'aejun's decision-making style was authoritarian and dogmatic to the extent that all employees were obliged to follow his decisions unconditionally. What was distinctive about Pak's decision-making style, however, was that he concentrated his decision making only on issues related to the management of the entire company and to extremely important international issues. At this level, decisions were almost entirely concentrated on Pak as the founder of POSCO.

Decisions relating to general business operations were delegated to the professional management team nurtured within POSCO, so that lower level managers could exert their creativity and autonomous decision-making abilities. In particular, Pak encouraged production and maintenance staff to come up with various suggestions aimed at reducing raw material and fuel costs, as well as enhancing work efficiency and product quality. Specifically, Pak insisted on zero tolerance of faulty workmanship, even at great cost. A good example of this occurred in 1977, when during phase three of facility construction, which had encountered many difficulties, Pak found faulty workmanship in the construction of the power generating and ventilating facility. He immediately summoned the contractor and the supervisor and ordered them to "blow up" the entire facility, which was 80 percent complete at the time. He also banned the contractor from ever receiving construction contracts from POSCO.[26] The Japanese supervisor responsible for the faulty work was sent back to Japan. This case, among others, set a clear example of POSCO workmanship, which led to the voluntary "zero defect" campaign among employees.

Transparent Information Management

It was general practice in the business world at that time that during the founding stage of a company the founder or their closest staff managed the most important information confidentially. Such a personalized method, however, was often extremely difficult to change when the company matured and required a more structured corporate information management system. From the very beginning, however, POSCO, under the watchful eyes of President Park Chung Hee and a range of politically sensitive institutions, both inside and outside the government, established a policy of transparency in each sector of management—from factory construction and production, to finance, personnel, and sales. This unusual set of circumstances, in many ways, drove POSCO to a high degree of transparency. Through the implementation of a balanced management method and strategy system, POSCO achieved the company's goals, while it maintained autonomy and transparency in information management. From the very beginning, a number of factors, including the external auditing and a verification system applied to public companies like POSCO by the National Assembly and the government, attributed to such a focus on the transparency of POSCO's information management system.

Even more crucial was Pak T'aejun's personal ability to guard against political interference in POSCO management. The public viewed this as being based on the principle of "zero defect perfectionism" and moral integrity.

However, this is not to say that Pak was free from political pressure, including during the founding stage. In fact, in April 1971, while the ruling Democratic Republican Party was frantically fundraising for the presidential election, Pak was under pressure, like most company presidents of both government-owned and private big businesses, to contribute political funds. He was pressured to contribute funds by paying a certain rebate level per ton whenever POSCO purchased raw materials or sold products. Believing that such pressure would frequently occur in the future, Pak sought help in person from President Park with an itemized written request. Pak's note included: the exclusion of pressure from political circles, the simplification of executive procedures for accessing the "Japanese Repatriation Fund," the approval of the discretionary power of POSCO to select facility suppliers, and guarantees from the government in the case of private contracts. President Park signed Pak's note and responded with written instructions that Pak should handle issues relating to POSCO independently and at his own discretion. This note was later known as Park's "Paper Horse Warrant."[27] This highly unconventional but equally decisive empowerment of Pak T'aejun's role in POSCO's management led him to incorporate a set of clear principles and mechanisms for transparent information in all sectors of POSCO from the outset. These included an efficient fund management and budget operation system, open competition for sales and purchasing procedures, as well as the consistent application of the merit system in personnel affairs. These principles have become the fundamental basis upon which POSCO has been able to develop and maintain its robust competitiveness in the global market and establish its respected corporate image up to the present.

The Priority of Staff Welfare

In the spring of 1968, once POSCO had completed purchasing its factory site, the number of staff increased dramatically, resulting in a housing crisis. The housing shortage became an issue because the movement of personnel at that time was extremely fluid. In the case of the small coastal fishing village of Pohang, where a large-scale steel industrial park was under construction, the demand for housing and school facilities was serious. The housing supply in Pohang was less than 60 percent of the total demand and the primary schools could not manage the student numbers even with a double-shift system.

Understanding the nature of steel mill construction, especially the long and strenuous day and night work shifts, on the part of workers forced to live away from their families for long periods, Pak T'aejun introduced the POSCO housing system. Such a system, he believed, would improve overall efficiency and that, once accommodation for employees and their families stabilized, workers could apply their full attention to their jobs. The establishment of the company's housing system, however, was not an easy task because POSCO at that time struggled with a lack of funds, to the extent that it could not even afford to pay employee salaries, let alone for the construction of a housing complex.

Once Pak obtained approval for the construction of company houses, he aggressively sought a bank loan without a mortgage. Against criticism from some political factions as well as some parts of the media, who argued that POSCO was trying to build an employee-housing complex ahead of a steel mill, Pak secured a bank loan of 2 billion *wŏn* from the Hanbit Bank (formerly Hanil Bank). This was only the beginning of POSCO's systematic construction of many public facilities, such as schools and recreational amenities, for the welfare of its employees. Almost thirty years later, POSCO's employee residential complex is still frequently cited as one of the best examples of a corporate valley.[28]

In many ways, Pak implemented a futuristic vision in which POSCO management actively anticipated the long-term effect of its decisions on employee welfare. POSCO, in other words, built houses for employees first and encouraged them to devote themselves to their work by helping them to establish their family lives, even at a time when POSCO struggled with financial difficulties. Similarly, as mentioned earlier, POSCO built its rail line in advance, which led to wide spread criticism from the political sector and the public. Yet, the construction of the railway enabled POSCO to increase transport capacity from five million to ten million tons. Thus POSCO management's forward thinking played a critical role in improving cost competitiveness by substantially reducing construction costs and timelines.

CONCLUSION

In the early stages of its economic development, the Republic of Korea tried to nurture the country's steel industry as the core driver of economic growth and strategically fostered it as an institution so that it could provide stable, high-quality steel supplies at low prices to manufacturing industries such as construction, automotive, shipbuilding, machinery, and electric home appliances. As a result, the South Korean economy enjoyed a surprisingly high rate of growth. The government-led, institution building of POSCO, promoted by President Park Chung Hee, proved to be a very efficient means to accomplish the goals of the Republic of Korea's development policies, particularly when large-scale investment with a high degree of public interest could not be easily covered by the private sector.[29]

To this end, POSCO was established to serve as a fundamental tool for the development of the national economy. Hence, the important circumstantial factors in POSCO's success can be found in the fact that the steel-making industry functioned in accordance with industrial features and policy goals desirable in mobilizing support from all sides, which were needed to realize the institution building strategy of POSCO against the backdrop of South Korean economic conditions at that time. In addition, strong leadership from President Park and Chairman Pak T'aejun was a crucial driving force behind POSCO's success. With the iron-will to promote the country's industrialization based on the steel industry, President Park helped POSCO enjoy maximum support from the government without lowering rationality and discretion in its management by protecting the company from political pressure and refraining from interfering in the company's inner management. Similarly, Pak T'aejun, with an extraordinary sense of mission based on "Steelmaking Patriotism," recruited and mobilized the most "suitable" human and material resources to establish the company. This was harmonized with other factors and greatly contributed to the success of POSCO, especially in the founding phase of the institution building process.

Another point that should not be neglected in discussion of POSCO's success is the culture and characteristics of the Korean people. When POSCO began construction, it was able to go far beyond established goals in a manner that could not have been expected at that time. This outstanding performance, despite the absence of the technology or experience required for the construction and operation of an integrated steel plant, was only possible because of excellent, well-educated, mentally resilient human resources. This indicates that fundamental factors such as culture and a people's characteristics are essential to a strategy's success and function as the backbone of any strategy for national development. Whether it is a nation or an organization, a system should have the ability to recognize the demands of a changing environment and cope with those demands in order to develop. This ability can only be achieved and developed when the organization's goals and visions are in accordance with environmental demands and also when the person with the highest authority is able to effectively plan and implement the changes in the system and structure so as to realize the organization's new goals and vision.

NOTES

1. The term "institution building" refers to a procedure aimed at establishing, nurturing, and protecting new norms and behavioral patterns in order to introduce and spread new values, roles, and changes in engineering and social technologies. It also includes all efforts and procedures needed to set up and operate policy plans to create or revamp official organizations until the intended changes are accepted with the support and cooperation of the surroundings.

2. Pak T'ae-jun became president of POSCO in 1968 and was appointed as its first chairman on March 2, 1981.

3. DKG Group was a joint venture of three companies based in West Germany including Demag, Krupp, and GHH.

4. *Widaehan saengae: Pak Chŏnghŭi taet'ongnyŏng hwiho rŭl chungsim ŭro*, 198. [Eds.]

5. The exchange rate in 1968 (US $1 = 274.8 Korean wŏn) is applied.

6. Because Korea Tungsten had available reserve funds for investment as well as a competent management team with experienced skilled workers, the company could offer eligible human resources to lead the steelworks construction project, which, in turn, helped the company to be selected as a contributing member to Pohang Iron & Steel Co. Ltd.

7. Since IBRD's evaluation reports enjoyed unquestioned high public trust in the world at that time, the opposition to the project exerted great influence on all KISA member countries, such that all became skeptical about South Korea's steelworks construction plan.

8. Han'guk Ŭnhaeng Chosabu, *Kyŏngje t'onggye yŏnbo*, 204.

9. In the Chosŏn period, a *map'ae* was a cast brass disk with a device of running horses. The king gave this disk to those officials that he personally appointed secret inspectors (*amhaeng ŏsa*) and sent into the provinces under cover to investigate corruption and rapacious governance. The disk, or warrant, authorized the appointee to act in the capacity of inspector. The more horses on the warrant, the higher the rank of the

inspector. The king only gave these appointments and associated warrants, to close officials he trusted. When a secret inspector caught corrupt officials in the act of whatever treachery, he could produce the "horse warrant" to show that he had been personally empowered by the king to investigate and arrest as necessary. Park's memo was called a *chongi map'ae*, or a paper horse warrant, to recall the trust and special authority kings placed in their close officials. [Eds.]

10. Yu Sangyŏng, "Han'guk sanŏphwa esŏ ŭi kukka wa kiŏp ŭi kwan'gye," 144.

11. The establishment and enforcement of the Industry Development Act (IDA) abolished the Steel Industry Promotion Act in 1986. The Promotion Act established for the realization of advanced industrial structures annulled the IDA in 1998.

12. In his interview with a researcher in 1995, Pak is said to have stated that only when this act is abolished would POSCO be able to extend its autonomy and the boundary of its activities. Yu Sangyŏng, "Han'guk sanŏphwa esŏ ŭi kukka wa kiŏp ŭi kwan'gye," 116.

13. For a detailed analysis of the government's HCI policy, see Hyung-A Kim, *Korea's Development Under Park Chung Hee*, Chapter 8.

14. Taniura Yoshio, "Kankoku no kigyōka to kaihatsu taisei," 47.

15. "Kin Gokuretsu Kankoku daihyō danchō ni kiku."

16. Byung Kook Kim, "The Leviathan: Economic Bureaucracy under Park Chung Hee," 3.

17. Kim Hangyŏl, an American-trained macroeconomist, is known to have been President Park's personal economic tutor as well as a friend. Kim died of cancer in January 1972. For details of Kim's influence in policy-making at that time, see O W., "Sanŏp chŏllyak kundansa." [A history of the industrial strategy corps], in *Han'guk kyŏngje sinmun* [Korean economic daily], May 31, 1993.

18. Pak Taejun has been spelled using the McCune Reishauer Romanization system. To reduce confusion, Park Chung Hee is spelled using the well-known English spelling [Eds.]

19. Yu Sangyŏng, "Han'guk sanŏphwa esŏ ŭi kukka wa kiŏp ŭi kwan'gye," 129.

20. O Wŏnch'ŏl, "Sanŏp chŏllyak kundansa."

21. In the making of this final decision, President Park is said have commented to Pak T'aejun: "Chŏng Chuyŏng [the owner of Hyundai] does well, but you are better at steel mill building. You do it [construct the Second Steel Mill]." Yu Sangyong, "Han'guk sanŏphwa esŏ ŭi kukka wa kiŏp ŭi kwan'gye," 135.

22. For a detailed analysis of Pak's idea of "Steel-Making Patriotism" see, Yun Sŏngman (Yoon Seokman), "P'ohang chech'ŏl ŭi kigwan hyŏngsŏng chŏllyak e kwanhan yŏn'gu."

23. Just two years after Pak's birth, Japan promulgated the Emperor system in 1932.

24. P'ohang Chech'ŏl Kongbosil, *Yŏngilman esŏ Kwangyangman kkaji: Pohang chech'ŏl 25-nyŏnsa*, 135.

25. The Seoul-Pusan highway cost 42.8 billion *wŏn*.

26. Seo, K. K., *The Steel King*, 420–1.

27. Other than those who knew about this Paper Horse Warrant, Pak kept it strictly secret until several days after President Park's assassination in October 1979, when he handed it over to one of the key members of POSCO to list it as part of POSCO history.

28. In July 1992, President of Moscow University, Victor A. Sadovnichii, visited POSCO and praised the complex by commenting, "It feels as if I am witnessing the realization of ideals which socialism has long been pursuing."

29. Korea Telecom and Korea Electric Power Corp. (KEPCO) can also be regarded as outcomes of the government-driven institution building strategy in that they also started off as public companies that provide national infrastructures (Korea Telecom was fully privatized in May 2002, whereas the privatization of KEPCO is still in discussion). However, there are differences between POSCO and the two companies: Korea Telecom and KEPCO provide final services aimed only at domestic demand, whereas POSCO produces and sells semi-final materials that can be directly or indirectly exportable.

3

The Cold War and the Political Economy of the Park Chung Hee Regime

TADASHI KIMIYA

No one can deny that the cold war influenced the political economy of the Park Chung Hee (Pak Chŏnghŭi) regime. First, President Park used the fact that South Korea had been both politically and militarily threatened by North Korea during the cold war to suppress anti-government movements and legitimize his authoritarian regime through promoting anti-communism. Second, President Park took advantage of the cold war that restrained South Korea as a divided nation to cement an advantageous relationship with the United States.[1] After 1965, Japanese foreign investment promoted by South Korea-Japan normalization and the demand for military procurement, produced by South Korean military involvement in the Vietnam War, contributed to South Korean economic development.

The policies of South Korea-Japan normalization and South Korean military involvement in the Vietnam War were promoted by the United States government because the United States regarded these issues necessary to strengthen the anti-communist bloc in the Northeast Asia. While it is important to point out that the cold war contributed to both the authoritarianism and economic development of the Park regime, it is even more important to notice Park's skill in taking advantage of the cold war. Park deliberately selected his economic development strategy by taking the cold war factor into consideration.

Following the coup d'état on May 16, 1961, the military junta concentrated on economic development. An export-oriented strategy was not initially adopted by the military junta. Rather the Park Chung Hee regime accepted it later—after it was the only strategy left. In addition, the Park regime intentionally took advantage of the cold war. Thus, while on the one hand the South Korean political and economic regime could be regarded as the one paying for the cost of the cold war, on the other hand Park manipulated this constraint into a benefit. To see this we need to accurately assess the costs and benefits the cold war brought to the Park political and economic regime.

THE INITIAL IDEA CONCERNING
ECONOMIC DEVELOPMENT BY THE MILITARY JUNTA

If the export-oriented industrialization strategy had been recommended by developmental economics textbooks at the time of the Park Chung Hee regime, the Korean government could have simply taken the strategy directly from the texts. Indeed, it is now mainstream academic thinking that for developing countries an export-oriented industrialization strategy is much more efficient, productive, and competitive than import-substitution industrialization strategies.[2] In the early 1960s, however, mainstream textbooks were influenced by mercantilist, nationalist, and Keynesian economics, rather than by neo-classical economics. In order to achieve rapid, autonomous, and genuine economic development, the import-substitution industrialization strategy was recommended the most often to developing countries.[3] One cannot assume that the Park regime would adopt an export-oriented industrialization strategy simply because it was the wisdom of the day.

In fact, the military junta initially adopted an autarkic industrialization strategy known in Korean as "inward-looking industrialization" (naep'ojŏk kongŏphwa).[4] This strategy was more of an import-substitution industrialization strategy than an export-oriented strategy. Two persons who played an important role in drafting the original Five-Year Economic Development Plan, Colonel Yu Wŏnsik, and Professor Pak Hŭibŏm, wrote about how this came about. According to their memoirs,[5] they had the clear intention to construct a self-reliant national economy by investing huge amounts of capital in basic industries. They were very critical of the United States aid policy at that time, and also of the Rhee regime's previous policy that made the South Korean economy too dependent on United States aid. They put top priority on the construction of heavy and chemical industries because they felt that heavy and chemical industries would forge a self-reliant national economy. They emphasized the importance of autonomy from United States influence and insisted that the South Korean government put more priority on national interest rather than cold war ideology as the basis for economic policy decisions. Since they thought that the government must take the responsibility of managing the economy for the sake of national interest, they argued for what they called "guided capitalism."

Yu and Pak played an important role in drafting the original Five-Year Plan published in the name of the Supreme Council for National Reconstruction in July 1961.[6] The Supreme Council's plan had many characteristics of an inward-looking deepening strategy. According to the plan, the government had to take charge of investment in the manufacturing industry, while South Korea could earn foreign currency by exporting primary agricultural and mining products. They advocated huge investments into the construction of heavy and chemical industries such as steel, machinery, and petrochemicals. In their plan they insisted that this economic development strategy was the only way to achieve economic self-reliance. This inward-looking deepening strategy was based on nationalism from above. Early on, both the chairman of the Supreme Council, Park Chung Hee and the founder of the Korean Central Intelligence Agency (KCIA), Kim Chongp'il, one of the most important planners of the military coup, endorsed this strategy.

THE UNITED STATES' RESPONSES
TO THE MILITARY JUNTA'S INITIAL IDEAS

The military government, however, could not carry out this strategy. The reason was partly due to the fact that the South Korean government was not autonomous or capable enough to carry out the strategy over the United States' objection. The United States was afraid that South Korean economic stability would be undermined if the inward-looking deepening strategy were to be adopted. The United States government had not seen the 1961 military coup d'état approaching. After it happened, the American embassy in Seoul tried in vain to restore the civilian government led by Prime Minister Chang Myŏn.[7] The government in Washington prevented the embassy in Seoul and the United States military in Korea from interfering in the South Korean domestic politics.[8] In addition, there was little internal opposition to the coup d'état.[9] Rather than try to overthrow the new regime, the United States proposed various conditions in exchange for validation of the new military government. Top among these goals was the "civilianizing" of the military government. The military junta thus promised to return political power to civilian politicians within two years.[10] However, the United States government was concerned that the Republic of Korea (ROK) would be more nationalistic, more authoritarian, and less amenable to the United States' influence than the previous governments.[11]

According to a report drafted by the Presidential Task Force on Korea,[12] the United States' top priority should be to make the Republic of Korea's use of United States' aid as efficient as possible in order to stabilize the South Korean political system and the economy. The United States advised the South Korean government not to invest large amounts of capital, other than social overhead capital, into new industries, but to make the most of human resources and existing factories. According to this priority, the inward-looking deepening strategy was not desirable because huge capital investment in the heavy and chemical industries would make the South Korean economy inefficient and unnecessarily unstable. When Chairman Park visited the United States in November 1961, the American government advised the South Korean government to scale down the First Five-Year Plan's annual growth target and adjust it to take resources and available capacity into consideration.[13] However, the U.S. government did not have a long-term, concrete vision for the Republic of Korea's economic development. Rather than directly dictate an export-oriented industrialization strategy, the United States only voiced its opposition to the inward-looking deepening strategy.

THE POLITICAL PROCESS:
ADOPTION OF EXPORT-ORIENTED INDUSTRIALIZATION

The consequence of American-Korean differences in economic policy was that the military junta could not carry through its inward-looking deepening strategy. The following four cases demonstrate the collapse of this inward-looking deepening strategy. Case one represents the Korean government's attempt to carry out a currency conversion to promote the inward-looking deepening strategy. The purpose of this conversion was supposedly to absorb "surplus" money into the government, transform it into industrial capital, and invest it in constructing heavy and chemical industrial sites and an integrated steel mill. The Korean government could not depend on the United

States government to carry out this strategy, because the U.S. government did not agree with it. And because it was difficult to rely on capital from other countries, the Korean government had no choice but to supply the money itself. A successful currency conversion might have given the Korean government the last chance to carry out the construction of large-scale heavy and chemical industries during the period of the First Five-Year Plan.[14] However, the currency conversion failed in the end.

The U.S. government put forth great effort into preventing the success of the currency conversion by threatening to withhold economic assistance and to take advantage of internal discord among the South Korean military junta.[15] The Park military government could not mobilize domestic support to overcome the United States' pressure because most of the South Korean business sector refrained from productive activities during this period and pressed the ROK government to release frozen money.[16]

In the second case, the South Korean government prioritized the construction of an integrated steel mill because they deemed such a mill indispensable for the promotion of the inward-looking deepening strategy.[17] The Park administration intended to depend on West German commercial loans at first,[18] but after the Van Fleet mission visited South Korea, the Park government decided that South Korea would depend on American Development Loan Funds (DLF) and commercial loans.[19] When the U.S. government failed to endorse the plan,[20] the South Korea government tried in vain to mobilize local capital.

Finally, the resumption of the financial stabilization plan prevented the Park administration from spending its financial budget on constructing an integrated steel mill. In the revised plan, the mill plan, which originally had been included in the First Five-Year Economic Development Plan, was eliminated.[21] It took ten more years before South Koreans would succeed in constructing the longed-for integrated steel mill, POSCO.

In the third case, the South Korean military government decided to resume a financial stabilization plan. This was to prevent the military government from investing huge amounts of capital in constructing heavy chemical industries. The financial stabilization plan was forced on the military government as a result of U.S. aid leverage.[22] Aid leverage had three forms: (1) organizing the timing and volume of the food aid provided under Public Law 480; (2) deciding which projects USAID would give the DLF; (3) determining whether or not the U.S. government would organize a South Korean consortium. The military government confronted the difficult decision of having to abandon the inward-looking deepening strategy in order to get aid. In any case, the internal struggles concerning the foundation of the Democratic Republican Party divided the military government at this time.[23] Under these conditions, the South Korean government could not but comply with the advice of the U.S. government.

In the fourth case, the military government at last decided to revise the original Five-Year Development Plan in December 1962. The Economic Planning Board (EPB), not the Supreme Council, revised this plan. The most conspicuous differences between the original and the revised plan were as follows.[24] First, the ROK government abandoned the principle of "guided capitalism" and decided to comply with the principle of a "free market economy." Second, the South Korean government emphasized the importance of the stabilization policy. Third, they revised the export plan. According to the original plan, primary products were expected to be the main export products, but the revised plan mentioned that the Republic of Korea had to specialize in exporting manufactured, labor-intensive products. Fourth, the military government scaled down the target of the annual increase in GNP (Gross National Product) per capita from 7.1 percent to 5.0 percent. This target of 5.0 percent was set according to the advice of USOM (the Korean branch of the USAID). The revised plan indicated that the South Korean economic development strategy changed from an inward-looking deepening strategy, to the labor-intensive, export-oriented industrialization model.

Among various factors that led to the failure of inward-looking development, the most important was the U.S. government's opposition. The U.S. government regarded the strategy as being inconsistent with American goals for the ROK economy. At this time, the ROK could not acquire capital from countries other than the United States. This was not for lack of trying. The Republic of Korea tried in vain to use European and Japanese "cards" against the U.S. government. European countries and Japan did not intend to cooperate with the ROK in implementing an inward-looking deepening strategy that was contrary to United States' desires. Pressure from the U.S. government, which took cold war factors seriously into consideration, promoted the failure of the inward-looking industrialization deepening strategy and the later adoption of the export-oriented industrialization strategy.

THE COLD WAR AND ITS IMPACTS ON THE "IMPLEMENTATION" OF THE EXPORT-ORIENTED INDUSTRIALIZATION STRATEGY

The cold war restrained opportunities for the Republic of Korea to structure economic decision-making and prompted South Korea to adopt the export-oriented industrialization strategy promoted by the United States, not the inward-looking deepening strategy that it preferred. How, then, did the cold war impact the "implementation" of the export-oriented industrialization strategy? Are there causal relations between the cold war factor and the "implementation" of the export-oriented industrialization strategy? Early in 1960s, the available funds for South Korea to import goods were mainly from U.S. aid. In order to promote export-oriented industrialization, South Korea had to multi-lateralize its sources of foreign capital.

In order to get as much capital as possible, not only from local sources but also from foreign sources, South Korea had to gain the confidence of foreign countries. South Korea also had to pioneer new markets for South Korean exportable goods. It is true that South Korea could take advantage of diligent and cheap labor to produce competitive manufactured exports, but South Korea had to compete with similar countries to acquire the foreign capital and secure reliable markets for its manufactured exports. The cold war in turn provided favorable conditions for export. South Korea sought to take advantage of the international environment through ROK-Japan normalization and South Korean military involvement in the Vietnam War.

KOREA-JAPAN NORMALIZATION AND ITS IMPACTS ON SOUTH KOREAN EXPORT-ORIENTED INDUSTRIALIZATION

ROK-Japan normalization was accomplished in 1965. It took fifteen years from the inception of negotiations until normalization was achieved, and the negotiations were some of the toughest not only for Japan but also for South Korea. On one hand, the South Korean government initiated the negotiations to normalize relations with Japan mainly because it wanted to complete the decolonization process by starting fully fledged diplomatic relations with the postwar "new" Japan. On the other hand, the Japanese government initiated the negotiations because it needed to resolve fishery issues between the Republic of Korea and Japan, and wanted President Syngman Rhee to abandon the Rhee

Line.[25] Japan also wanted to clarify the legal status of Koreans living in Japan. Because the purposes and agendas of Japan and the Republic of Korea were completely different, the negotiations could not be anything but difficult.

The hardest problem for the Republic Korea and Japan to solve was Korean property claims against Japan and compensation for the thirty-six years of Japanese colonial rule.[26] President Rhee demanded that in order to start new diplomatic relations with South Korea, the Japanese government must apologize and compensate for colonial rule by providing large amounts of money. For its part, the Japanese government insisted that it would pay just enough to meet South Korean legal claims against Japan. It was because of United States mediation that both governments began negotiations in 1951.

While each country's alliance with the U.S. could help bring the ROK and Japan together, these same alliances could prevent both governments from promoting the normalization process themselves. Both Japan and South Korea regarded their alliances with the United States as the most reliable, thereby making normalization unnecessary.[27] Both governments started negotiations, not because they thought normalization was necessary, but because the United States government told them to. One of the most important reasons why the normalization process in the 1950s had been very slow was that President Rhee was afraid that if the normalization were achieved, the United States would "sell out" South Korea to Japan, and the South Korean economy would once again be dependent on the Japanese economy as it had been under colonial rule.

This dynamic changed in the early 1960s when the United States changed its policy toward South Korea. Because the U.S. emphasized loans rather than grants, the United States needed more serious Japanese engagement with South Korea than before.[28] The U.S. government, while limiting its role to that of a catalyst,[29] a messenger, or a middleman rather than a mediator,[30] decided to play a more active role in promoting ROK-Japan normalization by persuading both governments to overcome domestic opposition and accomplish normalization.[31] In the 1950s, the U.S. regarded the military security and defensive capability of South Korea as most important, and had made light of South Korea's political and economic performance. By the 1960s, however, the U.S. government's top priority in terms of its policy toward South Korea was not military security or defensive capability, but political and economic stability. The U.S. determined that the most serious threat from North Korea was that of indirect infiltration. This could be accomplished by taking advantage of South Korean domestic political and economic turmoil, rather than direct military invasion.[32]

The Japanese government was also much more receptive to normalization with South Korea than before. The Ikeda administration decided to promote normalization with the Republic of Korea after the May 16 coup because the military government was much more positive in promoting normalization through containing domestic opposition. The Ikeda administration regarded a stable, anti-communist South Korea vital militarily, preferable politically, and profitable economically for Japan.[33]

Concerning the amount and the form of South Korean claims against Japan, there were huge and conspicuous disagreements between South Korea and Japan. The South Korean government insisted that it was entitled to legally receive all of the Korean claims against Japan to the amount of at least seven billion dollars.[34] However, the Japanese government insisted that the claims problem be resolved politically, not legally, because according to a purely legal procedure, the Japanese government would provide a smaller amount. The Ikeda administration decided to resolve these differences by providing money, goods, and services as economic aid or gifts in order to clear away the South Korean claims against Japan.[35]

The South Korean military government also decided to promote normalization by agreeing to the way the Japanese government proposed to resolve the claims problem.[36] The South Korean government agreed with the Japanese government in that the Japanese government should, over the course of ten years, provide three billion dollars as a grant, two billion dollars as a soft official loan, and more than three billion dollars as private foreign investments or commercial loans to clear away South Korean claims against Japan.

While opposition forces in South Korea insisted that the government not compromise so easily with the Japanese to solve the claims problem, the Park Chung Hee administration accepted the Japanese-initiated resolution in order to obtain economic cooperation and facilitate their industrialization strategy. The Republic of Korea's export-oriented industrialization strategy had elective affinity with the way in which ROK-Japan normalization was resolved as economic cooperation.[37] If the ROK military government had persisted in pursuing the inward-looking deepening strategy, such a resolution would have been regarded as irrelevant.

The United States, South Korea, and Japan agreed that the North Korean threat was now more political and economical rather than militaristic. The three governments also agreed that South Korea should focus more on political and economic security rather than military security. This attitude facilitated the Republic of Korea's adoption of export-oriented industrialization, and South Korea's decision to achieve ROK-Japan normalization through economic cooperation. Compared to the Rhee regime, the Park government gave more priority to achieving economic development and taking advantage of economic cooperation with Japan, rather than focusing on issues related to decolonization.

MILITARY INVOLVEMENT IN THE VIETNAM WAR AND ITS IMPACTS ON EXPORT-ORIENTED INDUSTRIALIZATION

No one can deny that military involvement in the Vietnam War contributed to an increase in exports and the accumulation of foreign currency for South Korea.[38] South Korea acquired foreign currency through military procurement in a number of ways during the Vietnam War. The Republic of Korea increased its exports to South Vietnam. The U.S. military increased the number of American troops and the ROK increased the number of Korean troops in Vietnam. American dollars were transmitted from South Vietnam to South Korea by South Korean military soldiers, who were given their overseas allowances by the U.S. government. South Korean expatriates working for Korean or U.S. firms in Vietnam also transmitted currency to the ROK. The chaebŏl, such as Hyundai and Hanjin, received orders from the U.S. military during the Vietnam War and brought some of their profits home. And finally, South Korean exports to the United States increased during the Vietnam War. Because the United States invested large amounts of capital into military industries during the Vietnam War, South Korean consumer goods were exported to the United States to take advantage of the shortage of consumer goods produced domestically. Even so, South Korea could not earn foreign currency in Vietnam without competing with Taiwan, Japan, and the countries of Southeast Asia.[39] Here, an investigation of Park's interactive strategies with the United States is especially instructive.

After the summit meeting with the United States President Lyndon B. Johnson (LBJ) in May 1965, it was not South Korea but the LBJ administration who initiated South Korean military involvement in the Vietnam War.[40] The Johnson administration felt pressured to persuade the South Korean government to dispatch its military troops according to the "Free World Assistance to South Vietnam" program, which was also called the "More Flags Campaign."[41] Johnson regarded other countries' military or nonmilitary involvement in the Vietnam War important because he feared that without outside support the United States would become internationally isolated in carrying out the war and may lose domestic support for the war. This vulnerability enabled the Park regime to negotiate for political, military, and economic compensation in exchange for sending its military troops to Vietnam on behalf of the United States.

Even so, however, it is not entirely obvious why South Korea, rather than other countries in Asia, sent the largest number of troops to South Vietnam. North Korea, after all, still threatened South Korea militarily, and United States troops still protected South Korea. Might not South Korea have too little defensive capability if it sent significant numbers of troops to South Vietnam? South Korea, moreover, had no alliance treaty with South Vietnam. SEATO member countries had signed treaties obligating them to defend South Vietnam from external military threats, but only a few countries among them sent their military to South Vietnam, and those that did, did so on a very small scale. What made the Johnson administration select South Korea among all of the other countries to fight against Vietnamese communists alongside the United States military?

Actually, it was the South Korean government which had been most enthusiastic about dispatching South Korean military troops to South Vietnam and Indochina—one of the hotspots between communists and anti-communists. Just at the time of the 1954 Geneva Accords, only one year after the Korean Armistice, President Rhee suggested that the ROK was prepared to dispatch military troops to Laos or Indochina in order to defend anti-communist Asian countries from communist aggression. At that time, the Eisenhower administration declined President Rhee's proposal with the reservation that in the near future it may be necessary to request the South Korean military troops be sent to Indochina.[42]

President Rhee's proposal had two motivations: (1) to obtain bargaining power with the U.S. and (2) to acquire prestige as an anti-communist Asian power. By doing the United States a favor, President Rhee hoped to get favorable terms from the United States on issues of normalization with Japan and corruption by appealing that he could contribute to anti-communism in Asia. President Rhee also wanted the political glory of being one of the most respected and powerful anti-communist leaders in Asia. At this time, however, the United States turned down Rhee's proposal because it was felt that it would be difficult for the U.S. government to get domestic and international support in stationing the U.S. military in South Korea while the South Korean military was being sent abroad.[43]

Rhee persisted, however, and made a similar suggestion to the U.S. government again in 1959. And, what is more surprising is that it was not only President Rhee but also Chairman of the SCNR, Park Chung Hee, who proposed sending South Korea's military to South Vietnam. When Chairman Park visited the United States in November 1961 after the May 16 military coup to get political and economic support from the Kennedy administration, Chairman Park suggested to President Kennedy that he was ready to dispatch Korean military troops, whether regular or voluntary, to South Vietnam if the United States government requested. Such a proposal surprised Kennedy, and both leaders agreed that they would consider the proposal at a later date.[44] We can validate, then, that South Korea had a more positive view of sending South Korean troops to South Vietnam than the United States. This is one of the reasons why the U.S. government selected South Korea as an ally during the Vietnam War.

Taiwan was the other promising candidate for fighting the Vietnam War. Generalissimo Chiang Kai-Shek was as positive as the South Korean leaders about sending troops to South Vietnam. He regarded the escalation of the Vietnam War as an opportunity for him to recover mainland China from the communists. The U.S. government, however, did not want to take the risk of escalating the Vietnam War into a Chinese civil war between the nationalists and communists. The United States, in fact, was very cautious about Taiwanese engagement in the Vietnam War.[45] This was one of the reasons why the U.S. selected South Korea as a member of the alliance fighting the Vietnam War. However, it is arguable that South Korean military involvement in the Vietnam War was mostly a product of South Korean policy makers taking advantage of the escalating cold war.

The motivation behind President Park when he decided to dispatch South Korean troops to South Vietnam, however, was not exclusively economic. It is a fact that South Korea received enormous economic gains from sending its military to South Vietnam, but the motivation in Vietnam involvement was militaristic as well as economic. South Korea sent troops to South Vietnam in order to prevent the United States from reducing its military in Korea. However, since South Korea gained more economically than other countries by sending its military troops to South Vietnam, one could argue that South Korea secured its economy by paying the cost of dispatching its military troops and fighting in the Vietnam War.[46]

CONCLUSION

The cold war constrained South Korea under United States hegemony and promoted the adoption of export-oriented industrialization by creating conditions under which the inward-looking deepening strategy failed. However, the Park Chung Hee regime succeeded in implementing the export-oriented industrialization by skillfully taking advantage of the cold war. It is true that the South Korean economy developed "in spite of" the cold war, but it is also true that the development of the South Korean economy was achieved "due to" the cold war. With respect to the relationship between the cold war and South Korean national interest, we can see the following double-edged aspects.

On the one hand, initially the Park Chung Hee regime did not possess autonomy nor were they capable enough to carry out an autarkic, inward-looking deepening strategy and overcome the constraints posed by the cold war. On the other hand, the Park Chung Hee regime exhibited the flexibility and capability to take advantage of the limitations posed by the cold war to carry out the export-oriented industrialization plan. In sum, President Park achieved the Republic of Korea's national interest in the form of economic development by viewing the cold war as a given and available resource.

As long as the cold war continued, South Korea could balance its national interests between these two poles. The escalation of the cold war while the Vietnam War heated up in 1960s, in fact, appeared to guarantee the continuation of this strategic balance. However, U.S.-China rapprochement in the early 1970s transformed the cold war in Northeast Asia. Because the United States-China confrontation was the main cause of the regional cold war in the 1960s, such rapprochement could not fail to influence neighboring countries such as

South and North Korea. The Park Regime responded to U.S.-China rapprochement by revising the constitution, installing the much more authoritarian Yusin regime, and promoting the Heavy and Chemical Industrialization (HCI) Program. In this new international environment, Park Chung Hee thought he could maintain balance by defining the national interest as being "relatively" more autonomous from the United States. This resulted in the installation of the Yusin authoritarian regime and the more autarkic HCI Program that included South Korea's construction of its own defense industries.

NOTES

1. For one of the most systematic analyses concerning the relationship between the cold war and South Korean economic development see Bruce Cumings, "The Origins and Development of the Northeast Asian Political Economy," 1–40.

2. Bella Balassa, *The New Industrializing Countries in the World Economy*.

3. Raul Prebisch, *Change and Development, Latin America's Great Task*.

4. Concerning the term, see Kimiya Tadashi, *Pak Chŏnghŭi chŏngbu ŭi sŏnt'aek*, 49–74.

5. Yu Wŏnsik, 5.16 *pirok: hyŏngmyŏng ŭn ŏdiro kanna*; Pak Hŭibŏm, *Han'guk kyŏngje sŏngjang ron*.

6. Kukka Chaegŏn Ch'oego Hoeŭi Chŏnghap Kyŏngje Chaegŏn Wiwŏnhoe, *Chŏnghap kyŏngje chaegŏn kyehoek*.

7. Telegram from American Embassy in Seoul to the Secretary of State, 1528 (May 16, 1961), National Security Files, Country File, Korea, Box 128, John F. Kennedy (JFK) Library, Boston, MA.

8. Telegram from the Acting Secretary of State to American Embassy in Seoul, 1316, (May 16,1961), National Security Files, Country File, Korea, Box 128, JFK Library, Boston, MA; Kim, Chŏnggi, "Kŭregori Hendŏsŭn ŭi hoego."

9. Telegram from American Embassy in Seoul to the Secretary of State, 1545 (May 17, 1961), 1569 (May 18, 1961), 1570 (May 18, 1961) and Telegram from Magruder to Lemnitzer, JSC, May 17, 1961, National Security Files, Country File, Korea, Box 128, JFK Library, Boston, MA.

10. Cho Yongjung, "Tak'yument'ari: kukka chaegŏn ch'oego hoeŭi"; Telegram from the Secretary of State to American Embassy in Seoul, 222 (August 5,1961), National Security Files, Country File, Korea, Box 128, JFK Library, Boston, MA.

11. "Park Briefing Book," National Security Files, Country File, Korea, Box 128, JFK Library, Boston, MA.

12. Presidential Task Force on Korea, "Report to the National Security Council,"

June 5, 1961, National Security Files, Country File, Korea, Box 127, JFK Library, Boston, MA.

13. Memorandum of Conversation, "ROK Government Economic Planning," November 16, 1961, National Security Files, Country File, Korea, Box 128, JFK Library, Boston, MA.

14. Concerning the planning process of the currency conversion, see the following memoirs. Yu Wŏnsik, 5.16 pirok; Ch'ŏn Pyŏnggyu, Ch'ŏnma ch'owŏn e nolda; Chung-Yum Kim, Policymaking on the Front Lines.

15. Telegram from American Embassy in Seoul to the Secretary of State, 1246 (June 8, 1962) and Telegram from the Secretary of State to American Embassy in Seoul (June 27, 1961), "Joint State/AID Message for Berger and Killen," National Security Files, Country File, Korea, Box 128, JFK Library, Boston, MA.

16. Yi Pyŏngch'ŏl, Hoam chajŏn, 128–30.

17. Pak Ch'unghun, Idang hoegorok, 176.

18. "Oeja toip ilch'a min'gan kyosŏpdan onŭl ch'ulbal " [The first mission of the private companies introducing foreign direct investments departs today], Tonga ilbo, February 8, 1962.

19. Concerning the role of the Van Fleet Mission, See Chunghwahak Kongŏp Ch'ujin Wiwŏnhoe Kihoektan, Han'guk kongŏp palchŏn e kwanhan chosa yŏn'gu 3, 28–33.

20. William H. Bruebeck, "Memorandum for Mr. MacGeorge Bundy, The White House, 'Accomplishments of American Investment Group Headed by General Van Fleet in Korea,'" (June 19, 1962), National Security Files, Country File, Korea, Box 127, JFK Library, Boston, MA.

21. Taehan Min'guk Chŏngbu, Kyŏngje Kihoegwŏn, Che-il ch'a kyŏngje kaebal o kaenyŏn kyehoek powan kyehoek.

22. U.S. Department of State, "Chapter 7, Part F, Korea," Administrative History of State Department, Lyndon B. Johnson (LBJ) Library, Austin, Texas; U.S. Congress, U.S. House of Representatives Investigation of Korean-American Relations, 166.

23. Telegram from American Embassy in Seoul to the Secretary of State, 504 (January 18, 1963), 528 (January 27, 1963), 538 (January 30, 1963), National Security Files, Country File, Korea, Box 129, JFK Library, Boston, MA.

24. Taehan Min'guk Chŏngbu, Kyŏngje Kihoegwŏn, Che-il ch'a kyŏngje kaebal o kaenyŏn kyehoek powan kyehoek.

25. In South Korea, the Rhee Line was called the "Peace Line" (p'yŏnghwasŏn).

26. Concerning the ROK-Japan normalization process, see Kimiya Tadashi, Pak Chŏnghŭi chŏngbu ŭi sŏnt'aek, 270–94; Yi Wŏndŏk, Han-Il kwagŏsa chŏri ŭi wŏnchŏm; and Ōta Osamu, Nikkan kōshō: seikyūken mondai no kenkyū.

27. Concerning triangle relations between the United States, South Korea, and Japan in the 1950s, see Ri Shōgen, Higashi Azia reisen to Kan-Bei-Nichi kankei.

28. Telegram from American Embassy in Seoul to the Secretary of State, 722 (November 17, 1961), National Security Files, Country File, Korea, Box 128, JFK Library, Boston, MA.

29. Telegram from the Secretary of State to American Embassy in Seoul and in Tokyo (July 13, 1962), National Security Files, Country File, Korea, Box 128, JFK Library, Boston, MA.

30. Telegram from American Embassy in Tokyo to the Secretary of State (July 26, 1962), Central File of the Department of State (Record Group 59), Decimal File, 694.95/7–2662, NARA (National Archives and Records Administration), College Park, Maryland.

31. The Department of State, "Normalization Agreement with Japan," Administrative History of State Department, LBJ Library, Austin, Texas.

32. Marshall Green, "Limited Hostilities in East Asia," January 27, 1960, National Security Files, Country File, Korea, Box 127, JFK Library, Boston, MA.

33. "232 Memorandum of Conversation, Washington DC, June 20, 1961, Subject Korea," Foreign Relations, 1961–1963, Volume XXII, Northeast Asia, Washington DC, U.S. Government Printing Office, 1996, 489–90.

34. Pae Ŭihwan, Porikkogae nŭn nŏmŏtchiman, 194.

35. Niinobe Akira, "Joyaku Teiketsu ni Itaru Katei."

36. "Kim pujang kwa Ilbon kowich'ŭng kwa ŭi hoedam" [The meeting of Kim Jong Pil, the director of the Korean Central Intelligence Agency, with high-ranking Japanese politicians], Taehan Min'guk Oemubu, oegyo munsŏ, tŭngnok pŏnho 796 [ROK Ministry of Foreign Affairs, diplomatic documents, registration no. 796], Kim Chongp'il t'ŭksa Ilbon pangmun, 1962, 10–11, [Kim Jong Pil's visit to Japan, October–November, 1962].

37. Concerning the argument in detail, see Kimiya Tadashi, Pak Chŏnghŭi chŏngbu ŭi sŏnt'aek, 270–94; Kimiya Tadashi, "1960-nendai kankoku ni okeru reisen gaiko no 3 ruikei.

38. Baku Konkō (Pak Kŭnho), Kankoku no keizai hatten to Betonamu sensō.

39. Concerning the comparison among the countries which were militarily involved in the Vietnam War, see Robert Blackburn, Mercenaries and Lyndon Johnson's "More Flags"; Kimiya Tadashi, Pak Chŏnghŭi chŏngbu ŭi sŏnt'aek, 323–28; Kimiya Tadashi, "Betonamu sensō to Betonamu tokuju."

40. Department of State, "Memorandum of Conversation between President Johnson and ROK President Park Chung Hee, U.S.-Korean Relations," May 17, 1965, National Security Files, Country File, Korea, Box 254, LBJ Library, Austin, Texas.

41. Chester L. Cooper and McBundy, "Memorandum for the President: Free World Assistance to South Vietnam," December 22, 1964, Declassified Documents Reference System (DDRS), Microfiche number, 1979–222B. DDRS is available through the Library Congress and other major university libraries in the USA.

42. Memorandum, "Discussion at the 185th Meetings of the National Security Council," DDRS, Microfiche number, 1985–1807; "Attachment: Political Aspects of Proposed ROK Offer of Troops to Laos Prepared by DOS, February 18, 1954," DDRS, Microfiche number, 1984–1803.

43. Joint Chiefs Staff (JCS), "Memorandum for the Secretary of Defense, Consideration of the ROK Offer to send a Division to Indochina, March 1, 1954," DDRS, Microfiche number, 1984–1576; National Security Council (NSC), "Minutes of the 187th Meetings of the NSC, Record of Actions by the NSC at its 187th Meetings, March 4, 1954," DDRS, Microfiche number, 1985–1911."

44. "Memorandum of Conversation, U.S.-Korean Relations, November 14,1961," "Memorandum of Conversation, Farewell Call of Chairman Park on President Kennedy, November 15, 1961," National Security Files, Country File, Korea, Park Visit, Box 128, JFK Library, Boston, MA.; "Message from CINCPAC to JCS: Possible Use of GRC and/ or ROK Troops in SVN, November 26–28,1961," National Security Files, Country File, Vietnam, Box 195, JFK Library, Boston, MA.

45. U.S. Department of State, "Use of ROK and GRC Military Forces Outside Their Homelands, February 4, 1965," Papers of James C. Thomson, Box 18, Far East: Baguio Conference, Baguio II, March 1965, Background Material (A), JFK Library, Boston, MA.

46. Kimiya Tadashi, Pak Chŏnghŭi chŏngbu ŭi sŏnt'aek, 295–330; Kimiya Tadashi, "1960-nendai kankoku ni okeru reisen gaiko no 3 ruikei."

SPECIAL ESSAY

4

How to Think about the Park Chung Hee Era

NAK-CHUNG PAIK

I found the invitation to provide a chapter in this volume too great an honor to resist, but I have many times since then regretted not having resisted it. Not only do I lack the expertise for reassessing the Park era, but I have not done—and have to this day shamefully failed to do—even an educated layman's readings on the subject. My title, "How to Think about the Park Chung Hee Era," reflects my painful sense of this predicament. I make no pretensions to tell you *what* to think of the era. I propose only to raise a few points regarding *how* we ought to go about the job. So please have patience with my very unscholarly performance, by taking it largely as a free-ranging essay by a literary man.

The "Park era" is not the same thing as Park Chung Hee himself, but feelings about the man inevitably play a large role in any assessment of the era. As is well known, feelings in South Korea today are quite divided, and, indeed, passionately so. Many of the people who went through that era dominated by that man still remain alive and active. They include both those who on the one hand either took an active part in his rule, or otherwise benefited from it and came to possess strongly vested interests, and on the other hand, the victims of that rule who suffered torture, imprisonment, enforced poverty or other deprivations of their rights, and the families and close friends of those so persecuted or even sent to their death.

Neither side would be the best qualified source for a dispassionate account. However, while any reassessment after twenty-five years should be as dispassionate as possible, I would like to stress, as an initial point of "how to think about the Park era," that no scholarly account would be adequate unless the scholar paid attention to these living voices, particularly those of the victims, for their voices were for a long time actively suppressed and, even when audible at last, would not easily translate into the "objective data" scholars prefer to deal with. Yet a serene disregard of their suffering as "collateral damage" in any march to modernization would not only be infuriating to those who had suffered, but would, in all probability, negatively affect the quality of the scholarly work in question.

Mine is hardly an instance of more savage persecution, but I will begin by telling you a little about it. I do so not to claim any intimate knowledge, much less to advertise such vicissitudes that I went through, but to let you know from what vantage point and out of what experience I am speaking. For I could make the second point, or suggestion, regarding "how to think": that each person should try to be as clear-eyed and candid as possible about his or her "subject position." Park's May 16, 1961, coup d'état took place when I was twenty-three, and I was forty-one at the time of his assassination. I had the first of many personal encounters with the regime's repressive apparatus when I was briefly detained for interrogation by the KCIA in 1965 for criticizing the government's jailing of the novelist Nam Chŏnghyŏn for writing an anti-American story. Such detentions, or "voluntary accompaniments" (imŭi tonghaeng) as they were officially called, grew more frequent after Park's second coup d'état, the event that virtually made him a lifetime president.

In 1974, I was expelled from my university post by the Ministry of Education for signing a petition for a democratic constitution, and managed to return only during "the Seoul Spring" (1980) following Park's assassination twenty-five years ago. During 1977–8 I was tried and convicted for publishing a "pro-communist book," a collection of reports on China written by Western and Japanese scholars and journalists compiled by my distinguished fellow dissident, Yi Yŏnghŭi. The publishing house Ch'angbi and its quarterly journal, Ch'angjak kwa pipy'ŏng (roughly translated as Creation and Criticism), went through other tribulations, including many suppressions and confiscations of published material, and the imprisonment of important contributors like Professor Yi and the poet, Kim Chiha. Neither the journal nor the publishing house, however, was shut down during the Park era: these shutdowns occurred under General Chun Doo Hwan (Chŏn Tuhwan) and the journal remained closed from 1980 to 1988 (i.e., until after the fall of the "Fifth Republic," following the massive popular resistance of June 1987). But all through these years I was never actually imprisoned, being given a suspended sentence even when formally tried and convicted. Nor was I ever physically tortured (with the exception of sleep deprivation, which should and does represent a form of torture). This probably accounts for the relative lack of rancor, or due intensity, depending on how you look at it, with which I speak of those years.

From such a vantage point or "subject position," then, I can say outright that I am proud of the achievements of South Korea's democracy movement, and that those achievements do not concern only the fields of human rights and democratic values in a narrow sense, but include long-term contributions to economic development as well. I shall come back to this later. I must admit, however, that the economy, generally agreed upon as marking the strong side of the Park era and Park Chung Hee himself, tended to be neglected by the democracy movement. While the democratic critics took a commendable lead in advocating labor rights and pollution control, exposing corruption, and denouncing what would later come to be termed "crony capitalism," they hardly offered a realistic alternative regarding how to develop South Korea's economy.

Most of the dissidents were hostile to Park's industrializing drive because of the repression involved, and many in the literary world were opposed because of the wanton destruction of native, mostly agrarian traditions. Such traditions represented no negligible concern, yet they had insufficient answers to the problems of coping with modernity or even Park's version of modernization. At the same time, the more radical sector of the democracy movement, influenced by Marxist and dependency theories, rejected the model of export-led growth, which drew on a large amount of foreign capital and advocated instead a more "self-reliant" (though not autarchic) development. In retrospect, however, there seems little doubt that Park's choice reflected a more realistic appraisal of the possibilities actually offered by the given conjuncture of the capitalist world-system and South Korea's standing within it.

All in all, the democratic movement at the time, and for a good while afterwards, did not give sufficient recognition to the extraordinary achievements of South Korea's economy in the Park era, nor to the record of Park Chung Hee as the competent, if high-handed and even cruel, CEO of "Korea Inc." But such recognition by itself, even coming from a former dissident, would not carry us far. It has by now become a platitude to say that, while

Park must be condemned as a dictator and gross violator of human rights, he deserves praise for leading the country out of poverty and building a strong, industrialized nation. How do we go beyond this all too facile "striking of balance" and particularize the manner in which the two contrasting appraisals are to be combined, specify the precise weight to be given to each, and determine the actual relationship between the two aspects? I certainly do not have a satisfactory answer. I shall only offer a suggestion, which would be my third point regarding "how to think about the Park era"; we should ask ourselves how those questions relate to our own contemporary agendas. For related to them they inevitably are, whether we realize it or not.

Here, then, are my agendas for this essay, which I shall indicate without trying to argue or validate them. First of all, I believe that despite some radical ecologists who reject economic development as such, South Korea needs to maintain a certain momentum of growth—not, indeed, to catch up with the richest nations, but in a spirit of self-defense within a world-system in which to stand still is to fall behind, and to start falling behind could easily mean to fall down for good and expose oneself to endless injustices and degradations. Our aim instead should be to avoid this fate so as, first of all, to preserve the democratic values we have so arduously achieved, and also to ensure ourselves some active role in reintegrating the Korean peninsula and building a better society than the division system now in force. This agenda calls not only for due acknowledgment of the economic growth that took place under Park, but for a serious study of what may still be viable in his economic strategies and how these may be combined with values that he contravened, namely, democracy and reunification.

I believe, moreover, that the new economic model needs to be eco-friendly as never before. Not only has environmental destruction reached a far more dangerous level throughout the globe since the Park's time, it has entered an entirely new, potentially terminal phase with the rapid industrialization of the entirety of East Asia, particularly China with its enormous size and population. If China's economic growth emulates the basic pattern set by Japan and adapted for latecomers by South Korea, as it threatens to do despite its professions of "socialism with Chinese characteristics," the earth as we have known it may well be given up for lost. For the sake of the whole of humankind as well as for their own well-being, Koreans must devise, or at least must begin to do so in tandem with the reunification process and with the creation of a wider framework for regional cooperation, a new economic paradigm radically different from the Park era (or any subsequent periods thus far). They must do so without disregarding or denigrating in the name of ecology the real needs of the people for development.

With these agendas in mind, I alluded in a recent newspaper column[1] to Park Chung Hee's "meritorious service in unsustainable development." Meritorious because, after all, not every dictator manages to deliver economic growth, and few indeed encourage such dramatic growth as in the South Korea of the Park era. But development along his way was unsustainable in a double sense. First, the Bruntland Report's notion of "a form of sustainable development which meets the needs of the present without compromising the ability of future generations to meet their own needs" may be debatable and open to various interpretations; there can be no doubt that Park's version, with its militarist ethos and unabashed environmental destruction, represented almost the diametric opposite of any "sustainable development." Secondly, and closer to home, that version was unsustainable in the sense that it could not go on for long, regardless of the meaning one gives to "sustainability."

To begin with, the Park Chung administration based its rule on military dictatorship in a society with strong traditions of civilian rule (decidedly more so than in Japan) and considerable popular aspirations for democracy, about which Bruce Cumings gives a compact and accessible account.[2] Thus, even apart from Park's shady personal past (running the gamut of pro-Japanese collaboration, communist ties, and betrayal of his communist colleagues in the army, and later, two coups d'état, the second of which abolished the constitution he had written after his first), Park's hold on power was inherently unstable and had to be buttressed by economic success. But ironically, this very success ultimately further threatened his power, for his slogan "Let's live well" (Chal sara pose)—meaning "let's live for once like the well-fed and well-clothed"—in essence represented the philosophy of a beggar, and people once out of poverty usually wish to live not by bread alone.

Anti-communism, which Park, perhaps to allay American suspicions of his past communist affiliations, elevated to "the first of national principles," was also an equivocal asset, given a divided nation of a long-shared history and strong, popular yearnings for reunification. Probably the single act of Park's rule that created the most spontaneous nationwide rejoicing was the July 4,

1972 joint communiqué by the two Koreas. What Park did, of course, was immediately to use it as a stepping stone to his second coup in October of the same year, turning the developmental state of the comparatively restrained authoritarianism of his earlier phase into something close to that of the private estate of an autocrat in the later "Yusin" phase.

Still, anti-communism in combination with economic growth served him well, so long as it was reinforced by the global conjuncture. While the East-West cold war would not come to an end for another decade after his death, already in the 1970s ideological confrontation decisively weakened, above all in East Asia, with America's (and subsequently Japan's) opening of diplomatic relations with China. It was as a defensive measure against these wider currents that the Yusin Constitution was promulgated. The defense did work for a time, in the sense that it shielded his presidency and CEO-ship from any more electoral challenges and allowed the economy to continue to perform strongly, at least through the mid-1970s. But the last years of the Park era saw increasing, almost endless domestic turmoil and international tension (not least with the United States). We all know how it ended.

Unsustainable as the whole thing was, however, it is on the basis of the growth and accumulation achieved through it that we can now contemplate a more sustainable, or at any rate less unsustainable, form of development. But what was the precise role of Park's democratic critics in it? Aside from the unquestionable contribution they made to winning democratic rights and institutions, did they only throw rocks and yell slogans while President Park and his followers were slaving to bring a good life to them, as is averred by some latter-day advocates of Park Chung Hee?

If a nation's economic development needs to go on for more than eighteen years—or say twenty-five, throwing in the brutal but still undoubtedly "developmental" dictatorship of Chun Doo Hwan—then those political critics who have worked to make it more sustainable must be given credit for economic contributions as well. During the 1970s, when South Korea's environmental movement made a cautious start in the name of "studying pollution problems," the very mention of industrial pollution would invite charges of siding with "the Reds." It was equally perilous to insist on minimal labor rights or to try to expose the illicit dealings of a politically favored business enterprise. Under the emergency decrees (the last of which really became a permanent decree, remaining in force from 1975 through the end of the Park era), even the mention of any violation of any one of the decrees would constitute a violation of an emergency decree. If such a state of affairs had gone unchallenged, not only would there have been no democracy, but economic development itself could well have become even less sustainable, resulting in a prolonged stagnation or decline as in many state-socialist countries, or being replaced by a fundamentalist religious alternative as in the Islamic Revolution of Iran.

Participants and inheritors of the democratic struggle in South Korea, therefore, have every reason to be proud of their input in the performance of the South Korean economy over the past quarter-century, and they need not be chary about acknowledging Park's "meritorious service" for the ambiguous yet undeniable thing that it is. Such acknowledgment is also necessary precisely in order to overcome the "Park Chung Hee nostalgia" of our day, which threatens not only the immediately pending democratic reforms, but also the larger task of creating a new paradigm of truly sustainable—or life-sustaining, as I prefer to put it—development.

That nostalgia, indeed, betokens the worst legacies of the Park era: its indifference to basic rights (including the rights of entrepreneurs to run their business without arbitrary government interference), insensitivity to human suffering, and ignorance of any individual or communal aspirations larger than the beggar's philosophy of "Let's live well." But these legacies will continue to exercise their pathological influence until the Park era has been adequately assessed and Park Chung Hee, too, has been given his due. Yet how to give him no more nor less than his due, and how to assess that crucial era in our modern history, are tasks that I leave to those more knowledgeable than I, many of whom, I know, are participating in this very volume.

NOTES

1. *Chungang ilbo*, August 12, 2004, 35.

2. See Bruce Cumings, *Korea's Place in the Sun*, Chapter 7, "The Virtues, II: The Democratic Movement, 1960–1996."

PART TWO—Political Thought,

Democracy, and Labor

5

Park Chung Hee's Governing Ideas:
Impact on National Consciousness and Identity

YOUNG JAK KIM

There is a good deal of research on the political leadership and ruling ideas of President Park Chung Hee (Pak Chŏnghŭi). Evaluations of him and his era are not only numerous but also diverse. Research on Park can be classified into two basic types: that which discusses the political nature of Park's rule in relation to democracy and authoritarianism and that which focuses on the rapid modernization and economic advancement of South Korea. Politically focused research generally depicts Park as an undemocratic authoritarian or even as a dictatorial leader and thereby negates and discredits Park's role in Korea's economic achievements. Research focused on modernization and development generally praises his leadership and characterizes him as a practical leader who successfully achieved the difficult task of modernization. This second type of research tends to be indulgent toward Park's authoritarianism as an "unavoidable cost." Each type of research seems to have its own validity, yet each alone is incomplete for assessing Park Chung Hee and his era.

Surprisingly, very few studies to date have focused on the structural characteristics of Park's governing ideals or have taken into account national consciousness and his feelings toward national identity—the core of his political philosophy. It is precisely these ideals and their impact on Park's political leadership and governing beliefs in modernization, democracy, and human rights that I propose to investigate in an attempt to draw a comprehensive understanding of the structural characteristics of his governing ideas. In spite of the tendency of previous politically focused research, I would propose a positive assessment of Park Chung Hee's governing ideas and practices.

THE PHASE OF "NATIONAL CONSCIOUSNESS"
IN PARK'S POLITICAL IDEOLOGY

Let me begin my analysis on President Park's political ideology by examining the purposes of his military revolution. The Revolutionary Pledge (*hyŏngmyŏng kongyak*) of the Supreme Council for National Reconstruction (*Kukka Chaegŏn Ch'oego Hoeŭi*), which took over in a military coup on May 16, 1961, can be a beginning point for understanding and analyzing, at least, the subjective intentions of the revolution. After taking power on that day, the revolutionary committee declared:

> In order to rescue the fatherland from extreme danger, the military has finally unleashed a serious of actions and assumed the administrative, legislative, and judicial powers of the state completely and has organized a military committee.[1]

They called it the "revolution for national salvation" (*kuguk hyŏngmyŏng*) or the "revolution for national reconstruction" (*chaegŏn hyŏngmyŏng*) and justified it by saying that it came in time to save the nation from collapsing.

"Nation" (*kukka*) and "national" (*minjok*) were key words in Park's political mission. The official name of the military government was the Supreme Council for National Reconstruction (*kukka chaegŏn*), and Park stressed the importance of nationalism in almost every statement he made. "We should concentrate all our energy on eliminating old evils, thereby promoting 'national morality' (*kungmin toŭi*) and national spirit, improving national life (*kungmin saenghwal*) in social, economic, and all other fields, thereby blocking Communist attempts at aggression and constructing a genuine welfare state."[2] Park's political ideals were so imbued with national consciousness and identity that he should be defined first and foremost as a nationalist and his political ideals and values should be placed within the framework of his nationalism-oriented political ideology. Despite the fact that he had served as a Japanese military officer during the colonial period and that he had once been close to the South Korean Labor Party during the early period of his military service in the Republic of Korea (ROK) Army, he was definitely a nationalist and strong anti-communist throughout his presidency.

It is noteworthy that Park never rejected the values of democracy, such as political freedom or economic equality, when he emphasized "national salvation" (national right to survival) or "national reconstruction." Rather, he identified those democratic values, at least in principle, as the ultimate goals of the "revolution for national survival," especially in the early stage of the revolution.

> The May 16 revolution is carried out in order to save this nation—and enable all our people to enjoy freedom, equality, and prosperity in the political, economic, social, cultural, and all other fields by reconstructing genuine democracy.[3]

This was, of course, an excuse for operating the Revolutionary Tribunal, a court through which many of the old civilian politicians were punished. However, this statement also implied that instead of rejecting the values of liberal democracy, Park regarded them as values to be pursued and restored. He considered them important but inferior in value compared to those of national independence and economic development.

"It would show an example of a newly emerging country, sloughing off subjugation and stagnation and successfully attaining political independence and economic self-sufficiency. It would thus prove that democracy is more instrumental than communism in efficient economic development."[4] In the previous sentence, Park indicated the superiority of democracy over communism, and that democracy is needed for other national goals. We will see, however, that strengthening the nation required restricting liberal democracy and when this happened it threatened the harmony between both nationalism and economic development and democracy.

A HIERARCHICAL ARRANGEMENT OF NATIONAL GOALS

President Park's political ideology and governing leadership can also be characterized by the fact that he arranged national goals in hierarchical order, with some more urgent than others, in regard to the nation's circumstances and limited capabilities. When he stressed the necessity of achieving national reconstruction, for example, Park also mentioned national goals such as modernization of the fatherland (choguk kŭndaehwa), economic development, the security of the nation (i.e., blocking communist aggression from the

North), recovery of genuine democracy (*chinjŏnghan minjujuŭi ŭi hoebok*), constructing a welfare state (*pokchi sahoe*), and reunification of the fatherland (*choguk t'ongil*). He never mentioned these goals as being equally important or urgent, but rather prioritized them in order of importance to South Korea's internal situation and external circumstances. During the 1960s President Park proclaimed:

> The sound development of democracy and the cultivation of our national strength for victory over communism, all depends on the success or failure in our economic constructions.[5] If the way to unification lies in the modernization of our fatherland, and if the way to modernization lies in the achievement of a self-sustaining economy, it follows that a self-sustaining economy is the first stage toward unification.[6]

He continued the same sort of statements in the 1970s:

> National strength is based on the nation's economic strength. The fundamental element for self-reliant national defense and in laying the foundation for unification is the national potential to achieve a completely self-sufficient economy.[7]

Park himself defined the priority of politics as follows:

> The priority of politics in a developing country such as Korea should be placed, above all, on economic construction. It is the fundamental condition for the growth of democracy in a developing country to achieve economic construction first to the extent where people are freed from worry about dietary life and clothing.[8]

It is quite clear that Park always kept a strategic way of thinking and arranged various national goals in hierarchical order: (1) promoting economic development (or modernization) and freedom from poverty (basic welfare) and strengthening of national power, (2) preserving national security, (3) reconstructing genuine democracy, and (4) achieving reunification.[9] According to Park, economic construction itself was an instrument for achieving other national goals, such as national security, democracy, and unification. He also believed that economic construction was a shortcut to victory over North Korea whether in a military clash or in an ideological competition for the prosperity and welfare of the people. Having mentioned above already well-known facts, I would like to point out that the conflict between Park and his political opponents was not merely a simple antagonism between "a military (authoritarian) dictator" versus "democrats," but rather a more complicated collision of different views on prioritizing national goals and setting strategies for achieving them.

Park's opponents, including liberal intellectuals and students, for example, always regarded genuine democracy as a prime goal of politics and accordingly asserted that had genuine democracy been recovered, the economic development together with national security could have more rapidly and effectively followed. President Park, by contrast, viewed it differently. He believed that such assertions were irresponsible and illusory. He especially rejected the "emotional approach" to unification shown by some politicians and intellectuals who advocated contacts with the North at a time when the North was still sending armed agents and commandos to the South.[10]

The above dispute leads us to partially discredit the existing theory that has evaluated Park and his opponents only from a limited perspective of liberal democracy and to extract a broader perspective of evaluating politicians and their political governance, not to mention Park's economic achievements. In order to evaluate Park and his opponents at the time, one should find out whose perception of the situation and circumstances conformed more to the reality of the time.

THE ANTAGONISM BETWEEN NATIONALISM AND DEMOCRACY

Different from his views in the early 1960s, when Park regarded liberal democracy as an ideology to be recovered, in the beginning of the 1970s he argued for an antagonism between liberal democracy and other national goals. At this time he rejected democracy and argued directly for the ch'onghwa system of total harmony (a type of corporatism) that would create the national unity and integration necessary for Yusin (national restoration or revitalization). This change in attitude was closely related to Park's perception of the internal situation, which was, in part, a natural by-product of his political ideology and practices and partly a product of the external circumstances.

The declaration of a state of emergency in 1972, then, actually meant the denunciation of liberal democracy that Park Chung Hee came to perceive as a political system of inefficiency and disorder. He argued, "Disorder and inefficiency are still widespread around us and political circles are beset with wrangling and discord."[11] He visualized liberal democracy as a vulnerable political system, one that he believed to have been proven unfit for the realities of Koreans achieving South Korea's national goals. As a politician who was goal oriented and tenaciously obsessed by the commitment to making South Korea great, he called for total dedication to this goal, putting aside the procedural formalities of liberal democracy. These means and procedures of liberal democracy, he felt, could be dispensed with as long as the people were included in a political system that served the purpose of attaining the grand goals of the corporatist nation. In other words, to him, "government *for* the people" was much more important than "government *by* the people."

By saying that "each and every citizen is called upon to take a square look at the stark reality facing the nation, focus thought and action on solidifying national security . . . "[12] Park implied that disputes about the political system of total harmony (ch'onghwa) would prove nothing but acts of politicking and political trickery. He believed that the system of general harmony was meaningful not only as a political system per se, but also as a means to achieving national integration. In spite of his efforts to build a corporatist system, radical demonstrations and party strife swept over the political scene. One presidential contender even went so far as to make such demands as the reduction of the standing army and the abolition of the Homeland Reserve Forces (hyangt'o yebigun). Park saw these demands as irresponsible, coming from his opponent's rash and illusory cravings for unification.

When Park declared a state of emergency in 1971, he put it thus: "We can no longer waste national energy simply to copy democracy."[13] "Yusin reforms afford us the last chance to 'indigenize democracy' (minjujuŭi ŭi t'och'akhwa) in Korea and pave the way for ourselves."[14] From that moment on, Park never hesitated to announce, when there was a chance, his view and belief that the national right to survival must be protected first in order to protect human rights. Choosing between individual human rights and the national right to survival was a matter of time and circumstances, not a matter of general theory. Park thus claimed: "Like others, we also want to enjoy all freedom, to do whatever we like to, and to maintain our freedom. If we could do all these, how nice it would be. But I regret to say that this is a fancy dream of a romanticist, who knows nothing about how things are going around him."[15]

His views on freedom and beliefs in democracy would be best expressed in the following rationale: "In order to protect 'big freedom,' we must have the wisdom of sacrificing and restraining 'small freedom' for a while. If not, we would be deprived of 'big freedom.'"[16] By big freedom, Park meant the freedom of a nation, and by small freedom, he meant the freedom of individuals. He continued to assert that sacrificing small freedoms for the sake of the big freedom is much better than zero human rights which is no freedom at all under communist rule. "There is and must be," he insisted, "a difference between countries in the degree of freedom which should be allowed and which should be restricted, according to the situation, the historical situation and environment, and the special social condition of each country."[17] Park's nationalistic tendency and his emphasis on the collective freedom of the nation were accelerated by the collapse of South Vietnam and Cambodia. After the fall of these two countries, he warned protesters opposing him.

I would like to know what freedom those Vietnamese and Cambodians who accused their governments of oppressing freedom and democracy before the fall of their countries are enjoying now. In [South] Vietnam and Cambodia today, basic human rights are totally denied and hundreds of thousands of innocent people are [sic] massacred.[18]

To him, liberal democracy was not only ineffective in achieving economic development but also made the nation vulnerable to subversion. Park indirectly but candidly admitted that he was negating liberal democracy when he asserted the following:

The national right to survival is an inviolable *natural right*—and the supreme value orientation of our society today is for national survival and national defense. *Only when the survival of the 35 million people and the security of the Republic of Korea are guaranteed, can freedom of every citizen be promoted and democracy developed. It is nonsense to talk about freedom and democracy without such a guarantee.* To guarantee the survival of the 35 million people is to protect human rights in the best way in this society.[19]

This does not necessarily mean, however, that Park was negating all kinds of individual freedoms and human rights in general. To him, just like the democracy problem, the problem of freedom and human rights was a matter of time and circumstance. In fact, there are various kinds of freedoms and individual human rights among which the priorities should be given according to the situation. For example, out of Franklin D. Roosevelt's "Four freedoms,"[20] Park suppressed the "freedom of speech" and "freedom of political association and demonstration," but he endeavored to attain "freedom from want" and "freedom from fear" and said, "It is our solid aim to construct a society free from poverty and famine and from disease and illiteracy."[21] "Poverty, communism, and corruption are the great enemies of our society."[22]

The "human rights" President Park had in mind were to solve basic problems, such as the absence of food, housing, and clothing for all citizens. He claimed, "If modernization means better food, better clothing, and well-being only for a limited number of people, I would reject such modernization."[23] For such purposes, he reiterated calling on businessmen to "throw away the selfish idea of seeking your own interest only, without paying attention to wages and working conditions"[24] in the latter part of his rule. For him, with the lack of the basic human right to survive or to sustain a basic living, individual human rights such as "freedom of speech" and "freedom of association" were meaningless. Park depended on the haves—mainly big businessmen and entrepreneurs—achieving economic development in order to attain the basic human rights for the masses—the have-nots. Ironically, Park confronted strong resistance from the masses. Another difficult question to answer is whether the downfall of Park Chung Hee was a consequence of the failure of his economic development plan to sufficiently satisfy the masses, or if a corollary of his economic success created a "crisis of rising expectations" and toppled his government.

EVALUATION

The above analyses on Park's political ideology show that he was a nationalist rather than a democrat. He has been defined as an authoritarian leader. He could even be depicted as a dictator, as many people from a liberal democratic viewpoint have done. Accusing him of being a non-democratic politician is easy, and it is easier to condemn his measures to oppress individual human rights. There are grounds for these accusations and condemnations. Nevertheless, what should be further considered is whether liberal democracy should be the only basis or the supreme criterion for evaluating political leadership. Is there really no room for defending Park's views on democracy and the relationship between individual human rights and the national right to survival? Even when we criticize President Park for his defection from liberal democracy, the question of whether or not his governing ideas had anything to do with democracy in the broader sense remains to be examined. Quite clearly, he was not a democrat in terms of means and procedures of liberal democracy, namely "government by the people," but he might be classified as a democrat in the sense that his governing ideas and practices belonged to the "government for the people." He endeavored to attain positive freedoms such as "freedom from poverty," "freedom from disease," and "freedom from illiteracy," and succeeded in those cases. In this sense, Park's political ideology and practices, what he called "Korean democracy" or "indigenous democracy," can be defined as a "basic democracy" or a type of "guided democracy" which is very often found in the early stages of the third world modernization.

One way of defining politics or political leadership, I think, is that political leadership involves the art of arranging the order of various national goals and allocating the adequate means and resources to achieving these goals according to a nation's situation and capability. Furthermore, democracy could take different forms and the extent of individual freedoms could vary according to events and the state of affairs. If one admits the above political axioms, evaluations of Park's political ideology and leadership should be based on whether or not his arrangement of the hierarchy of national goals, which regarded economic development as a prime goal, was proper in view of the actual situation of the Republic of Korea at that particular time. In other words, how much of his political ideology and deeds defected from genuine liberal democracy and restricted the small freedoms—the negative freedoms of Isaiah Berlin?[25] How much of Park Chung Hee's ideology considered the "big freedom"—the national right to survival—the "positive freedoms" such as "freedom from poverty," to be more urgent? Could this be defended in view of the situation in South Korea at the time, and how much should be reproached even accounting for this special situation?

These questions may not be easily answered. However, raising these questions may be a start to reconsidering and reevaluating Park's political ideology and his leadership, which would lead us to overcoming the two extreme dogmatic views of him. As for me, I would like to dare say that Park, though he was authoritarian, should be defined as a patriotic nationalist and successful practical politician. I also dare to express my judgment that Park's political leadership was a very adequate one in the sense that his arrangement of hierarchical order of national goals was in fact appropriate considering the economically underdeveloped, socially disordered, politically turbulent, and externally threatened situation in South Korea up until the promulgation of the Yusin reform in October 1972.

To defeat the above "political axioms" on which my assertions are based, the opponents to my assertions should prove, through historical examples, the hypotheses that multiple national goals, which very often conflict with each other in developing countries, can be achieved all at once, and that if democracy comes first, other national goals such as national security, economic development, welfare of the people, and the unification of a divided country, can be achieved more effectively. Park, nevertheless, should be only partly defended in the case of the authoritarian Yusin system, because he carried his defection from liberal democracy and restriction of small freedoms too far and attempted to create a permanent presidency through a constitutional amendment.

The blame for this should be placed, of course, mainly on Park himself. But even in this case, it might be fair to say that partial responsibility lies with his political opponents neglecting internal and external situations. Park seemed to do this when he criticized "the educated ignorance" of the intellectuals and students who persisted in valuing Western liberal democracy and dreamed of a fancy unification, and South-North rapprochement through measures such as the abolition of the Homeland Reserve Forces founded in April 1968. Park and his opponents exploited each other's defects as being too "nationalistic" in the case of Park and too "liberal democratic" in case of his opponents. Between the two, a vicious circle of confrontation and repression emerged. The assassination of Park was the logical culmination of this process. The Republic of Korea had to wait ten more years, however, for the victory of the liberal democrats. The Korean people are now certainly living in an age of democracy and enjoying many more small freedoms. But I am not quite sure if we are under a more democratic leadership, in the true meaning of the word, with an appropriate arrangement of national goals and harmony of small (negative) freedoms and big (positive) freedom. This is an important question to be examined further in the future.

NOTES

Editorial note: In some instances the editors were unable to obtain full citations from the author due to the seriousness of his present illness.

1. "Proclamation by the Committee, May 16, 1961."

2. "Kungmin toŭi chaegŏn mit kungmin kyŏngje chaegŏn ŭl wihan chido inyŏm kwa silch'ŏn yogang" 213–20; see also the "Retirement from Active Service Ceremony and Address," August 30, 1963.

3. "Address at a Ceremony of the Revolutionary Tribunal," July 12, 1961.

4. Park Chung Hee, *Our Nation's Path: Ideology of Social Reconstruction*, 196–97.

5. Pak Chŏnghŭi, *Minjok ŭi chŏryŏk*, especially chap. 4 "Toyak ŭi 60-nyŏndae."

6. Taet'ongnyŏng Pisŏsil, "Sinnyŏn mesiji," *Pak Chŏnghŭi taet'ongnyŏng yŏnsŏl munjip* 3:17–20. Hereafter noted as PCHTY.

7. "Such'ul chinhŭng konggwanjang hoeŭi yusi," PCHTY 8:126–28. .

8. "New Year News Conference," 1972. The term, welfare state, that he used at that time meant the situation where the people are freed from the worry about basic needs. See PCHTY 9: 24–25.

9. The order of democracy and unification seems to have reversed in the 1970s. Ibid.

10. Park may have had in mind the many armed attacks when he emphasized threats from the North. They included: the North Korean commandos' attempt to infiltrate the Presidential Blue House (Ch'ŏngwadae) on January 21, 1968; the capture of the USS *Pueblo* on January 23, 1968; the hijacking of a KAL plane on December 1, 1969; tunnels discovered under the DMZ on November 15, 1974; and the attempt to assassinate President Park on August 15, 1974, which killed the first lady.

11. "Declaration of a State of Emergency," October 17, 1972. PCHTY 9:323.

12. "Message to Law-Enforcement Officers," January 21, 1972. PCHTY 9:71.

13. "Statement Announcing Draft Revision to Constitution," October 27, 1972, PCHTY, 9:334.

14. "UN Day Message," October 24, 1972, PCHTY 9: 328.

15. "Armed Forces Day Message," October 1, 1974, PCHTY 11:208.

16. Ibid.

17. "New Year Press Conference," June 14, 1975.

18. "Speech at Justice Ministry," February 4, 1977; also see "The Road to National Survival," 112.

19. "Speech at the Justice Ministry," February 4, 1977. Italics added.

20. As is well known, President Franklin D. Roosevelt's four freedoms were freedom of speech, freedom of worship, freedom from want, and freedom from fear.

21. "A Message to the North Korean People," October 3, 1961.

22. "Che 6-tae taet'ongnyŏng ch'uiimsa," PCHTY 4:279–83.

23. "Taet'ongnyŏng kija hoegyŏn," PCHTY 5:27–57.

24. "Che 13-hoe 'kŭlloja ŭi nal ch'isa," PCHTY 8:123–25.

25. Isaiah Berlin, *Two Concepts of Liberty*.

6

Democracy in South Korea: An Optimistic View of ROK Democratic Development[1]

JAMES B. PALAIS

INTRODUCTION: THE PESSIMISTIC VIEW
ON THE FUTURE OF SOUTH KOREAN DEMOCRACY

Most of the English literature on democratic development in South Korea is pessimistic. While almost all scholars agree that democracy has been achieved at the minimalist level, i.e., fair elections appear to have become the only method for choosing political leaders—the long-term prospects for "consolidated democracy" are suspect for a number of reasons. "Consolidation" requires the adoption of attitudes and values similar to those of Western democratic states that have endured over a period of two hundred years. The reasons presented for this pessimistic view consist of the following arguments:

Corruption

Because there is too much corruption among politicians and government officials, the public has either lost, or will lose, confidence in the political system. Moreover, state-capital (the chaebŏl) collusion in effect prevents democracy.

Bossism

The history of politicians and political parties shows the prevalence and endurance of leader-follower groups. The leaders take their followers in and out of parties, rendering parties unstable. This is another reason for growing disgust with politicians.

Parties focus on personalities rather than issues: Voters are either confused or disgusted because they are not presented with clear-cut policy differences and either have or will lose confidence in parties, and by extension, the democratic system.

Regionalism

The voters vote according to regions without caring what positions candidates from the region take on different issues.

Exclusion

Exclusion of groups like women, farmers, workers, and the poor and homeless from party membership and leadership, and failure of the parties to respond to the demands of those groups prevents "consolidation" of democracy. The ingrained, conservative force of Confucianism obstructs if not opposes democracy: This is seen most clearly in masculine prerogatives; discrimination against women; and favor for collectivism, tying the individual to the family or group, versus the individualism that is necessary for democratic politics. In this context, the ROK presidency is too powerful for healthy democracy.

Failure of ROK Presidents to Achieve Goals

The failure of recent presidents to achieve economic prosperity and democratic development has led to nostalgia for past dictators whom the public believes were more efficient than democratic presidents. Political progress toward "consolidated" democracy takes too long. Because democratic progress is slow, the public loses faith in the democratic system.

Before analyzing each of these propositions, however, it is necessary to consider the relationship between dictatorship and democratic development, particularly between Park Chung Hee's (Pak Chŏnghŭi) dictatorship and the growth of democratic forces during his regime.

Park Chung Hee and Democracy

One of the factors in the development of democracy in South Korea that has not been adequately appreciated is the importance of the struggle both against dictatorship and for democracy and human rights that took place from 1945 to 1987. South Korea did not become democratic (at least with respect to voting, elections, free speech, and association) in 1987 because the U.S. granted the model of a democratic constitution to the Koreans in 1948, or successfully chose democratic leaders in 1945. The U.S. was unable to find middle-of-the-road liberal democrats to provide political leadership in 1945. For that reason, it ended up supporting Rhee and right-wing anti-communists, many of whom had collaborated with the Japanese during the colonial period because in the cold war, U.S. presidents were more concerned about maintaining stability in South Korea against communist expansion than they were about promoting democratic procedures.

Syngman Rhee (Yi Sŭngman) manipulated the constitution, the electoral system, and the national assembly as a means of consolidating his power, and he corrupted the administration of justice to punish his political enemies. Yet some of the national assemblymen tried to pass decent laws under the terms of the constitution, and others—both in the assembly and outside in the world of newspapers and publishing—did their best to combat dictatorial methods. I witnessed some of those things when I was in the army in Korea in 1957 and 1958. When Park Chung Hee seized power in 1961 and established a military junta to rule the country for two years, he did not appear interested in re-establishing civil government, but the Kennedy administration pressured him to doff his military garb for civilian clothes and run for president. In the ensuing decade Park began a program to create an industrial and commercial country out of a traditionally agrarian one, and succeeded beyond anyone's imagination.

If he had been born in the Chosŏn Dynasty, he would have been counted as one of the greatest kings in Korean history, but he was born in the twentieth century under the aegis of U.S. hegemony, a United States. Which, with its allies in Britain and Russia, had just defeated the axis powers. He was tolerated by many in the U.S. government because he was succeeding in bringing Korea out of backwardness into modernity and was needed as a counterpoise to communism and an outer defense of Japan. But many in the

United States despised his despotic methods, and a lonely few in South Korea continued the fight against those methods. I witnessed some of those struggles when I worked on my Ph.D. dissertation at Seoul National University from 1963 to 1965, in particular the student demonstrations against normalization with Japan that culminated in the Normalization Treaty of 1965. During that era I met Chang Chunha, the publisher of *Sasanggye*, the leading independent journal of the time. My friend, Marshall Pihl, had been living in Chang's house for a number of years even before I arrived in Korea, and I watched as Chang disappeared from his home for months on end to escape the police.

I also watched as Park cracked down on student demonstrators, sending troops into the college campuses for the first time since 1945 to prevent students from organizing on campus; students lined up to march downtown in protest. I watched Park introduce new methods of interdicting students on the way to Kwanghwamun and the space in front of the Sich'ŏng (City Hall) by inventing the use of helmets, masks, and shields for police to block students, and recruiting army recruits as plain-clothes cops to spy on students. I heard about students dragged by police onto buses where they were beaten silly by the police lest the public see the police doing this on the streets. I read of students suffering torture under interrogation at Namdaemundae[2] and of some students turning up dead after a demonstration.

And I watched as the small group of intellectuals, professors, and honest opposition politicians protested against overwhelming odds, against the instruments of coercion wielded by Park. Even so, the system of elections established in 1963 miraculously showed that opposition politicians were able to increase their votes against Park's government party because the rural farmers from the countryside were migrating into Seoul and other towns, and experiencing the effects of social mobilization that increased their political consciousness. By 1971, Kim Dae Jung (Kim Taejung) was almost able to defeat Park. But Park had already decided to extend his presidency in 1967 beyond the two-term limit, and in 1971, he decided on amending the constitution to eliminate any serious possibility that he could be defeated at the polls. It appeared that the country had been on the verge of opening to democracy, but Park decided to close off the opportunity.

At first I thought he did it only to eliminate Kim Dae Jung from the political arena, but more recently it appears he was motivated by his fears that the

United States was withdrawing support for South Korea. He determined that it was necessary for him to protect the country by launching a major heavy industry and petrochemical project to provide the basis for major economic development and the beginnings of an arms industry. But his fears were probably unfounded. At the end of the 1970s, President Jimmy Carter tried to withdraw U.S. troops from South Korea to punish Park for his violations of human rights, but the forces in the United States, which continued to maintain support for Park despite his dismal human rights record in order to maintain political stability to defend South Korea from communism, were too powerful for Carter to overcome. Carter's failure only proved that Park's fear of U.S. abandonment was exaggerated.

Nonetheless, he established the Yusin dictatorship that was far more comprehensive than his regime in the 1960s; he stopped labor union activity altogether, put liberal politicians out of commission, banned academic critics from jobs in universities, and filled the jails with student protesters. All these tasks were achieved by the use, or by the threat, of force, but the objects of suppression bided their time until the opportunity for renewed struggle appeared again after the establishment of the Chun Doo Hwan (Chŏn Tuhwan) regime in 1980. Then the struggle emerged once again.

Democracy was gained by a long struggle against overwhelming odds, a struggle that culminated in 1987. Martyrs to freedom and democracy were created along the way, but the achievement of free elections and liberalization of the press and association was won by a heroic segment of the Korean people by their own effort. For the most part, the U.S. government supported dictators to maintain a stable status quo, occasionally intervening to save a prominent figure like Kim Dae Jung from death, but leaving hosts of lesser known protestors to languish in jail. Some have credited the middle class with achieving the democratic breakthrough, but the middle class does not deserve that much credit. The middle class remained quiescent throughout the period of struggle, joining the students, intellectuals, and professors only at the very last stage of protest. The students took the most risks, followed by workers, and then intellectuals, professors, and reporters behind them. Because of the efforts of such individuals and the suffering they endured for thirty years, the denouement of their struggle in democratic elections guarantees the kind of stability that cannot be gained in any other way.

WESTERN THEORETICAL MODELS—
FLAWS IN WESTERN EXPERIENCE

Much of the literature in English (and much in Korean as well) in the field of political science gives short shrift to the intensity of the struggle for democracy in South Korea, and instead takes Western models (both in theory and practice), as well as the "third-wave" of democratization in Eastern Europe and Latin America, as a basis for judging the quality and longevity of South Korean democracy. As a result there seems to be a tendency to demand that South Korean democracy converge with the Western theory of democracy or the perceived "consolidation" of Western democratic states. I am not a specialist in world politics, in U.S. politics, or in U.S. history. I did major in U.S. history so many years ago that I can hardly remember what I learned. Yet I read the *New York Times* every day. It strikes me that U.S. political history has revealed, and in many cases still does reveal, flaws in its democratic system that are quite similar to, and perhaps even worse than, problems that South Korea faces today. Let me list them.

Corruption

Corruption among political leaders, government officials, and police, exists in every state in the United States, perhaps in a matter of degree. In major U.S. urban areas it tends to be worse than in rural areas. Elections in the United States along with economic transactions have been vulnerable to corruption, such as paying men to vote, tampering with the ballot boxes, excluding minorities from voting, using the courts to interfere in elections, falsifying company books to hide indebtedness to obtain more loans, violating stock market rules by insider trading, and overcharging the government for services rendered. None of this seems to have led to pessimism about the high quality of American democracy.

Corruption was endemic in the Chosŏn Dynasty, and also in South Korea after 1945. One could ascribe this to the Confucian obligation of reciprocity, making gifts to someone who can do you a favor. Since 1987, however, there seems to be a visible increase in prosecutions for corruption by the Prosecutor's Office for people at the highest level of society: chaebŏl executives, politicians, and sons of presidents. Maybe the increased rate of prosecution will reduce the level of corruption, but even if it does not, corruption will not disappear from democratic politics. Democracies always have to deal with it.

Bossism

Bossism in U.S. history is quite similar to leader-follower (patron-client) relations in South Korean politics. The Tammany Hall crowd in New York City, Mayor Richard Daley in Chicago, James Curley in Boston, the Prendergast crowd in Kansas City, Missouri, and a number of others in other cities ran machines that controlled the votes of whole communities. Some of the votes were real, others fictional. The bosses stayed with parties rather than moving around from one to the other (except for the Teamsters in more recent times), but the boss system was anything but ideal with respect to democratic theory. One could say that the United States failed to "consolidate" democracy during that era, or that Korean bossism is simply one of the real flaws that occur in any democracy over time. One recent scholar in an article on Korean politics published in 2003 remarked that:

> Boss politics is still strong. Inter-party relationships are based and centered on such key personalities as Kim Dae Jung, Kim Jong Pil, and Lee Hoe Chang. Even former president Kim Young Sam formally returned to politics in July 1999. . . . With Kim Young Sam's return, the three Kims are all very influential as they had been in the previous four decades. . . . [I]t is quite certain that the legacies and effects of the politics of the three Kims will stalk and haunt the political future in Korea for a long time.[3]

In 2004, however, Kim Dae Jung was kicked out of his party's presidency and his party was left with only nine seats in the national assembly elections of 2004. Kim Dae Jung, Kim Young Sam (Kim Yŏngsam), and Yi Hoech'ang were disgraced by a number of things, including jail sentences for their sons. Kim Jong Pil's (Kim Chongp'il) party was eased out in the recent elections as well. Yi's party is now in the minority. The three Kims and Yi are now out of politics.

Regionalism

Almost all observers believe that regionalism in South Korea is antithetical to democratic politics, but there are mitigating circumstances that explain regionalism on the basis of real issues, and there are similarities to U.S. politics. David Kang has argued convincingly that regional voting began only in 1987, and not before. He also pointed out that it is difficult to determine why voters in a region vote, because sometimes they may do it on rational rather than irrational grounds.[4] I would also add the observation that the solidarity in voting in Chŏlla Province for Kim Dae Jung versus the similar support among Kyŏngsang Province voters for the successors to Park Chung Hee and Chun Doo Hwan's parties can be explained in a rational way, because Park had poured all his industrial development investment into Kyŏngsang and short-changed Chŏlla. The Chŏlla people demanded their fair share and believed they could only obtain it by winning political power. The Kyŏngsang people desired to retain their economic advantages rather than lose them. Both sides had reasons for their votes.

In addition, Kang also compared South Korean regionalism to the machine politics of the United States,[5] which did not invalidate democracy—at least in his mind. In addition, regional voting has also characterized U.S. politics: Southern Democrats voting against Republicans because they opposed the freeing of slaves by Lincoln, but in the late 1900s the Southern Democrats shifted en masse to the Republicans against the racial, religious, and economic liberalism of Northern Democrats. Furthermore, rural people have generally voted Republican, against urban residents who vote Democratic. In short, regionalism may be less than ideal, but it is not restricted to South Korea and does not mean the end of democratic procedure.

EXCLUSION OF WOMEN
AND OTHER GROUPS FROM POLITICAL PARTICIPATION

The pessimists seem to lose sight of the fact that liberal democracy in the United States and Great Britain in the nineteenth century failed to grant the franchise to all people. Not only were African-Americans and women not given the vote, but even voting rights of men were limited by the possession of property, poll taxes, and the like. African-Americans were not recognized as whole people until manumission by Lincoln in 1863, and their voting rights were soon taken away during Reconstruction. The civil rights movement reversed some of the discrimination in the 1950s, but other devices like intimidation and violence were used to prevent people of color from voting or even registering to vote, and recently tampering with ballot boxes occurred in Florida in 2000. Women did not get the franchise in the United States until 1920, close to 130 years after the founding of the Republic. As for running for office and being elected to office at both the national and local levels, some results only began to appear in the 1980s and 1990s. Maybe U.S. political scientists have not been vociferous enough in pointing out the flaws in U.S. democracy. Maybe Korean political scientists should realize that U.S. democracy is further from the perfect model than they think.

State-Capital Collusion Prevents Economic Democracy

The argument has been made that "the institutional drag of the 'developmental state,' forged during the dictatorship of Park Chung Hee, has impeded democratic consolidation." And that "state-capital collusion . . . has made the Korean chaebŏl not only economically inefficient and anti-competitive but also deeply entrenched and reform resistant."[6] These two propositions should be reconsidered. Some chaebŏl were economically inefficient, to be sure, but others had to compete against international competition which required efficiency. Samsung electronics, Hyundai shipbuilding, and POSCO's cheap steel, for example, appear to be efficient enough to capture market share in the world market against international competitors.

Despite the criticism in some circles of the chaebŏl's excessive power, Park Chung Hee's determination to create large companies to compete internationally may turn out to be very prescient, because big capital and high productive capacity to reduce costs may be the only way for South Korean companies to compete internationally against the MNCs [multinational corporations] of the West and Japan. Of course, the chaebŏl have fought to maintain their privileged position. They do not seem to be concerned with the equal distribution of wealth or raising wages that raises their costs, contrary to the wishes of democratically elected presidents like Kim Dae Jung. But are South Korean chaebŏl an exception to the behavior of big business around the globe? Ralph

Nader, for example, has been preaching that the United States has been captured by the big moneyed interests. If one is not convinced by Nader, just consider how undemocratic the robber barons of the late nineteenth century were in the United States.

The U.S. government either left big business alone or provided them aid. Andrew Carnegie took off to Europe while the Pinkertons and the cops were beating the heads of his steel workers. How often is it that big money cannot get its way in "consolidated democratic" societies? Workers and humanitarian idealists will be battling the chaeböls of the industrial/democratic world for a long time to come. That either means that democracy refers only to political procedure, or that the absence of equitable distribution and power in democratic societies will render such societies beyond democratic "consolidation" permanently.

THE ROK PRESIDENCY IS
TOO POWERFUL FOR HEALTHY DEMOCRACY

The argument has been made that South Korean presidents remain too powerful even after the transition to democracy in 1987. The evidence indicates that Kim Young Sam twisted the law by prosecuting Chun Doo Hwan and Roh Tae Woo (No T'aeu) after the statute of limitations had run out, and that Kim Dae Jung used state prosecutors and the National Intelligence Service (the old KCIA) to hound opposition parliamentarians out of the national assembly and used coercion to pass legislation. The effect was to emasculate the legislature.[7] The statute of limitations in South Korean constitutions, however, was devised by dictators to protect they and their minions from prosecution in the courts. How valid, how legal are constitutions manipulated by dictators? How sacrosanct are they, especially after they have been amended at least nine times since 1948? Few nations emerging from dictatorship to democracy in the late twentieth century have been able to punish their dictatorial tormentors, but Kim Young Sam did so by putting moral justice over legal nicety. And has the United States always preserved legal principle over the bias of judges? Consider the Supreme Court's decision over the election recount in Florida in the presidential election of 2000, for example.

Criticizing excess presidential power makes theoretical sense, but in the South Korean case, one suspects that a weakened president and strengthened national assembly would result either in deadlock or inaction in a time of crisis, given the current fragility of political parties. Besides, the emergence of a majority party like Yŏllin Uridang (Our Open Party), of which the president is not a member, may already signify an advance in the national assembly's power brought on by the unpopularity of the three Kims. Presidential power may have evoked a beneficial and contrary reaction. Open elections may well allow the dialectic to function without bloodshed and open the path to a two or three-party system based on liberal versus conservative policies in the economy and polity.

Failure of ROK Presidents to Achieve Goals

Some have believed that the failure of presidents Kim Young Sam and Kim Dae Jung to achieve economic prosperity and democratic development leads to nostalgia for past dictators whom the public believes were more efficient than democratic presidents. That feeling definitely became manifest after the economic crash of 1997, but to what extent were the presidents responsible for the economic meltdown? In the United States, presidents usually are held responsible for poor economic performance even though they usually feel that their predecessors were responsible for an economic downturn while they also claim credit for an upturn that began before they were elected. Despite nostalgia for Park Chung Hee, it is obvious that U.S. toleration for South Korean protectionism during the cold war era and WTO toleration thereafter, against free-market principles, is no longer possible.

Both Kim Young Sam and Kim Dae Jung realized that pressure for dismantling protectionism at the expense of agriculture and some native industries is unavoidable. Outsourcing of Korean factories to China has already become a serious problem because of cheaper labor costs, and South Korea has no choice but to move its way up the product cycle to high-tech products or suffer serious decline. While this takes place, bankruptcies and layoffs will continue, but the state has yet to meet the challenge of providing an adequate safety net for the unemployed. In this situation, nostalgia for Park's dictatorial developmentalism is like whistling in the wind. Retreating to protectionism would only lead to retaliation by other countries in the form of increased tariffs and a big drop in exports.

Parties Focus on Personalities Rather than Issues

There is no question but that political parties have been organized around
personalities. The dictators (Rhee, Park, and Chun) formed parties as a means
of satisfying the Americans, but they ruled through the bureaucracy, army,
police, and the KCIA (after 1961). Opposition politicians formed parties, or
left the parties they belonged to, to form other parties, but they had a single
agenda: ending dictatorship. They sometimes espoused radical policies, even
though there was no chance they would be adopted into law. For that reason,
the formulation of policy took second place, but when Kim Young Sam and
Kim Dae Jung were elected to office in 1992 and 1997 respectively, they abandoned some major policies that they had espoused when they were in opposition. Kim Young Sam did much for democratic development by dismissing
military officers associated with past dictators. But he abandoned the working
class by backing globalism to the hilt.

Kim Dae Jung took money from Roh Tae Woo to run a separate campaign
against him in 1987, splitting the opposition vote. When Kim was elected
president in 1997, he abandoned the low-wage workers, the unemployed, and
the homeless by hewing to the IMF line on retrenchment without offering any
resistance. Maybe he had no choice, but he hardly put up a struggle. He also
bribed Kim Jong Il (Kim Chŏngil) of North Korea to hold the summit meeting
in P'yŏngyang in 2000 and had the Hyundae Asan Corporation launder the
transfer of funds.

In the run-up to the 2002 presidential elections, most parties looked like
amalgamations of party leaders with their retinue of followers. Some liberals,
fed up with Kim Dae Jung, had joined Yi Hoech'ang's conservative
Hannaradang. Kim Dae Jung was recruiting conservative politicians and ex-
bureaucrats and others in his attempt to win votes from areas other than
Chŏlla Province. When Kim Dae Jung's candidate, Ro Moo Hyun (No
Muhyŏn) won the presidential election of 2002, the parties began to disinte-
grate. Politicians with a liberal orientation deserted the old parties to form a
new Yŏllin Uridang based on issues rather than personalities. President Roh
has no party affiliation. Maybe the first step has been made toward parties
based on policy rather than personality.

HOW MUCH CONVERGENCE WITH
WESTERN DEMOCRACY CAN ONE EXPECT?

The pessimists are skeptical not only of South Korea's current level of democracy, but also of the future prospects for "consolidation"—that is, the adoption of values associated with democracy in the West. This expectation is related to the old problem of convergence—whether or not Asian states will converge with the conditions of "consolidated" Western democracies. The evidence seems to suggest that complete convergence is a pipe dream, but that does not mean that an East Asia variant of democracy is not possible. The pessimists' argument is that the ingrained, conservative force of Confucianism obstructs if not opposes democracy.

In particular, Confucianism is important for defending masculine superiority in family control, property ownership by the male head of household, the control of children after divorce by the husband, and the restrictions against female participation in politics. Furthermore, Confucian collectivism ties the individual to the family or group and prevents the emergence of individualism, which is necessary for democratic politics. Confucianism, however, in the modern world has already changed. Confucians tolerate the profit motive and commercial and industrial activity even though they dislike it. They no longer control the educational curriculum, and can only fight a rearguard action against science and technology. They have retreated somewhat on the power of eldest sons, divorce, and the remarriage of widows.

On the other hand, Confucianism ancestor worship has made inroads into the Christian community. Respect for parents, elders, superiors, teachers, upper classmen, and employers, along with the necessity to provide for relatives in need of monetary support, is still very strong. Status consciousness that dominated the dynastic period has reared its ugly head again in a capitalist era. These customs are difficult to remove and will persist. They will most likely color the nature of democratic procedure for a long time to come. The democratic system will combine with a value system that will differ from Western practice in many ways. Democracy and a degree of family solidarity and collectivism will undoubtedly coexist.

ROK/U.S. RELATIONS AND DEMOCRACY

One unresolved problem remains, however. Nationalism has been a powerful phenomenon in the twentieth century, and yet South Korea remains heavily dependent on the United States for military defense, trade, and emergency support in time of economic crisis. Dependency on a foreign power (China) under the tributary system was one of the powerful legacies of the Confucian past. South Korea has gained security at the sacrifice of national sovereignty, but a radical assertion of sovereignty might make the country vulnerable. U.S. sanctions against North Korea could lead to a war that would destroy both democracy and millions of lives, or a U.S. pullout that would also threaten both security and the democratic process. Either of those possibilities could pose a greater threat to South Korean democracy than internal defects in its democratic system.

How Much Time Does It Take
for Major Political and Cultural Change to Occur?

Let us assume that "consolidated" democracy could possibly occur in South Korea in the future. How much time would that take? Most political scientists seem to lack historical perspective on that question. They are impatient if things do not occur overnight, as they did in the industrialization of South Korea in a couple of decades. Democratization is much more difficult than rapid industrialization, because it requires changes in deeply ingrained attitudes, beliefs, and conventions. Korea has undergone three similar changes of immense scope before. The first was the adoption of Chinese standards of centralization and the adoption of Chinese writing and thought from some time in the fourth century BCE to the sixth century CE.

The second was the adoption of the universal religion of Buddhism and its superimposition over native animism and shamanism from the mid-fourth century BC through the seventh or eighth centuries and its continuation to the end of the fifteenth century, and later. The third was the adoption of the Song Dynasty version of the Confucian Learning of the Way (tohak) and its displacement of Buddhism from around 1300 to 1700. Since these transitions took 300-1,000 years, is it likely that democracy (let alone Christianity and new religions) will occur in a few decades only? Furthermore, these kinds of major transformations do not proceed in straight lines. There are ups and downs, and at any point the future of the new trend may appear dim. The pessimists (who would like the development of "consolidated" democracy to take place in South Korea) are disheartened, but significant events have occurred already: the escape from dictatorship has been achieved with minimum violence, a civilian president was elected in 1992, the military appears finally ready to recognize civilian rule, a member of an opposition party was elected president in 1997, the beginnings of a free press occurred, and a vital civil society with a plethora of NGOs working for the reform of individual issues has emerged in spades after 1987.

Years ago Gregory Henderson deplored the inability of Koreans to form voluntary associations, which he thought was the key to democratic development, but now voluntary associations have become the equivalent of a popular sport.[8] Contrast the South Korean democracy with that of Japan: democracy was imposed on Japan after suffering horrendous damage in WWII, a dominant party has been maintained to date with hardly any change, and no meaningful election of a candidate from an opposition party to the post of prime minister has occurred. If South Korean democracy is judged by comparison with the real state of affairs in the United States and other democratic countries, it may look much better than the pessimists believe.

NOTES

1. The late Professor Palais passed away in 2006 before this article could be edited, so we have made changes only for grammar and style, and have not updated references to the contemporary politics of 2004 when this article was written.
2. The original reads Namdaemundae; presumably Namdaemun Kyŏngbidae (Namdaemun Police Garrison) is meant.—Eds.
3. Sunhyuk Kim, "Civil Society in Democratizing Korea," 105.
4. David C. Kang, "Regional Politics and Democratic Consolidation."
5. Ibid., 179.
6. Samuel Kim, "Korea's Democratization in the Global-Local Nexus," 35.
7. Ibid., 37.
8. Gregory Henderson, *Korea: The Politics of the Vortex*.

7

Labor Policies and Labor Relations during the Park Chung Hee Era

HAGEN KOO

As in most other areas, the Park Chung Hee era (Pak Chŏnghŭi) left a mixed legacy in labor policy and labor relations. On the one hand, his labor policy was successful in the sense that labor was effectively mobilized and harnessed to his industrialization program with minimal friction. Given that export-oriented industrialization depended heavily on the low-wage, hard-working, and disciplined labor force, the major objective of Park's labor policy was to ensure such a favorable labor market for export-led industrial development. Labor supply was well maintained, manpower training was adequately performed, and wages were kept under control. More importantly, the Park government maintained a high level of industrial peace throughout the period of rapid economic growth until the end of the 1970s. Throughout this period, there was not a single occasion when any large-scale labor disturbance hampered export production. South Korea thus offered a very favorable investment climate for foreign capitalists. Both foreign and domestic capital were assured of industrial peace and of consistent state policies about labor issues.

On the other hand, Park's labor policy may be considered a failure from humanist and societal points of view. It was a highly authoritarian and repressive system. It systematically denied workers the right to organize and defend their interests collectively through representative organizations. Obsessed with economic growth, the Park administration turned a blind eye to the incredible degree of labor exploitation and abuse in the workplace and left no adequate outlets for workers to air their concerns. Thus, the system bred much disaffection and resentment among workers. An historical evaluation of Park Chung Hee's labor policies, therefore, depends on which side one takes—that of capital, labor, development, or economic justice. It was a good system from the capitalists' point of view and from the viewpoint of economic growth. But it was a bad situation from the workers' point of view, and from the human rights' perspective. Considering this, it would be fair to regard Park's labor policies as half success and half failure.[1]

From a long-term perspective, however, I would argue that the Park Chung Hee (Pak Chŏnghŭi) government's labor policy was largely a failure, and an unfortunate one. It was so, I contend, not simply because it was undemocratic and repressive, but also because it established a system that was effective in the short term but counterproductive and not sustainable in the long run.[2] The structure of the control system had broken down by the end of the Park era through internal contradictions and labor resistance. And it left an undesirable legacy for the succeeding labor regimes that plagues today's industrial relations system.

This chapter examines labor policies and labor relations during the Park Chung Hee era by focusing on the dialectic relationship of mobilization and demobilization of labor. Park's consistent policy was to mobilize workers economically as an element of production, and demobilize them politically as a possible threat to security and national development. But he did this in a rather crude and shortsighted fashion, relying primarily on security forces, with little regard to developing a mature industrial relations system. The consequence of his narrow developmentalist and security-oriented approach was the growing alienation of workers from the system and the mobilization of workers at the grassroots level in alliance with democratic forces in society. Eventually, both Park himself and the working people had to pay a great price for the crude labor system Park installed during this period. Furthermore, Park's labor policies bequeathed to succeeding generations a pattern of habits and behaviors—on the part of capital, labor, and the state—which rely too heavily on mistrust, uncompromising confrontations, and violent means of dispute resolution. To a great extent, the highly contentious and mistrustful industrial relations that seem to characterize the South Korean industrial system today is attributable to the pattern established during Park's developmental decades.

PARK'S LABOR POLICIES

It seems that Park Chung Hee and his associates came to power with no clear vision or ideas about the industrial relations system they planned to develop. Their main concern was to maintain political and social order and to prevent organized labor from becoming a source of political instability or an obstacle to economic development. Most probably, military leaders came to power with a certain degree of arrogance and immaturity with regards to labor, because industrial labor at the time was not a serious power to be reckoned with.[3] Park's leadership might have thought that organized labor could be easily molded into shape with a little manipulation and ideological control.

Although Park Chung Hee's labor policies are generally described as harsh and oppressive, it is necessary to recognize that his earlier policies were not so authoritarian and restrictive of labor rights. In the 1960s, workers were relatively free to organize themselves, bargain collectively, and engage in collective actions. While Park's approach to organized labor was heavy handed, during this period he showed no intention to restrict workers' basic rights of organization and collective activities.[4] Park's policies, however, took a sharp turn at the end of the 1960s and became increasingly authoritarian and repressive during the Yusin period (1972–80). It is thus useful to divide the Park period into two periods: the relatively liberal 1960s and the repressive 1970s.

Laying Down the Framework: The 1960s

One of the first measures which the military junta took after it seized power on May 16, 1961, was to dissolve the Federation of Korean Trade Unions (FKTU, Taehan Noryŏn). Immediately after that, the newly created Korean Central Intelligence Agency (KCIA) selected some thirty labor representatives and trained them to organize new unions.[5] Of them, nine members (the so-called Nine Member Committee) were entrusted with the task of reorganizing the national union. They finished the task swiftly and founded the new Federation of Korean Trade Unions (FKTU or Han'guk Noch'ong) on August 30, 1961. Subsequently, other labor leaders, recommended by the Nine Member Committee, were selected to engage in organizing industrial- and regional-level unions. The new FKTU was organized along industry lines, and officially sanctioned unions were given exclusive representation rights. Only one union was allowed to represent a given enterprise or a given industry. Legally, these enterprise unions were organized as union shops, although compulsory membership was never enforced or even encouraged in practice.

The overall union structure that came into existence during the Park period thus resembled the state-corporatist model in terms of state sanctioning of unions, exclusive representation rights of official unions, and industrial union structure.[6] The real nature of the South Korean union structure, however, was far from a genuine state corporatist model. In the ROK, official unions were neither encouraged, nor allowed, to represent workers. Industrial unions were not given much authority or resources to regulate and represent the interests formed at the local union level. There were few horizontal linkages among local unions within the industry, and virtually all the collective bargaining was conducted at the enterprise-union level. Most of all, the state was basically uninterested in taking organized labor even as a junior partner into its policy-making process.

Nonetheless, the Park leadership at the beginning of its regime was willing to respect the constitutionally protected rights of the working people. The new labor laws adopted in 1963 were based on the first labor laws adopted during the Syngman Rhee (Yi Sŭngman) government in 1953. Like the earlier ones, the new labor laws guaranteed the three basic rights of labor: freedom of association, collective bargaining, and collective actions. One major change was the addition of a restrictive clause regarding unions' political activities. The new labor law prescribed that labor unions would not collect political funds from its members or use union dues for political purposes. The main motivation of the Park regime in restructuring the union and labor laws at this time was more political than economic, that is, to keep organized labor depoliticized and disconnected from political opposition groups.

By and large, the 1960s represented a relatively liberal period for labor-union activities. Although there were many administrative restrictions imposed on union organization, union-organizing efforts were not severely repressed, collective bargaining occurred regularly, and labor conflicts were handled without too much heavy-handed government involvement. During this period, as Ogle observed, "open conflict was allowed, and to some degree recognized as an inherent part of the process."[7] He noted that the representatives of the Urban Industrial Mission (UIM), which became the regime's anathema in the 1970s, were routinely invited to participate in the FKTU's educational meetings during the 1960s.[8] The situation began to change toward the end of the 1960s. The South Korean economy ran into the first crisis of the export-oriented industrialization in the late 1960s, caused by serious balance-of-payment problems and widespread business failures in foreign-invested firms. Frequent labor disputes occurred in response to layoffs, delayed payments, and plant closures.

Between 1968 and 1971, several notable labor disputes occurred, including labor protests at the foreign-invested firms, Signetics Corporation and Oak Electronics in 1968, a large-scale, industry-wide strike by textile workers employed at sixteen cotton textile firms, a prolonged strike at the government-run Chosŏn Shipbuilding Company in 1969, and a hunger strike at a subsidiary of American Pfizer.[9] The rising level of labor activism in the export sector, especially in foreign-invested industries, posed a clear threat to Park Chung Hee's development program when the external economic climate was unfavorable. In response to this emerging crisis, Park took several extraordinary measures to improve the investment climate for foreign capital and the financial structure of domestic firms. In 1969, Park proclaimed Provisional Exceptional Law Concerning Labor Unions and the Settlement of Labor Disputes in Foreign-Invested Firms. It imposed severe restrictions on labor organizations and prohibited strikes in foreign-invested firms. This action marked a major turning point in the Park regime's labor policies. It was only the beginning of a series of labor-repression measures, which the Park regime was going to implement in the following years.

Imposing Wholesale Repression: The Yusin Period

Several factors contributed to the rise of the dictatorial Yusin regime. The worsening economic condition, growing political opposition, Park Chung Hee's near defeat to Kim Dae Jung (Kim Taejung) in the 1971 presidential election, the upcoming North-South meetings, Nixon's visit to China in 1971, and the partial withdrawal of U.S. military forces from South Korea all caused great concern for Park Chung Hee and his political elites. Park's response to all these economic and political challenges came in a harsh authoritarian manner. In December 1971 Park declared a state of emergency and proclaimed the Law Concerning Special Measures for Safeguarding National Security

(LSMSNS). This emergency decree effectively closed all the political space and put a clamp on civil liberty. The immediate target of the measure was organized labor.

Article 9 of the LSMSNS specified (1) workers seeking to exercise their rights on collective bargaining and collective action must file an application to the appropriate government agency and must follow its regulatory decision and (2) the president has the right to take special measures to restrict the actions of the labor organizations engaged in government organizations or regional government offices, state-owned enterprises, public-interest enterprises, and other enterprises which have a serious impact on the national economy.[10] In essence these emergency security measures suspended two of the workers' three basic rights guaranteed by the constitution: the right to bargain collectively and to engage in collective actions.

In March 1972 the government introduced another restrictive measure, the Collective Bargaining under National Emergency measure. This measure expanded the range of enterprises defined as belonging to the public interest, which were then barred from union actions; it also placed further restrictions on the activities of industry-level unions. The culmination of all these authoritarian legislative actions was the installation of the dictatorial Yusin system in October 1972. The Yusin Constitution bestowed upon Park Chung Hee a lifetime presidency with unchecked executive power. But, for the working people, the Yusin Constitution and labor-law revisions introduced in 1973 and 1974 made little difference. For organized labor, all the repressive measures had already been put in place with the National Security Measures proclaimed in 1971.

While severely restricting union organization and union activities, the state also tried to reconfigure the union structure from an industrial union structure to an enterprise union system. This move was partly based on the realization that industrial unions are not the most reliable tools for maintaining control on local unions. As labor volatility grew, state planners began to fear that industrial unions may become an unwelcome base of labor power. Labor planners thus shifted their policies and tried to destroy industry unions and contain union activities within company-controlled enterprise unionism. The dominant character of the Yusin regime's labor policy is nicely described by Song as follows:

> If [the Park regime] employed an indirect method of co-opting the upper
> echelon of the union leadership and having them control industrial unions
> and their members during the 1960s when it had a lingering attachment to
> the idea of democracy, in the 1970s it had no hesitation to cast its attach-
> ment to democratic ideals and sought to control labor through supra-consti-
> tutional measures and by mobilizing the repressive administrative power.[11]

What characterized Park's labor regime during the Yusin period was its security-oriented approach to labor and its heavy reliance on the threat of violence in controlling labor activism. The state tried to control labor activities through security forces rather than through legal and bureaucratic means. Park Chung Hee was not known for his patience in dealing with his political opponents. Labor activists were his enemy. He and his political elites seemed to have a strong conviction that those who were responsible for labor unrest, or those who tried to organize workers into independent unions in violation of labor laws, were influenced by, or linked to, communism. While ignoring customary violations of labor-practice laws by management, the state was quick and ruthless in cracking down on labor agitation. While workers' pleas for government protection against labor abuses were most commonly ignored, employers' requests for intervention to block unionization efforts were quickly responded to by the state. The inevitable consequence of such strong anti-labor state actions was a growing level of politicization and strong resentment against both the state and capital among workers.

IDEOLOGICAL MOBILIZATION

The Park government, of course, did not only try to demobilize labor and keep it as an atomized and pliable productive force. It also tried to mobilize laborers as motivated producers and as cooperative partners in increasing productivity in the workplace. Economic and ideological mobilization of workers was as important as their political demobilization. From his early days, Park Chung Hee was intent on mobilizing the working population with the ideologies of nationalism and developmentalism. The repeated slogans of *minjok chunghŭng* (restoring national glory) and *Chal sara pose* (Let's try to live well) were not just empty words: they represented Park's utmost desire and governing ideology. Accordingly, ideological mobilization

of industrial workers constituted an important part of the Park government's labor policies.

A major intent of the ideological mobilization of workers was to encourage
them to work hard, to cooperate with managers to build an efficient economic
system, and to restrain their demands until the economy had grown large
enough to distribute the fruits of their labor. The first thing that Park's leadership did to mobilize workers on the ideological and discursive levels was to
label them as *sanŏp ŭi chŏnsa* (industrial warriors) or *sanŏp ŭi yŏkkun* (builders of
industry). Workers were likened to soldiers fighting for national defense and
national glory in the global economic war. Given the importance of exports in
the nation's development strategy, factory workers were also called *such'ul ŭi
yŏkkun* or *such'ul ŭi kisu* (chief producers of exports). Working with dedication
to promote exports was celebrated as a patriotic act that workers must be
proud of. Ideologies of nationalism and developmentalism were wrapped up
in a strong military rhetoric in order to shape the motivation and self-identity
of the rapidly growing proletarian population engaged in export industries.

To what extent these nationalistic and developmental ideologies were effective in shaping the identity and consciousness of the working class during this
period is not clear. Most probably, they influenced the public presentation of
workers rather than their inner feelings or self-identity. Yet, it is interesting to
notice that nationalistic and developmental language was frequently used by
workers and workers' organizations. For example, workers at the Wonpoong
Textile Company who built one of the most independent and aggressive
unions in the 1970s issued the following union resolution in 1973:

- We are the warriors of industrial peace and will make our utmost effort to
  increase productivity.

- We will make every effort to improve our working conditions with strong
  solidarity among ourselves.

- As champions of the working people, we will do our best to improve the
  quality of the union.[12]

In all likelihood, state-defined worker identity had only a limited effect on
the true identity and consciousness of the workers. Although workers used
these words themselves, due in large part to the lack of any other positive

language describing themselves, they must have had a great deal of doubt and suspicion. As one worker wrote, "Who dares, with a shred of sincerity, to use those words like 'industrial warriors' or 'pillars of export' to call us, when we are not even allowed to express our own feelings?"[13] Their daily working life and the way they were actually treated by society belied such an exalted image of industrial workers.

State leaders themselves must have realized that they could not depend on just a vacuous, symbolic exaltation of workers in order to assure continued labor submissiveness and industrial peace. The rise of labor volatility in the late 1960s and the growing interconnection between laborers and intellectuals must have made Park's leadership aware of the necessity of finding a more powerful organizational form of ideological mobilization and control of the working people. The Saemaŭl Factory movement played a vital role in this regard.

The Saemaŭl movement was originally a rural movement implemented in the early 1970s, a massive government-directed, agriculturally cooperative effort to improve productivity and rural standards of living.[14] Its major emphasis was to culturally or spiritually uplift the farming population by encouraging the cultural values of diligence, self-help, cooperation, and community spirit. With growing confidence drawn from the successful results of this program in rural areas, Park expanded this movement to all sectors of society.

The Saemaŭl Factory movement constituted a vital component of Park Chung Hee's nation building program. It was formally implemented in 1973 with the same themes (or "saemaŭl spirit") borrowed from the saemaŭl rural movement: "diligence, self-help, and teamwork." Additionally, the Saemaŭl Factory movement put new emphasis on increased productivity and labor-management cooperation. The themes of the movement are well articulated in many of Park Chung Hee's speeches:

> The Saemaŭl movement as practiced in offices and factories is nothing different [from the one now being practiced in the countryside] for its basic spirit remains the same: diligence, self-help, and teamwork. In a business corporation the entire personnel, from the president on down, should work together to reduce waste and improve efficiency, and devote their whole energy to increased productivity. There should be close labor-management cooperation, with the company president making an utmost effort to improve

pay and welfare for his employees and the latter fulfilling their duties with a sense of responsibility and sincerity, doing factory work like their own personal work, and caring for the factory as if it were their own. In such a corporation, productivity will be high, thanks to the family-like atmosphere, and the workers will be well taken care of as due return for their faithful service.

. . . . Thereby complete harmony between employees and employers would be made possible, and on this basis efficiency and productivity can be promoted. . . . Therefore, this movement, as the labor-capital cooperation movement uniquely developed in our country, will become a driving force to build up national strength.[15]

In addition to the general themes transplanted from the rural *saemaŭl* movement, we can see that a critical idea promoted in the Saemaŭl Factory movement was that of familism or enterprise family ideology. The major slogan of the Saemaŭl Factory movement was this: "Treat employees like family. Do factory work like your own personal work." This idea of the family-enterprise system basically denies the reality of conflict relations between labor and management and seeks to promote pseudo-family relations among all members of an enterprise. It borrows the rhetoric of a traditional patriarchal family—the employer is likened to a father, the worker to a son, and the manager to an elder brother. From the mid-1970s, one could find a large sign at every South Korean factory gate that read, "Treat employees like family members, do factory work like my own work!" This family enterprise ideology was frequently wrapped up within the national development ideology, in which labor cooperation and hard work were deemed essential to building a strong nation and were often elevated to the status of a citizen's sacred duty.

The South Korean Chamber of Commerce and Industry coordinated the Saemaŭl Factory movement. The key organizational components of the movement were *saemaŭl* leaders and *saemaŭl* work teams. The *saemaŭl* leaders were in charge of carrying out the movement under the direction of the top manager of the company. The *saemaŭl* work teams were composed of eight to fifteen workers and were involved in a wide range of production-rationalization programs. At the national level, *saemaŭl* educational centers played an essential role in training and indoctrinating *saemaŭl* leaders. There were twelve factory *saemaŭl* education centers throughout the country, and these centers, between 1973 and 1979, trained a total of 46,531 high-level managers.[16] Labor unions, at all levels, were required to provide ethical training consonant with the *saemaŭl* movement. The FKTU established its own educational center in 1975 and functioned as a major vehicle of *saemaŭl* education. The union leaders were taught the following subjects: "the *saemaŭl* spirit and the labor-union movement; Yusin doctrine; the ideal posture of union leaders; church doctrine (indicating UIM and JOC activities) and the labor-union movement; North Korea's situation; South Korea's national security and unification; South Korea's economic prospects; and Koreanized labor-capital relations."[17]

It is important to realize that the Saemaŭl Factory movement was not simply a cultural or spiritual movement implemented in the factory setting. Its origin was more mundane and economic. The predecessor of the Saemaŭl Factory movement was the managerial attempts to copy the Japanese model of quality control circles as early as 1970. Various attempts were initiated at large firms to implement the Japanese style of production technology, but they remained sporadic and unsystematic in the early years. Then the 1973 oil shock presented a greater impetus to the rationalization movement at large manufacturing firms. The Saemaŭl Factory movement was partly a response to this managerial demand. It was thus very appropriate that the Ministry of Commerce and Industry was the central agency in charge of this movement.

From the workers' point of view, the Saemaŭl Factory movement activities required them to work extra hours without compensation—they had to come to work earlier than their regular schedule, attend numerous extra meetings, and stay longer hours after regular work hours, most of which were not remunerated. Naturally, the level of workers' grievance with the program was very high, and it worked as an important source of their increasing class awareness in the late 1970s and the 1980s.

Supplementing the Saemaŭl Factory movement was the Labor-Management Council, composed of the representatives of management and labor. Joint labor-management councils were first established in the late 1960s but only became important institutions after an amendment to the Labor Union Law in March 1973. The manifest function of this bipartite organization was to foster cooperative relations between management and labor and to boost labor productivity. The law stipulated that workers' demands relating to wages, working conditions, and other grievances be handled by bipartite councils, which would weigh these issues against the primary concerns of increased productivity and labor-capital harmony. The government required that these councils be established in all the firms where unions existed. In essence, bipartite councils were anti-union organizations that took over many functions of labor unions and undermined laborers' organizational strength.

INDUSTRIAL RELATIONS AND LABOR RESISTANCE

One of the interesting puzzles in South Korea during the developmental decades is the continuous growth of labor discontent and resentment toward an industrial system that undoubtedly brought noticeable improvement to the working population. The decade of the 1970s in particular brought rapid wage increases. Not only did wages increase dramatically but the increase rate surpassed the rate of productivity. This was also the period of accelerated job creation in the industrial sector and, as labor economists argue, marked the end of unlimited labor supply. Such a macroeconomic performance was more than enough to justify Park Chung Hee's basic orientation toward labor relations: workers must be willing to restrain their wish to exercise their political rights and cooperate with managers to increase productivity, and then all will be rewarded with the fruits of economic growth. The statistics of wage growth and income distribution during Park Chung Hee's reign was clearly supportive of such developmental faith.

Unfortunately, however, workers were not happy with the way the South Korean economy was going and the ways the industry treated them. Their disaffection was partly due to low wages, which was the situation for a large proportion of workers employed in the labor-intensive sectors of industry. But more important sources of their grievances were harsh working conditions and extremely poor industrial relations. Exceptionally long work hours, hazardous working conditions, arbitrary exercise of power and contemptuous attitudes of managerial employees toward production workers, rampant sexual harassment—all of these were common features of most work places and caused great distress to helpless workers. Workers thus constantly cried for "humane treatment." Chŏn T'aeil's self-immolation in 1970 dramatized this problem. His deep sense of frustration and anger was widely shared among the majority of factory workers.

State planners were, most likely, not unaware of these problems but did not bother to confront them in any serious manner. There were only occasional and sporadic efforts to enforce laws on unfair labor practices. Park Chung Hee, from time to time, made speeches telling employers to treat their workers like family members. He also forced top industrialists to implement company welfare programs, like dormitories for workers, mess halls, company savings and loan associations, scholarship programs, and the like. In large-scale firms, these were part of the Saemaŭl Factory movement. However, it does not seem that Park Chung Hee and his economic planners really understood the magnitude of labor suffering or that the developmental policies were, to a great extent, responsible for industrial despotism and, consequently, a source of widespread labor resentment.

A chief merit of Park Chung Hee's developmental state, as Amsden clearly recognizes, is that the state exercised its disciplinary power over both capital and labor to ensure proper performance.[18] Park indeed had a puritan work ethic and a keen performance orientation. In exchange for state subsidies and protection, capitalists were expected to perform according to the state's performance criteria. But Park's criteria narrowly concerned export performance. Those export manufacturers who helped the state achieve the export target each year were rewarded with low-interest investment funds and exclusive investment licenses. Such a development policy encouraged an expansionist-investment strategy among South Korean capitalists, which resulted in serious consequences for industrial relations.

As long as industrialists were primarily concerned with meeting export targets and with capturing new profitable investment ventures by proving quantitative success in export markets, they would have minimal interest in developing a stable and committed workforce or in cultivating workers' skills and productivity by offering high wages or other incentives. While they tried to maximize profits by exploiting cheap labor, South Korean capitalists made minimum investments in improving work safety or developing company welfare systems. Nor did they invest much in manpower training of their workforce. Rather, it was the state that took primary responsibility in providing training and skill upgrading through state-run technical and vocational schools.

In retrospect, the Park era was a capitalists' heaven: not only was the international market condition favorable but the developmental state was also completely pro-capital. The state did practically everything for the capitalists as long as they successfully carried out the state's development plans. The state authority occasionally reprimanded the employers whose firms were involved in serious labor disputes but did not waste time in taking care of troubles in order to restore "industrial peace." In any event, Park's leadership failed to alleviate the high degree of labor exploitation and despotic exercise of authority in the South Korean industry.

When workers' deepening discontent and resentment began to surface in a more organized fashion from the mid-1970s, the Park government was too shortsighted and too inflexible to modify its labor policy. It just increased the level of repression on labor activists while co-opting upper-level union leaders. It also tried to block the formation of independent unions which challenged the official, government-controlled FKTU. Park's political elites refused to look at the emerging grassroots union movement as a genuine worker struggle for self-protection but saw it rather as a product of agitation by external political forces. They were either reluctant, or incapable of devising a more effective long-term strategy to deal with this problem other than intensifying the old methods of the cooptation, intimidation, firing, and blacklisting of union activists coupled with the exercise of violence.

The consequence of such a security-oriented and exclusionary approach of control led to the polarization of the South Korean union structure. At the national level, the official unions became the instruments of the state's corporatist control of organized labor; at the grass-roots level, workers strived to create independent unions outside the official union structure. This is the "democratic union movement" that has become the main object of worker struggles since the Yusin Period. This was clearly a reaction to the dominant state strategy of labor containment. The Park regime's labor strategy had turned the majority of existing unions into co-opted and powerless organizations, which were not simply unable to represent the interests of workers, but also frequently worked to suppress and distort laborer demands. Unlike corporatist systems in other countries, the Republic of Korea's ostensible state-corporatist system did not employ a combination of inducement and control, but relied primarily on control without offering benefits; in other words, it used only the stick and not the carrot to keep unions under control. Official unions were deprived of any useful and legitimate role to play for rank-and-file workers. Consequently, worker struggles converged in an attempt to create an alternative organization in opposition to the official union structure.

By the last years of Park's rule, it became increasingly clear that his labor regime was breaking down. The official union structure became ineffective and discredited, the Saemaŭl movement lost its ideological grip on workers, and the police and security agencies were incapable of controlling the expanding networks of grassroots activists and the growing level of worker identity and consciousness. Then came the economic recession caused by the second oil crisis, mounting foreign debt, and decreasing exports due to growing protectionism abroad. Labor disputes increased in frequency, and the intensity of conflicts also increased noticeably. Most frequently, these conflicts occurred in the labor-intensive sectors of export manufacturing where female workers were predominantly employed. As is well recognized, this early stage of the labor movement was led by young female workers who suffered double or triple doses of oppression and exploitation in the workplace.[19]

But no one would have imagined that a labor protest by some two hundred young women workers at a wig factory would have brought about a political crisis that would eventually put an end to Park Chung Hee's rule. The labor conflict that occurred in 1979 at the wig manufacturing firm, Y.H. Trading Company, represents the nature of industrial conflicts and the mode of state control that was characteristic of the Park Chung Hee period.[20] Established in 1966, the Y.H. Trading Company was one of the major wig exporters to the United States. Its founder, Y.H. Chang, emigrated to America in 1970 and established another trading company, leaving the management of the South Korean wig factory in the hands of his brother-in-law. Rather than concentrate on the wig business, the new manager diverted profits from Y.H. Trading Company to buy a new shipping company.

A third manager also made side investments in electronics and film production companies. Thus, Y.H. Trading Company exemplifies the expansionist-accumulation strategy and how it can hurt employees. The continuous outflow of capital made Y.H. Trading Company's business unhealthy, especially because the worldwide wig market began declining in the 1970s. By the late 1970s, the total number of employees decreased from 4,000 to 1,800. In March 1979 the management announced a plan to close the plant, which triggered a strong reaction from the union, one of the new breed of independent unions formed in 1975. A series of sit-in demonstrations followed. As conflict between the management and the union escalated, several outside organizations became involved. Not only religious leaders and intellectuals, but also representatives from democratic unions at Wonpoong, Tongil, Control Data, Pando Trading, and Tonggwang textile companies attended the Y.H. union meetings. The Y.H. workers' strike intensified as the announced date of the plant closing approached. The police were called in and were ready to break up the strike by force. Facing an imminent police attack, the strikers decided to move to another, safer place to continue their struggle. Surprisingly, the place they chose was the headquarters of the opposition party, the New Democratic Party (NDP) in downtown Seoul.

On the morning of August 9, 1979, 187 Y.H. workers stormed into the NDP building and occupied the fourth floor of the building as their new demonstration site. The NDP headquarters was immediately surrounded by police, and tension rose as then NDP President Kim Young Sam (Kim Yŏngsam) declared his support for the striking workers. A highly emotional and tense confrontation between the strikers and the police lasted for two days. At dawn on the third day (August 11), some one thousand riot police broke into the building. They smashed windows, threw over furniture, and applied indiscriminate violence to NDP party members, opposition congressmen, and newspaper reporters, as well as to the desperately resistive Y.H. workers. In the midst of this police violence, one worker fell to her death from the fourth floor. Kim Young Sam was taken away by force.

Although Y.H. workers sacrificed much and achieved nothing, their valiant effort contributed tremendously to the externalization and politicization of labor movements, and to the fusion of both labor and pro-democracy political struggles. The Y.H. incident had greater political repercussions than just its impact on the labor movement. The New Democratic Party, which had been more or less aloof from the labor movement so far, became inadvertently involved with labor conflict. Party politics plunged deeply into crisis when the ruling party ousted Kim Young Sam from his congressional seat, charging him with inciting violence and social instability. Mass demonstrations occurred in Pusan, Kim's congressional district, and spread to the neighboring industrial city, Masan. Participants in the street demonstrations were not just students but also included workers, the unemployed, and ordinary citizens, who had become deeply disaffected with the Park government's authoritarian practices. The recessionary state of the South Korean economy during this period helped escalate the political unrest. As political protests intensified and spread across the country, a crack began to occur within the ruling group, and serious rivalries developed among Park's aids, which eventually led to Park Chung Hee's assassination by his own CIA chief on October 26, 1979.

CONCLUSION

A key accomplishment of Park Chung Hee's labor policies was their internal consistency. His economic policies were consistently based on the same principle of placing national goals above individual ones, putting economic growth before distribution, protecting capitalists' interests before that of labor. Park's orientation toward labor was also consistent, which may be characterized as productionist and instrumental—he looked at industrial labor primarily as an element of production and as an instrument of economic development. And his chief concern was how to maintain the labor force and labor market in the most optimum condition for rapid economic growth. He had a firm belief that the best, and the only, way to improve the living standards of the working people was to achieve economic growth. Workers thus were expected only to work hard, cooperate with management to improve productivity, refrain from making political demands, and always be mindful of the nation's security situation in a hostile world. Park and his economic planners rarely looked at laborers in human terms, as rights-bearing citizens. If the human side of labor came into consideration, it was mainly their potential to disrupt the nation's economic plan. Military leaders had a deep suspicion about the real motive of the labor movement. In short, Park Chung Hee's labor policies pursued the goal of mobilizing and demobilizing labor simultaneously—that is, mobilizing labor's productive economic power and demobilizing their potential political power.

The Factory Saemaŭl movement was the most important mechanism implemented by the Park regime for the mobilization of workers. It established an impressive array of bureaucratic apparatuses to mobilize workers for increased productivity and cooperation with management. The demobilization of labor was based primarily on the draconian emergency measure proclaimed in 1971, the Law Concerning Special Measures for Safeguarding National Security, and a whole battery of other security-oriented measures. Both approaches were highly authoritarian and heavy handed, and they were possible because the state possessed an enormous amount of power to mobilize and demobilize the population. And these policies were effective as far as enforcing the world's longest work hours and maintaining a high level of industrial peace, despite some volatility in the labor arena.

In the long run, however, the labor-relations system that the Park government developed was neither an effective nor a rational system. Apart from humanistic considerations, the system involved too many internal contradictions and weaknesses, and the system broke down by the end of Park's rule. We can identify several of its internal weaknesses. First of all, Park's ostensibly state-corporatist system of labor control was a faulty one. Although it adopted the same organizational structure as other state-corporatist structures, its actual operation, as described above, was quite different. Rather than foster unionism and use officially sanctioned unions as a mediating mechanism in state-labor relations, the Park government was uninterested in allowing official unions to function as legitimate organizations of labor representation.

State power was primarily interested in co-opting and manipulating the leadership of the official unions while suppressing unionization efforts in general. While the corporatist strategy of labor control is supposed to be based on both incentives and constraints in dealing with unions, the Park government relied primarily on constraints rather than on incentives, in other words, on sticks rather than on carrots. In the end, the Park government's repressive and manipulative approach to unions led to the alienation of the majority of the working people from the official union structure and to the emergence of grassroots independent unionism.

Second, Park Chung Hee's approach to labor mobilization based on traditional values of family, cooperation, hierarchy, and community was bound to fail, as the value orientation of industrial workers was rapidly changing. Park's attitude toward workers may be correctly described as paternalism, and he must have genuinely wanted to create a paternalistic business system. A major objective of the Saemaŭl Factory movement was to train managers to create such a system. In this regard, Park Chung Hee clearly wanted to emulate the Japanese model of enterprise paternalism. Unlike the case of Japanese paternalism, however, Park's economic planners made little effort to force employers and managers to improve their company welfare system and to treat their workers with more respect.

The Factory Saemaŭl movement exacted longer working hours and greater compliance from workers but enforced very little reciprocity from employers. In short, the South Korean economic elites made little effort to give substance to the rhetoric of enterprise family and family-like industrial relations—in contrast to what the Japanese economic bureaucracy did to develop their paternalistic business system in the early decades of the twentieth century.[21]

The third, and the most serious failing of Park Chung Hee's labor regime, was its neglect to develop a better legal and institutional foundation for mature industrial relations; instead, the government relied heavily on security-oriented control by the police, the KCIA, and military security forces. During the Yusin period, the constitution, labor laws, and the Bureau of Labor Affairs played minor roles in controlling labor. Instead, the major agency of labor control was security agencies, and the main method of control was not legal procedures but intimidation and violence used by these agencies. Hardly any attempts to create or maintain independent union organization were free from hostile actions by the police or the KCIA. And only a handful of large-scale labor protests occurred without the exercise of violence by the police, the *kusadae* (save-the-company corps), or management-backed male workers hired to fight against resistant female workers. Violence or the threat of violence was an integral part of labor control and labor activism during the period of the Park Chung Hee regime and his military successors. Protesting workers themselves often resorted to violence, throwing rocks and Molotov cocktails, using iron pipes, or even committing self-immolation. The sad reality was that an industrial authority based on violence bred violent resistance from the workers.

In short, Park Chung Hee's labor regime left an unfortunate legacy. It was a legally and institutionally underdeveloped system of labor control. It encouraged managerial despotism in industry and made capitalists ill prepared for the growing power of labor by overprotecting capital against labor. Its reliance on security ideology and the constant threat of violence encouraged a militant and violence-prone resistance movement on the part of the working class. The militant, uncompromising, and violent pattern of South Korean labor activism that many people deplore today derived from the repressive and security-oriented approach of labor control that was laid down during the Park Chung Hee period. Furthermore, the strong mistrust among labor, capital, and the state formed during the authoritarian period continues to act as a major obstacle to building a productive and cooperative industrial relations system in the age of globalization.

NOTES

1. Song Hogŭn, "Pak Chŏnghŭi chŏngkwŏn ŭi kukka wa nodong: nodong chŏngch'i ŭi han'gye" 199–234.

2. Here I agree with Professor Paik Nak-chung who critiques in Chapter 4 of this book the legacy of the Park Chung Hee era in terms of "unsustainable development," rather than simply on moral or ideological grounds.

3. Kim Chun, "5.16 ihu nodong chohap ŭi chaep'yŏn kwa 'Han'guk Noch'ong ch'eje' ŭi sŏngnip"; Song Hogŭn, "Pak Chŏnghŭi chŏngkwŏn ŭi kukka wa nodong."

4. Park Y. K., *Labor and Industrial Relations in Korea: System and Practice*; Jangjip Choi, *Labor and the Authoritarian State.*

5. Jangjip Choi, *Labor and the Authoritarian State*; Kim Chun, "5.16 ihu nodong chohap ŭi chaep'yŏn"; Song Hogŭn, "Pak Chŏnghŭi chŏngkwŏn ŭi kukka wa nodong."

6. Philippe C. Schmitter, "Still the Century of Corporatism," 7–53; Jangjip Choi, *Labor and the Authoritarian State.*

7. George E. Ogle, *South Korea*, 17.

8. Ibid., 88.

9. Jangjip Choi, *Labor and the Authoritarian State.*

10. Kim Samsu, "Pak Chŏnghŭi sidae ŭi nodong chŏngch'aek kwa nosa kwan'gye," 183–212.

11. Song Hogŭn, "Pak Chŏnghŭi chŏngkwŏn ui kukka wa nodong," 222.

12. Wŏnp'ung Mobang Haego Nodongja Pokchik T'ujaeng Wiwŏnhoe, *Minju nojo 10 nyŏn: Wŏnp'ung Mobang Nodong Chohap hwaltong kwa t'ujaeng*, 83.

13. Tongil Pangjik Pokchik T'ujaeng Wiwŏnhoe, *Tongil Pangjik Nodong Chohap undongsa*, 49.

14. For a detailed description of the Saemaŭl movement, see Hyung-A Kim, *Korea's Development under Park Chung Hee*, 133–47.

15. Park Chung Hee, "Saemaul: Korea's New Community Movement," Presidential Address, National Conference of Saemaul Leaders, December 9, 1977, Cited from Jangjip Choi, *Labor and the Authoritarian State*, 183.

16. Hyung-A Kim, *Korea's Development under Park Chung Hee*, 143.

17. Jangjip Choi, *Labor and the Authoritarian State*, 186–87.

18. Alice Amsden, *Asia's Next Giant.*

19. George E. Ogle, *South Korea*; Seung-Kyung Kim, *Class Struggle or Family Struggle?*; Hagen Koo, *Korean Workers*; Soonok Chun, *They Are Not Machines.*

20. For a more detailed description of this event, see Hagen Koo, *Korean Workers*, 89–96.

21. Andrew Gordon, *The Evolution of Labor Relations in Japan.*

PART THREE—Cultural Influence and Civil Society

8

Rural Modernization under the Park Regime in the 1960s

CLARK W. SORENSEN

When one looks back at the various Park regimes—the military junta (Supreme Council for National Reconstruction 1961–3), the semi-democratic Third Republic[1] (1963–72), and the authoritarian Yusin Republic[2] (1972–9)—from our vantage point in the early twenty-first century, the various periods tend to blur together. One tends to think of Five-Year Plans, the turn to export orientation with labor-intensive light industrialization, the development of vocational high schools, or perhaps the toxic combination of the Yusin Constitution, labor repression, and the Heavy and Chemical Industrialization Program of the 1970s. As we all know, South Korea emerged into the eighties as an urban industrial economy, participating more and more in international chains of production and transfers of capital and technology. Educated, urban residents demanded, and eventually got (though not during the lifetime of President Park) democratic reforms, the right to travel, and a relatively free press, so as to build a vibrant, modern, and, even to an extent, a cosmopolitan society.

Such "collective memories" of the Park regime are popular today in certain sectors of Korean society,[3] but these memories tend to be anachronistic and teleological. They are teleological of course, because they interpret the past in terms of its "purpose" in creating the present. These memories are anachronistic because they neither correspond to the consciousness of Park and his associates during the sixties and seventies when they were active, nor to the consciousness of most Koreans during those times. The basic problem is that these collective memories generally ignore the rural sector, and the importance of the rural sector in the thinking of Park and the economic and social planners of his time.

THE IMPORTANCE OF THE RURAL SECTOR TO PARK

Today the rural sector in South Korea contributes a bare 4 percent of GDP, and rural workers are less than 14 percent of the workforce.[4] Park and his planners, of course, had looked forward to the day when the Republic of Korea would be an industrial society. (This is hardly unique to Park's era: even Yi Kwangsu in 1916 could imagine Korea becoming industrial and commercial).[5] The reality of the 1960s and 1970s, however, was that South Korea was still largely a rural country with most labor in the agricultural sector. At the time of the May 16, 1961 coup that brought Park to power, South Korea's population was 56.5 percent rural. This rural population would continue to grow for almost a decade to peak in 1968 at 15.9 million people. The rural population began to decline rapidly after that, but as late as 1975 nearly two in five South Korean residents were still rural, and there were more agricultural than industrial workers in South Korea.

For most of the Park regime, then, the rural agricultural sector absorbed the largest portion of the South Korean labor force, and supported the largest number of families. Being able to provide economic stability, even prosperity, to this huge peasant sector[6] was a critical need for a developmental state like South Korea under Park because the authoritarian regime could prove its legitimacy only through the ability to promote economic growth and well-being. Park's electoral support, moreover, continued to be heavily dependent on the rural sector until the end of his life. During the Third Republic (1963–72), when the president was directly elected, Park was able to win handily in 1963 and 1967 but barely squeaked by against Kim Dae Jung (Kim Taejung) in 1971.

As the burgeoning industrial cities created by successful industrialization filled with laborers who were exposed to new ideas, the cities became more demographically important and voted against the Park regime in greater numbers. Park and his Democratic Justice Party (DJP) became more and more dependent upon the dwindling number of rural voters the longer he was in power. The DJP polled a majority of Seoul and Pusan dwellers in 1963. By 1971 the DJP had lost all cities and could poll majorities only in rural areas.[7] The move to indirect elections for president, and to more heavy-handed repression in 1971–2, thus was, at least in part, a response to the declining importance of the rural sector—the bedrock of Park's political support.

The New Village movement, begun in 1971, was designed in part to shore up Park's rural support, and was central to Yusin development strategy. The New Village movement, in fact, can be paired with the Heavy and Chemical Industrialization Program as one of the two legs of Park's Yusin Period development strategy. Park was personally and deeply involved in the drafting and implementation of both programs. A meeting on the New Village Movement (*saemaŭl kwallyŏn hoeŭi*) was held at the vice ministerial level once a week, the Blue House Secretariat directly participated through the Dynamic Village Development Committee (*idong maŭl ŭl kaebal wiwŏnhoe*). Park paid personal attention to the movement, both by making personal decisions about the use of resources, and by making many speeches to New Village organizations.[8] We need only recall the gleeful way that Park offered rice to North Korea in his New Year's press conference of 1977, the year South Korea first achieved self-sufficiency in rice production, to realize this. The importance of rural development for legitimizing the Park regime, moreover, can be seen in the way the regime trumpeted at home and abroad the successes of the Saemaŭl movement, probably even more than the successes of the various export drives and industrialization movements. Just before Park's assassination in October 1979, a bureaucrat writing the preface for an English-language collection of Park's speeches on agricultural development, for example, gushed:

> The Saemaŭl (or New Community) movement which President Park Chung Hee personally initiated and has led is spreading rapidly throughout our land; it is a spiritual revolution which has achieved the immense task of modernizing the rural community in Korea, and is the chief driving force behind the bold bid to accomplish national regeneration for Korea.[9]

Foreign scholars and dignitaries, indeed, frequently showed an interest in Park's rural development efforts. Foreign politicians and scholars were regularly led to the Saemaŭl movement training center established in the early seventies near Suwŏn, and then returned home to write articles in their home press about the Park regime's successful community development program. The Saemaŭl movement was even one of South Korea's first political exports: experienced movement leaders were sent to Africa to teach villagers there how to modernize, renew themselves spiritually, and pull themselves up by their own bootstraps. An example of a foreign reporter who became impressed by the rural development efforts of the Park Regime is Richard Critchfield. Chapter 20 of his 1981 bestselling book, *Villages*, was devoted to the Korean village of the "Valley of the Swallows," (Cho Dong Kok), which he visited for five weeks in April and May, 1980.

In Toynbeean fashion, Critchfield had divided his world of villages into six major "cultures": Christian, Islamic, Hindu, Malay-Javanese, African tribal, and post-Confucian. Critchfield used Cho Dong Kok to evoke post-Confucian culture as he wove together stories about village life in each of the six cultures. The term post-Confucian, which Critchfield appropriated from a Roderick MacFarquhar article in *The Economist* (1980), was supposed to refer to villages where Confucian ideals of "individual perfection and a harmonious social order" are still relevant. He noted that by 1980, farm labor was being done largely by women and older men, but he praised the rise in rural standards of living in the seventies, the disappearance of spring hunger (*porikkogae*), the advent of television, and the appearance of motor tillers. Park, he observed, was generally respected in the village. (This was a period just a few months after the president's assassination).[10] Critchfield attributes most of the improvement in rural standards of living to Green Revolution technological innovation by U.S.-trained South Korean PhD scientists who developed dwarf, high-yield varieties of rice, but he also praises the Park regime's integrated rural development efforts.

The government likes to give credit also to its Saemaŭl movement, launched by Park in 1970. Villagers were exhorted with a Confucian-style slogan—"self-help, cooperation and diligence"[11]—to build roads, bridges and wells, and, most spectacularly, to replace their old thatched roofs with brightly painted tile or metal ones, completely changing the appearance of the countryside. At first there was some coercion from over-zealous local officials—laggards might come back to find their home open to the sky. Today, however, the Saemaŭl movement is generally praised—even by the student dissidents—for showing that once villagers get capital, technology, and access to markets, a government drive to get local officials to work better can do wonders.[12]

RURAL DEVELOPMENT IN MEASURING THE PARK REGIME

Given the importance of the rural sector in the Park regime's developmental programs, an assessment of these programs must be an essential aspect of evaluating the Park regime as a whole. As one who had contact with Korea's students during the eighties, however, I would not agree with Critchfield's notion mentioned above that "dissident students" generally praised Park's rural development efforts. On the contrary, there was a great deal of criticism of coercive methods that did not take into account the peasants own needs and desires, and of initiatives that exposed peasants to the vagaries of the market and drove peasants deeper and deeper into debt. (The new roofs that Critchfield praised are an example of debt-inducing change that did little to change people's standard of living, though it did enrich the suppliers of roof material). And the years following Critchfield's upbeat report about Korean rural development did not bear the fruit he expected. The villages continued to "hollow out"[13] as able-bodied young and middle-aged workers migrated to the cities. Already by the late seventies, moreover, the new varieties of rice were proving susceptible to disease. In the fall of 1980, just after Critchfield left Cho Dong Kok, cool weather forced yields of rice down by 30 percent.[14]

The oil shocks of the seventies raised the price of fertilizer, squeezing the Green Revolution cultivators who had become increasingly dependent on industrial inputs, and the Chun government that followed Park after his assassination was not able to keep crop prices rising fast enough to maintain standards of living in rural areas comparable to those in the rapidly growing urban areas. Although the South Korean agricultural authorities have continued year after year to plug away at finding new technical and marketing opportunities for South Korea's farmers, these farmers are today less than 13 percent of the South Korean labor force, and are substantially poorer than urban workers. The villages have continued to age as young people move out for better opportunities elsewhere, and the vibrant social and ritual life that used to characterize Korea's villages at a time when life there was otherwise impoverished is a thing of the past. For these reasons, other scholars such as Boyer and Ahn (1991) evaluate Park-era agricultural policies, particularly the New Village movement, as failures.

Park-era agricultural development programs, then, were important to the regime, and were used by the regime as important evidence of developmental success. This rural development has been evaluated both as a great accomplishment and as a dismal failure. In hindsight, it seems clear that Park-era agricultural development policies never really managed to create the foundations for a truly vibrant, rural economy. Perhaps this would have been an impossible task, since most industrial economies have had declining rural sectors. In evaluating Park regime efforts at rural development, however, one should recognize that the goals of the Park regime were broader than simply raising the rural standard of living. The political goals of the Park regime have already been alluded to, but Park was also of peasant origin and able to connect with people in the rural sector.

In a 1967 campaign speech for example, Park was able to truthfully say, "I was born as a son of the peasantry, as a poor peasant. From when I was small I experienced, until it penetrated into my bones, the hardships our peasants have, and the fact that there are such difficult problems in our villages, so coming into the government I determined that more than anything else I must speed the revitalization of our villages."[15] The writer of the preface to Park's speeches on rural development quoted above, moreover, does not speak of standards of living, but rather primarily of three things: "spiritual revolution," "modernizing the rural community," and "accomplishing national regeneration." Economic and rural well-being, though undoubtedly goals of the government, may be too narrow a lens through which to view the rural regeneration efforts of the Park regime. Perhaps it would be valuable to review rural development programs from a wider perspective. Since I happened to be doing fieldwork in a village in Kangwŏn-do during the height of the New Village movement in 1976 and 1977, I feel well-placed to do so.[16] In this paper, however, I will not concentrate on the New Village movement of the Yusin Period, which has been widely written about,[17] but on the sixties. I am interested here particularly in origins of the ideas and institutions of integrated community development in South Korea, and of the ideas about the deficiencies of Korean peasant mentalité.

TO COMPREHENSIVE COMMUNITY DEVELOPMENT

Rural development in South Korea did not begin with President Park, and land reform preceded the advent of programs of integrated rural development. High tenancy rates had been a legacy of the Japanese colonial period, and were especially prevalent in the rice-growing areas of South Korea. At liberation in 1945, tenant farmers cultivated more than 60 percent of the agricultural land of South Korea.[18] Although the agricultural lands that had once been owned by Japanese, had been confiscated, managed, and eventually sold to tenants in 1947 by the American occupation authorities, these lands were only about 12 percent of South Korea's agricultural land. This left about half of the land still tenanted. North Korea, though it had a less serious tenancy problem than the South,[19] performed thorough land reform in the spring of 1946 through uncompensated expropriation from landlords and free distribution to cultivators.[20]

South Korea did not pass its land reform based on compensated expropriation from landlords and sale to cultivating tenants until 1949, and it was not carried out until 1950. Much has been made of the deficiencies of the 1950 land reform: the Korean War broke out just as the land reform was about to be implemented; the authorities were not able to prevent private sales of land during the land reform period; the redemption price for land was too high; the government was tardy in paying former landowners; the administration of the land reform was corrupt; farm size after land reform was too small to provide an adequate living standard; land reform was not accompanied by the improved provision of farm inputs; and many small-scale farmers were not able to make a go of it and sold their land.

However, the fact remains that at the end of the land reform period in 1955, tenancy rates declined from over 60 percent to less than 5 percent. Farmland was now mostly in the hands of those who cultivated it, giving farmers more incentive to work, invest, and improve their techniques. Former tenant farmers, relieved of the need to pay 50 percent of the crop to landlords, experienced a modest rise in their standards of living. Limited access to agricultural inputs, both because of lack of availability and because of farmer poverty due to low grain prices—created partly because of cheap imports of PL480 grain[21] from the US—kept productivity gains in the 1950s and early 1960s modest. Nevertheless, from this time forward, rural, social, and political power remained in the hands of owner-cultivators, rather than non-cultivating landlords and educated yuji who avoided manual labor.[22]

The slow growth of the agricultural sector in the 1950s made it clear, at least to outside economic planners, that land reform had not been a panacea. The "balanced growth" theories current at the time suggested that if South Korea was to wean itself from the high levels of foreign assistance it required after the Korean War, the rural sector would require drastic improvement. Accordingly, international aid and development circles promoted the benefits of "integrated rural development." Beginning in 1953, the Ministry of

Education, with the help of UNESCO and UNKRA,[23] initiated a rural school project, and the Ministry of Education began emphasizing the construction of rural schools from 1960. The Agricultural Cooperative Law (Nongŏp hyŏptong chohap pŏp) and the Agricultural Bank Law (Nongŏp ŭnhaeng pŏp) passed in 1957. The former provided improved production factors (such as fertilizer) to the peasantry, while the latter provided rural credit. The Department of Reconstruction formed in 1958 and created the Agency for Rural Revitalization (Nongch'on chinhŭng ch'ŏng) in the same year.

The Agency for Rural Revitalization (ARR) organized demonstration development projects in hundreds of villages from 1959 and eventually reached thousands of villages nationwide by 1963. As with economic planning in general, which began in the late 1950s before the advent of the Park regime,[24] agricultural developmental planning did not have to wait for the military coup of 1961 to begin. However, under the First Five-Year Plan (1961–6), a substantial plan created before the Park Regime took power, the Park regime introduced administrative changes that increased the effectiveness of rural development and structured rural development throughout the 1960s and 1970s: (1) efforts to straighten fields and improve irrigation were strengthened and left within the Ministry of Agriculture and Forestry (Nongnimbu); (2) the old Agricultural Cooperative Law that had not been implemented as an obligation was replaced by a new Agricultural Cooperative Law on July 29, 1961, that combined the Agricultural Cooperative with the Agricultural Bank. This reorganization commenced the Park regime's emphasis on self-help as it called for "autonomous self-help agricultural cooperative tasks based on the peasants themselves" (nongmin chasin e ŭihaesŏ chajujŏk imyŏ chajojŏgin hyŏptong chohap saŏp).[25] It also made the parastatal[26] Agricultural Cooperative (Nongŏp hyŏptong chohap) the main source of agricultural inputs and agricultural credit, and one of the main sources of agricultural marketing in South Korea; and (3) the Agricultural Extension Office (Nongŏp chidoso) continued to be active.

These reforms created the basic framework within which rural development took place during the Park regime. A couple of characteristics of this framework are noteworthy at this point: (1) as was characteristic of the South Korean governmental structure at that time no single agency was assigned primary responsibility for rural development in the sixties, but rather a variety of agencies competed among each other to promote rural development: the

Agricultural Cooperative, the Agricultural Extension Office, and the Agency for Village Revival. These agencies had overlapping responsibilities and competed for influence and resources within the bureaucracy and among planning agencies. Straightening of fields and extending irrigation works was the responsibility of agencies within the Ministry of Agriculture and Forestry, as was agricultural extension work. In addition, by the mid-sixties, three different general rural development projects to improve village life and attitudes were the responsibility of three different agencies. The Ministry of Education had a program to create "rural development districts" centered on primary schools. The Agency for Rural Revitalization had a separate Rural Development Project (chiyŏk sahoe kaebal saŏp). Concrete activities to provide agricultural input, credit, and assistance in the marketing of agricultural products were the responsibility of the Agricultural Cooperative. (2) The language of self-help and autonomy was present from the start of these programs. A declaration of this sort was Park's famous speech on Agriculture Day (Kwŏnnongil), June 6, 1970, "Heaven helps those who help themselves" (hanŭl ŭn sŭsŭro tomnŭn cha rŭl tomnŭnda).[27] . . . "The peasant who tries to make a living for himself, who works diligently, is usually helped by heaven as well. But heaven cannot help the peasant who doesn't have a strong spirit of self-help (chajo chŏngsin), and the government and neighbors can't help him either."[28]

In spite of this rhetoric of self-help, however, Park-era development programs always operated largely from the top down. Straightening fields and irrigation construction projects were determined at provincial and county levels. Township level bureaucrats primarily participated in these projects in order to solve problems of land exchange and compensation among peasants getting new straightened fields or irrigation. At the Agricultural Extension (Nongŏp chidoso), priorities were set nationally, and implementation was done by "persuasion" of reluctant farmers through local field workers—what Burmeister (1987) called "directed innovation," rather than the "induced" innovation that would be indirectly motivated through manipulating pricing and marketing structures. The Agricultural Cooperative, during the period in question, was indeed a membership organization (not all peasant farmers belonged, though the most substantial two-thirds did), but it often used coercive techniques to implement policy set by government higher-ups. Many crops (such as tobacco, ginseng, and silk cocoons) were government monopolies in which the peasants got their seed (eggs, in the case of silkworms)

from the Agricultural Cooperative and were required to sell their crops to the
co-op as well.

During the later Yusin Period (which will not be dealt with in detail in this
chapter), villagers were often told by the Agricultural Co-op the quota of fertilizer that they were "required" to buy, and since rural credit was also controlled
by the Agricultural Cooperative, the peasants were in no a position to say no.[29]
My one experience of a program of the Office of Rural Revitalization was a
lecture by an urban professor in 1976 to an audience of peasant men, women,
and unruly children. The professor passed out an impressively scientific pamphlet (that I still have) filled with Chinese characters that explained why certain
agricultural practices are better than others (though the lecture had been on
modern family and child rearing). As we left the village hall one old villager,
noticing the pamphlet in my hand, asked me incredulously, "Can you read
that?" I said I could (not mentioning that I would need the help of a diction-
ary). He shook his head, "Well I can't!"[30] and walked off.

THE HISTORICAL ROOTS OF
PARK-ERA RURAL DEVELOPMENT POLICIES

The characteristics of the rural development bureaucracy of the 1960s and 1970s
confirm the corporatist character of the government at the time: decisions were
made at the highest level, and the role of local government was primarily to
feed information to the central authorities (so they could make policy) and to
mobilize the peasantry to participate in approved ways with government priorities. Although there were concrete programs to invest in rural areas—particularly during the Yusin era that is not dealt with in detail in this paper—there
was a palpable emphasis on "spiritual revitalization" and "self-help." These
characteristics, in fact, were not unique to the Park regime, but rather have
roots in colonial-era rural development programs, right down to the name of
the agencies involved and the developmental slogans that were used.

As has been shown elsewhere,[31] rural development had already been a
preoccupation of the Japanese colonial authorities from the early twenties.
From 1920 until 1934 (when they discontinued the program in the wake of the
world-wide agricultural depression) the Government-General promoted several rice production plans (that mostly involved reclamation of new land, and
improving irrigation facilities). These were initially done in cooperation with

large-scale landlords, particularly those large-scale Japanese and Korean landlords who were rationalizing and increasing their production. As agricultural prices deteriorated in the late twenties, and rural unrest became more and more serious, however, the Government-General began retooling its agricultural policies to address a wider range of problems.

The Decree on Korean Agricultural Associations (*Chōsen nōkai rei*) was published in 1927, and from 1928 these associations (dominated by Japanese and Korean landlords) mediated and settled tenancy disputes. A credit union (*kinnyū kumiai*) was set up to provide rural credit, but soon developed a bad reputation among Korean peasants for lending money to landlords which they re-lent at higher interest to tenants, and for foreclosing on debts and confiscating land (a process that became acute in the early thirties when the agricultural depression was most severe).[32] Thus, by the early thirties, rural Koreans were already familiar with government efforts to penetrate and mobilize the villages for economic and political reasons. The movement that shows the most parallels with Park-era agricultural development efforts is the Government-General's Rural Revitalization Movement of the early thirties. As Shin and Han point out, this movement shows classical corporatist tendencies in which "government sanctioned intermediary associations that link colonial subjects more effectively to the regime"[33] were created. These kinds of associations by their nature do not represent the economic interests of their members, but are created by the state for purposes of control and mobilization.

The rural revitalization movement began under Governor-General Ugaki[34] in November 1932, when the second rice production program was winding down. According to Shin and Han, the term "Korean Rural Revitalization Movement" (*Chōsen nōson kōkō undō*) was chosen under the influence of the Korean Peasant Society (*Chosŏn nongminsa*).[35] Unlike the previous rice production movements, however, Ugaki was convinced that spiritual, in addition to material considerations must be brought to the fore. This notion fit in with the growing emphasis on *kokutai* and military spiritualism in Japan, but it also reflected notions of the need for spiritual revitalization in rural Korea, as well. The program was organized with Councils for Rural Revitalization (*Nōson kōkō iinkai*) at all administrative levels with the top Government-General administrators' *ex officio* members at each level.

The Financial Cooperative (*Kinnyū kumiai*) and Mutual Aid Associations to Increase Production (*Siksan kye*) were also included in the councils. Notably, the government tried to bypass existing local leadership (*yuji*, local landlords, et cetera) to focus on "educated youth" who would have more "modern" notions.[36] During the colonial period (1910–45), of course, educated Korean youth would have been educated in Japanese-medium schools where they would have been subjected to Imperial Japan's assimilationist pressures and pejorative discourses about Korea, as well as modern, scientific knowledge. The slogans of the movement focused on self-help and cooperation: "rebirth through one's own efforts" (*charyŏk kaengsaeng*); "cultivate healthy beliefs" (*kŏnjŏnhan sinangsim*); "mutual help between rich and poor, wise and stupid" (*pinbu chiu sangbo ŭi midŏk*).[37]

Self-help in the Rural Revitalization campaign of the thirties was basically a method to promote rural development without asking for capital investment from the center.[38] During the movement, moral exhortation was used to discourage peasants from "wasting" their money on consumption so that they could save it for investment. Sumptuary regulations— encouraging peasants to wear straw sandals rather than rubber ones (rubber was needed for the war effort), and white (or black) rather than luxurious dyed clothes—were important parts of the program. Peasants were discouraged from taking out loans (for a wedding, say) so they did not get caught up in cycles of indebtedness. For political reasons, of course, the colonial regime discouraged peasants from becoming agitated by the "tendencies of cultural life" (that is, of course, left-wing thought).

In addition to discouraging consumption, the movement emphasized intensifying labor. More efficient use of labor in the village might free peasants for mobilization into war industries elsewhere. Thus, women were encouraged to engage in field labor.[39] A second form of intensification was the mobilization of the entire village into gangs (*ture*) rather than using more informal networks of labor exchange (*p'umasi*) to cultivate fields.

COLONIAL RURAL REVITALIZATION,
POST-WAR RURAL DEVELOPMENT

One of the most striking aspects of community development strategies of the fifties and sixties in South Korea are the continuities with the colonial period. South Korea's first integrated rural development ministry, the Rural Revitalization Agency (*Nongch'on chinhŭng ch'ŏng*), followed the name of

Governor-General Ugaki's program. While I cannot prove that it was modeled on Ugaki's program, activities reiterated many of the same sayings and ideologies of the Ugaki program: rebirth through self-help, frugality in consumption, avoidance of waste on extravagant ceremonies, success through village cooperation, and living a clean, modern life. Park's speeches in the sixties on agricultural development are also full of this kind of rhetoric. To give just one example:

> Where there is faith there is a future; where there is [a] will there is a way. Our firm faith that through our own strength (*uri him ŭro*) we will try to live better, our will to build our locality into a rich and good-living paradise will convert dried up wilderness into fertile soil; and making denuded mountainsides into fertile parks we shall without fail end up opening the autonomous, self-reliant (*charip chajon*) road of national revival (*minjok chunghŭng*).[40]

These are the themes that echo throughout the speeches of Park and the literature of rural development: self-help and autonomy. Sometimes these are expressed through the Sino-Korean terms "self-help" (*chajo*), "self-done" (*charip*), "self-surviving"[41] (*chajon*), "own strength" (*charyŏk*)—simple Koreanizations of the pronunciation of the Chinese characters of originally Japanese terms. More often Park uses both these and native Korean expressions such as "through our own strength" (*uri him ŭro*), "by our own efforts" (*uri sŭsŭro*), and so forth.

PEASANT MENTALITÉ

Along with the self-help talk, a striking characteristic of Park's rural development rhetoric is the emphasis on changing attitudes. "Heaven helps those who help themselves,"[42] has already been mentioned. He was even more explicit when speaking to cabinet secretaries, mayors, and governors: "Whether rural people live well, or live poorly, that is whether the income of peasants and fisher folk grows, depends upon whether the peasants discard their traditional consciousness and agricultural management, and how they pick up and make part of their life (*saenghwalhwa*) new agricultural management and technology that leads to development."[43] Note here that the "problem" of rural development is not defined in material terms—lack of access to factors of production, too little investment, distorted material incentives—but

in spiritual terms. More than anything else, he emphasizes "traditional peasant consciousness" as an impediment to development.

This attitude is not one that was held by Park alone during this period.
One could turn to innumerable treatises on rural development published in
South Korea during this period that proceed on the same assumptions. A
typical example culled from my personal collection of such books is Hwang
Kapson's *Theory of Rural Development* (1973). Pride of place is featured in his
chapter titled "Factors Inhibiting Agricultural Growth" in the section on
Korean Peasants' Consciousness and Values. Korean peasants, he says, have
a pre-modern consciousness that is based on affectivity rather than rationality.
Citing Western authorities as far-ranging as Spengler, Hwang continues that
spiritual values—ideology, values, and consciousness—are more important
than material conditions. Hwang cites traditionalism and conservatism
(familism, blindly following officials), belief in fate and destiny, and dependency as the main problems, while listing material conditions (such as frag-
mentation of farms) and technology well down on the list.

We find similar rhetoric about peasant fatalism in the speeches of Park. For
example, in a speech to regional officials in 1970, Park complained that, " . . .
the majority of peasants and civil servants, too, have done farming complain-
ing about drought saying it has to rain, and if rain doesn't come have fatalistic
conceptions that there is nothing human strength can do, and because of having this vice they cannot overcome, this year the government has had to hurry
up to set up policies."[44] The belief in the deleterious *mentalité* of the peasantry
is so widespread in the East and West that it would be futile, I think, to try to
trace these ideas to specific sources. Although there is a certain element of
plausibility in some of them, over all they do not correspond particularly well
with the *mentalité* of the peasants I knew in the seventies and eighties, making
me think that these ideas about the peasantry are discursively constructed.
However, the main point I want to make here is that *if one assumes peasant poverty is caused by peasant consciousness rather than material conditions, successful rural
development must depend on an educated intelligentsia to provide "modern knowledge,"
and on leadership to inspire the peasantry to change their traditional ways.* This was
indeed the emphasis of the New Village movement of the 1970s.

Rural development in the sixties was not so one-sided as one might
assume given the remarks mentioned above. There *were* important programs
dealing with material conditions—above all, the Agricultural Extension that

concentrated on developing new crops and seed types and the Agricultural Cooperative that focused on providing modern factors of production, capital, and marketing facilities to South Korea's peasants. There were also rural electrification and road building programs. These programs, combined with the price supports relied more heavily on by the Park regime in the seventies, provided the main material support to raising rural productivity and standards of living. Nevertheless, the amount of capital introduced to rural areas was minimal compared to the amount that went into industrialization. Park really did expect the peasants to "pull themselves up by their own bootstraps" just as Governor Ugaki had, and for similar reasons. Capital was just too short for the government to want to spend very much on low-return rural investment—in the case of Ugaki because of the depression of the thirties and Japan's military buildup for the invasion of China, in the case of Park because of the urgent need to build industrial capacity and military strength.

THE ROOTS OF PARK'S RURAL DEVELOPMENT STRATEGY

The parallels in rhetoric, assumptions about peasant *mentalité*, and emphasis on self-help in the Rural Revitalization movement of the 1930s and the Rural Development projects under the Park regime is quite striking and shows the way that Park's programs were embedded in Korean history. I am *not* arguing, however, that because President Park was educated by the Japanese military in Manchuria he favored Japanese-style development movements. Nor am I arguing that agricultural revitalization originating in Japan was applied to Korea in the colonial period, and then revived after liberation by South Koreans. If anything, in fact, the direction of influence seems to flow the opposite way, from Korea to Japan. If this seems surprising, we should remember that colonial governments do not have to deal with countervailing sources of power to nearly the same degree that domestic governments do. India often served as a laboratory for government action that was then applied to England, and it would not be surprising if a similar kind of process was at work in the Japanese Empire. The governor-generals of Korea, who ruled by decree and had to deal only with a few prominent Koreans and Japanese settlers, had much more autonomous authority to experiment with government programs than even prime ministers in Japan, who had to deal with a variety of centers of power including the military, the bureaucracy, industrialists,

party politicians, and local elites. Korea, thus, could well have been a laboratory for Japanese social experiments.

There is some evidence that this was the case. The name and many of the
slogans of the colonial Rural Revitalization movement seem to have Korean
sources, particularly the agrarians organized around the Society of Korean
Peasants (Chosŏn Nongminsa). Secondly, Korea's Rural Revitalization movement seems to *precede* similar movements in Japan by at least half a decade,
and when these movements were introduced into Japan the introducer was a
former governor-general of Korea. While the Rural Revitalization movement
of Korea got off the ground in 1932, it was really only after 1936 that these
intensely controversial mobilization tactics that bypassed local elites and were
used in Ugaki's Rural Revitalization movement in Korea could be applied to
Japan. It is interesting to note that two governor-generals of Korea, Saitō
Makoto and Ugaki Kazushige, both became prime ministers of Japan during
the period of military cabinets, and in both cases *after* their stints as governor-
generals of Korea. Saitō, after serving more than ten years as governor-
general of Korea, became prime minister of Japan from 1932 to 1934, during
which period he introduced some elements of rural revitalization, including
the slogan "rebirth through our own efforts" (*charyŏk kaengsaeng*).

Ugaki, under whose administration Korea's Rural Revitalization movement was initiated, after serving as governor-general of Korea from 1931 to
1936, became prime minister of Japan in the same year he relinquished his
position of governor-general of Korea. Was this just in time to apply what he
learned in Korea to rural Japan? Further research should clarify this point.
What interests me most about these problems, however, is the conception of
the peasantry that lies behind them. Again and again, whether one is reading
about the colonial-period Rural Revitalization movement, or the New Village
movement of the seventies, one comes across the same images: peasants as
conservative and averse to innovation, peasants as prodigal people who do
not think of the future, peasants as members of an *Urgemeinschaft* who traditionally cooperate with one another, peasants who waste their money on
unnecessary rituals, and peasants as backward people holding the country
from progress. These images do not correspond to what I saw of peasants in
the seventies and eighties. Did the peasants change, or were these images
fantasies of the urbanites? Above all, why would some bureaucrat in 1979 still
think that a spiritual revolution among the peasantry would achieve the task

of modernizing the rural community, and that this would accomplish national regeneration for Korea?[45]

The emphasis on spiritual regeneration of the peasantry, present from the beginning of South Korea's rural development efforts in the 1950s, was taken up by Park and extended systematically as he consolidated his power. What was a rhetorical tendency during the sixties when Park and the EPB emphasized "balanced development" (meaning balance between industrialization and rural development), was even more systematically incorporated into the New Village movement of the authoritarian Yusin period (1972–9). This rhetoric that is so characteristic of Park, and so abundantly found in his speeches, however, does not seem to originate with Park himself. Rather it seems to have been "common knowledge" among Korean developmental elites that Park was able to harness to politically mobilize the rural sector. The approach to development that combines this rhetoric with systematic attempts to mobilize "young modern leadership" in the villages to induce social change has its origin in colonial Korea. It seems to be neither a totally Japanese-imposed movement without Korean input, nor an indigenous Korean movement free of Japanese influence and coercion. Rather, the Rural Revitalization movement of the thirties and South Korea's post-liberation rural development efforts both seem to show typical colonial and post-colonial hybridity.

The colonial movement combined Japanese governing structures with Japanese and Korean intellectual input that was also influenced by existing Western notions of the rural backwardness of peasants. By the time South Korea began creating its own rural development programs in the 1950s, this originally "hybrid" thinking about rural problems seems to have become indigenized. It no longer seemed new: it just seemed to be common sense. In the 1950s, even North Korea used the slogan "Rebirth through our own efforts" (charyŏk kaengsaeng), pioneered by the colonial Rural Revitalization movement, for the Ch'ŏllima movement, its mass mobilization effort.[46] Thus, although much of Park's rhetoric and programs seem on the surface to have a "Japanese" flavor, rather than call it Japanese I would rather simply call it post-colonial.

CONCLUSION

The success of the Heavy and Chemical Industrialization Program in the seventies during the heyday of the New Village movement helped contemporary rural development in some respects by providing domestic inputs—for example, fertilizers to help Korean peasants raise their productivity. Its success also undermined rural revitalization, however, because urban living standards constantly grew more rapidly than their rural counterparts, so that the young—including the leaders trained by the New Village movement training center—kept leaving the countryside rather than providing the rural leadership that would create prosperous rural villages. For a short time in the seventies, high crop price supports kept rural incomes comparable with those of the urban areas. South Korea had, however, an export-dependent economy so that pressures of GATT—especially the Uruguay Round—made it impossible for Park's epigone to withstand the pressure to loosen the restrictions on agricultural imports necessary to keep domestic prices high.

The excessive concentration of industry in Seoul and the southeast, and the poor development of rural transportation infrastructure made it difficult for rural people to move into part-time farming as has been the tendency in Japan. In spite of Park's best efforts then, rural living standards in South Korea have fallen way behind those of urban areas. As the young and mobile move out, the rural work force has gotten older and older. Now, even those young men who remain in rural areas are finding it increasingly difficult to even find brides—rural life is hard and poor—so much so that progressively more rural men are turning to the internet and seeking marriage partners in places like Vietnam and the Philippines.

NOTES

1. In the constitution of the Third Republic, the president was directly elected to four-year terms, and could appoint his cabinet without the advice and consent of the unicameral legislature. The 173-seat legislature could not revise the junta's previous legislation, political independents were not allowed to run, and incumbents who changed parties, or whose parties dissolved, lost their membership in the assembly. Gregory Henderson, "Constitutional Changes," 32.

2. In the Yusin Constitution, the president was indirectly elected by the National Council for Reunification, a 2,359-person electoral board. One-third of the legislature was appointed by the president, and the rest was elected in multi-seat constituencies. Emergency measures were enacted to allow suppression of most dissent. Gregory Henderson, "Constitutional Changes," 33.

3. The 1999 publication of *The Sayings of Park Chung Hee* under the title "We, too, can do it," (Uri to hal su itta) is only one example of this phenomenon.

4. Han'guk kyŏngje kihoegwŏn, 2000, *Han'guk t'onggye yŏn'gam.* Year 2000 Census figures.

5. See, for example, Yi Kwangsu, "Nongch'on kyebal" [Rural enlightenment and development]. In *Maeil sinbo* November 26, 1916–February 18, 1917.

6. By calling Korea's rural population at the time "peasants" I do not intend to disparage them. I simply mean that they were small-holding farmers for whom "agriculture is a livelihood and a way of life," who produce *both* for home use, *and* for market sale on small family farms. See Robert Redfield, *Peasant Society and Culture,* 18.

7. Hong Nack Kim and Sunki Choe, "Urbanization and Changing Voting Patterns."

8. Park's collected speeches are available in several formats. Some on the New Village movement in English can be found in Park Chung Hee, *Saemaul: Korea's New Community Movement* or in Korean in *Saemaŭl undong: Pak Chŏnghŭi Taet'ongnyŏng yŏnsŏlmun sŏnjip* both published in 1978. Less well-known speeches are also available in Korean in his collected speeches published by the Presidential Press Secretary's Office starting in 1965. All of these sources organize Park's speeches by date, so I have generally cited the date and title of the speech, rather than specific editions. In most cases the translations are mine.

9. Ibid., i.

10. It is ironic to think that the period in which Critchfield was investigating his Korean village corresponds almost precisely with the few weeks of demonstrations leading up to Chun Doo Hwan's declaration of martial law and the Kwangju Uprising. None of this is mentioned in Critchfield's book.

11. *Chajo, hyŏptong, kŭnmyŏn.*

12. Richard Critchfield, *Villages,* 269.

13. Critchfield's observation of the aging and feminization of the agricultural work force was evidence for this phenomenon, though he did not interpret it this way.

14. Larry Burmeister, "The South Korean Green Revolution."

15. Park Chung Hee, "Chŏnju yuse yŏnsŏl" [Chŏnju campaign speech] 1967. 4.18.

16. I have many field notes about New Village movement activities that I have never analyzed.

17. Vincent S.R. Brandt and Man-gap Lee, "Community Development," for example.

18. Tenancy rates in North Korea, which has a smaller proportion of irrigated riceland than South Korea, were only about two-thirds of that of South Korea at the time of liberation.

19. In 1931, for example, most southern provinces had tenancy rates greater than 60 percent while northern provinces mostly had tenancy rates lower than 60 percent, with North Hamgyŏng coming in at 20.6 percent. Rents also tended to be lower in the north.

See Hoon K. Lee, *Land Utilization and Rural Economy in Korea*, Table 67, 155, passim.

20. Much of the benefit to peasants of the North Korean land reform was appropriate by the North Korean state through a 25 percent tax-in-kind levied in the fall of 1946.

21. U.S. Public Law 480 provided for the cheap sale of surplus U.S. grain to countries with food shortages.

22. Many former landlord families, traumatized by the "shame" of having their land confiscated (even if they were eventually compensated) migrated to urban areas or gradually sold their land to finance education for their children who then made urban rather than rural careers. Field interviews Kyŏngnam Haman County 1985–6.

23. UNKRA, the United Nations Korea Reconstruction Agency was a UN agency set up after the Korean War to assist the rebuilding of the devastated South Korean economy.

24. David H. Satterwhite, *The Politics of Economic Development*.

25. No Chang-sŏp, et al, *A Study of Rural Society*.

26. The term "parastatal" comes from Larry Burmeister, "The South Korean Green Revolution." Koreans usually say "half civilian, half official" (*panmin pan'gwan*).

27. By replacing "*hanŭl*" (heaven) with "*hanŭnim*" (God) —a term derived from an honorific for heaven—one can easily turn this phrase into, "God helps those who help themselves." "Hanŭl ŭn sŭsŭro tomnŭn cha rŭl tomnŭnda" June 10, 1970. Many of the slogans of Park are reminiscent of Weber's Protestant ethic.

28. Park Chung Hee, "God Helps Those who Help Themselves," *Saemaul*, June 10, 1970.

29. I know this from my own field notes, and this is also confirmed by Brandt and Lee, *Community Development*.

30. I took this to mean that he did not know the difficult scientific vocabulary, rather than to mean that he was totally illiterate—something that was uncommon among even rural males by the seventies, though many of the oldest women were still illiterate. To be fair, the pamphlet actually provides well grounded scientific information adjusted to the needs of the farmers of this region. However, a peasant would probably have required at least a high school education before being able to read and understand the pamphlet. In the late seventies and early eighties, however, there were no high school graduates in this fairly poor and remote village. Those villagers who had been able to complete high school had all migrated to the cities where there was more economic opportunity. It was only in the late 1980s that a few graduates of agricultural high schools (*nonggo*) whose fathers owned substantial tracts of land settled back in the village. A sample from the pamphlet is translated below:

> If one considers the status of absorption of nutrition in Poiodeae [grasses like wheat and barley] according to their growth cycle, much Nitrogen is absorbed over the early and middle growth periods, and although the rate of absorption of

Phosphoric Acid is low in the early growth period it rises rapidly from the middle growth period and displays its highest absorption rate at the time of ripening. Potassium shows a comparatively even rate of increase in its rate of absorption spanning the entire growth period. Republic of Korea, Nongŏp chidoso, 1976–77 *Tonggye maul ŭl yŏngnong*, 50.

31. Andrew Grajdanzev, *Modern Korea*; Sangch'ul Suh, *Growth and Structural Changes*; Gi-wook Shin and To-hyon Han, "Colonial Corporatism."

32. Han Toyhyŏn, "1930-yŏndae nongch'on."

33. Gi-wook Shin and To-hyon Han, "Colonial Corporatism."

34. Ugaki Kazushige was governor-general from 1931 to 1936.

35. Shin and Han give no reference for this statement, and I have not yet been able to document it.

36. Gi-wook Shin and To-hyon Han, "Colonial Corporatism."

37. Han Tohyŏn. "1930-yŏndae nongch'on."

38. Ibid.

39. My field experience leads me to believe that traditionally middle and upper class women refrained from field labor (except for vegetable patches). This was the pattern in San'gongni that I observed in the seventies. However, in other parts of the country more exposed to modernization, female labor was already common for transplanting, even in the seventies. Rural interviews in Haman-gun (near Masan) in the eighties led me to believe that in South Kyŏngsang Province, so many males had migrated to Japan by the late thirties that female labor was common in rice cultivation there by that time.

40. Pak Chŏng-hŭi, "Che 12 hoe chungang 4H kurakpu kyŏngjin taehoe ch'isa," [Welcoming remarks to the twelfth central 4-h club competitive congress] November 29, 1966.

41. The term *chajon* is difficult to translate into a pithy English phrase. It implies reliance on the self in the struggle for survival (*charyŏk saengjon*).

42. Park Chung Hee, *Saemaul: Korea's New Community Movement*, June 10, 1965. "Che 17 hoe kwŏnnongil ch'isa" [Welcoming remarks for the seventeenth farmer's day]

43. Ibid., December 5, 1968. "Kungmin kyoyuk hyŏnjang sŏnp'o tamhwamun" [On the spot proclaimed statement on the people's education].

44. Pak Chŏng-hŭi, "Chidoja rŭl chungsim ŭro mungch'in saemaŭl kakkugi undong" [The new village decoration movement united centering on leaders], a speech given to a regional officials' meeting on drought policy on April 22, 1970.

45. Ibid., i.

46. See its use, for example, in Kim Il-sŏng's speech "Modŭn him ŭl yŏsŏkkae koji ŭi chŏmnyŏng ŭl wihayŏ," 424.

9

Compressed Modernization and the Formation of a Developmentalist *Mentalité*

MYUNGKOO KANG

INTRODUCTION

South Koreans have struggled to overcome hunger and poverty for the past forty years. Despite the economic crisis of 1997–8, South Korea is now on the threshold of being one of the world's most advanced economies. Millions of Koreans who are now over sixty years old have gone through historical turmoil. They have witnessed the transformation from a pre-modern to modern society in terms of individual living standards; from the devastation and poverty under Japanese colonial rule and during the Korean War, to new lifestyles encompassing cars, apartments, department stores, and overseas travel. Few societies have changed from a pre-industrial to a knowledge-based economy within one generation. Such rapid change has been referred to as "compressed modernization" (*apch'uk chŏk kŭndaehwa* and *apch'uktoen kŭndaehwa*).

The rise of many South Koreans above the hunger and poverty level is attributable to industrialization and modernization. Even though there remain such problems as serious inequality, unemployment, a lack of transparency, as well as instability in the market system, many South Koreans have finally reached the minimum living conditions necessary for a decent life. Nonetheless, many obsessively believe that they should enjoy an even more abundant life. The middle and lower classes are eager to ascend to a higher social status. At the same time, each stratum of society struggles to live better than the other. They have no time to ask themselves what a better life is, or why they should want to live well. What is a better life to South Koreans? Only one clear criterion exists—materialistic affluence. They either have it or are eager to have it so that they do not need to envy others. The problem at this point is that they put being wealthier than others before the substantial quality of their own lives.

Being a winner in any kind of situation is considered to be a means to acquiring material prosperity. This prevailing idea is not limited to a few individuals or groups. South Koreans from lower to higher social strata are preoccupied with the desire for a better life. Developmentalism denotes a state of mind, behavioral style, and a structure of feeling that infatuates most South Koreans in this way. It is relevant to call such a state of mind a developmentalist *mentalité* because it forms a structure of feeling that makes up the psychological infrastructure inherent to South Korean society and goes beyond values or attitudes. I use the term *mentalité* as the Annales School defines it, meaning a kind of mindset that has been formulated in a society and shared by its community members over a long historical period, such as four or five hundred years.

This chapter examines how a developmentalist *mentalité* formed in the family system, as well as bureaucratic and corporate organizations, during the Park Chung Hee era and how this mentality is related to the formation of individual and collective identities. A developmentalist *mentalité* serves as a system of ideology and affect that consolidates modes of behavior as well as ways of thinking. Due to this developmentalist *mentalité*, civil virtues and morals of solidarity and tolerance have been replaced with avaricious desires for material possession and an indiscriminate, competitive, survival *mentalité*. As researchers point out, the developmentalist *mentalité* is a behavioral framework and a way of thinking in a society where all people compete with one another just like a war of all against all. Based on the belief in the need to get more profit and privileges, rent seeking has been established as a "rational" rule of the game instead of reasonable investment and transparent management between bureaucrats and enterprises. How can this perverse rule of the game be changed? This study assumes that though the developmentalist *mentalité* has acted as a catalyst for social vitality, it has also become a social ill from which South Koreans suffer. To explore how the forms of developmentalist *mentalités* work in different organizations, this study reviewed nearly two hundred academic articles that deal with issues related to compressed modernization since the Park Chung Hee regime. By analyzing these secondary sources, the study tried to identify a variety of forms of developmentalist *mentalités* in bureaucratic and business organizations and in individual and collective identities.

A CRITICAL REVIEW OF SOUTH KOREAN ECONOMIC GROWTH

Indicators of High Economic Growth

South Korea has witnessed continued economic growth since the 1960s. The Park Chung Hee military government strongly pushed ahead with economic development plans in a bid to obtain popular support because it had come into power by staging a military coup and therefore lacked political legitimacy. South Korea subsequently achieved high economic growth (7.8 percent) during the first economic plan period from 1962 to 1966, 9.6 percent from 1967 to 1971, 9.2 percent from 1972 to 1976, 5.8 percent from 1977 to 1981, and 8.7 percent from 1982 to 1986.[1] In line with economic growth, the GNP jumped about 200 fold from $2.3 billion in 1962 to $458 billion in 1995, and per capita GNP increased 116 fold from $87 to $10,076 over the same period. Secondary industries also rose accounting for 36.6 percent of GNP in 1995. They changed the labor market, household income, and the overall economy, as well as economic growth, while they accounted for only 8.7 percent of GNP in the early 1960s. With the growth of East Asian New Industrializing Countries (NICs) since World War II, the extent of South Korean economic growth is evidenced by its internationally accredited high growth rate. Figure 9.1 compares the economic growth rates of South Korea with other advanced capitalist countries and indicates that South Korea achieved far higher economic growth rates than advanced Western countries (as one would expect, given the extremely small economic base in South Korea in the 1960s). Over the past thirty years, South Korea has recorded an average growth rate of 8.38 percent compared with 2–3 percent, common among advanced Western countries.

As shown in Figure 9.1, the growth rates for the South Korean economy were significantly higher than those of Western capitalist economies. South Korea was outpaced only by Taiwan in growth rates. According to Lee (1980), early in the 1960s the Kennedy administration regarded South Korea as a country with little possibility of becoming industrialized due to a low level of technology and few natural resources. However, in 1966 South Korea began achieving economic self-reliance and industrialization that would enhance its status in the international community. Economic takeoff was facilitated by U.S. aid and support for economic reform, diplomatic and economic normalization of relations with Japan, and returns from participation in the Vietnam

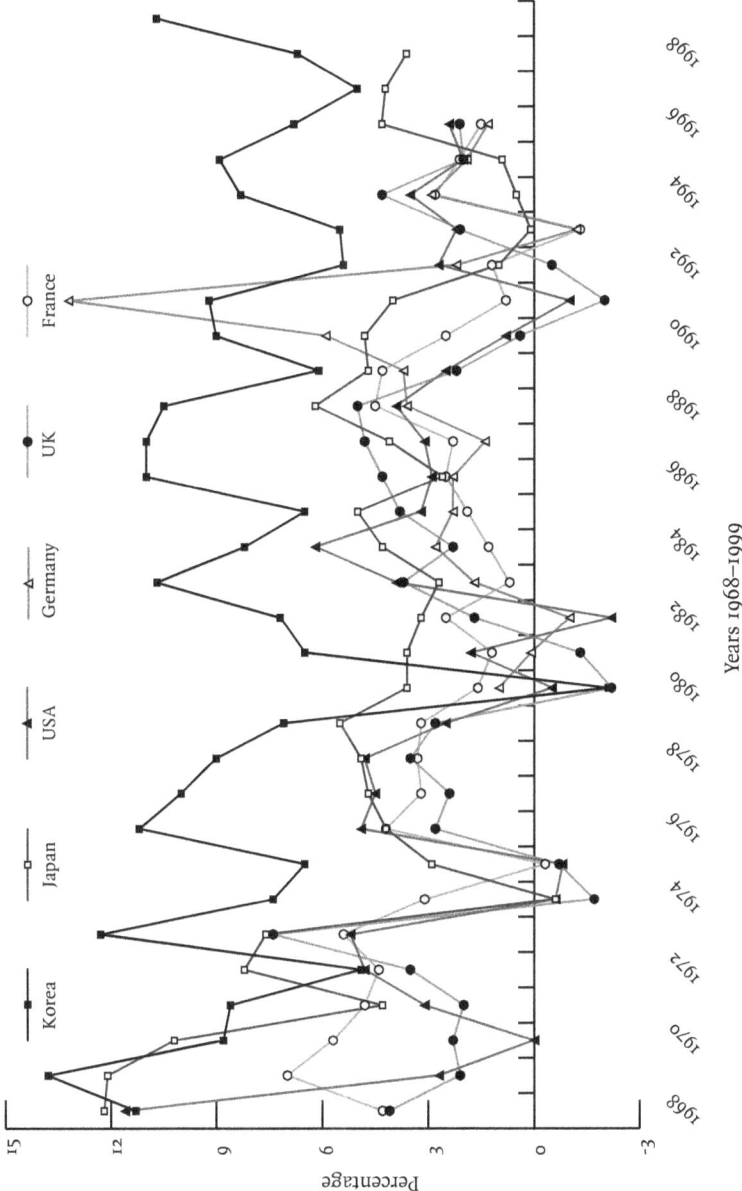

Figure 9.1 Comparative Annual Rate of Economic Growth

Figure 9.2 Annual Comparison: Scale of Trade Ratio to the Previous Year

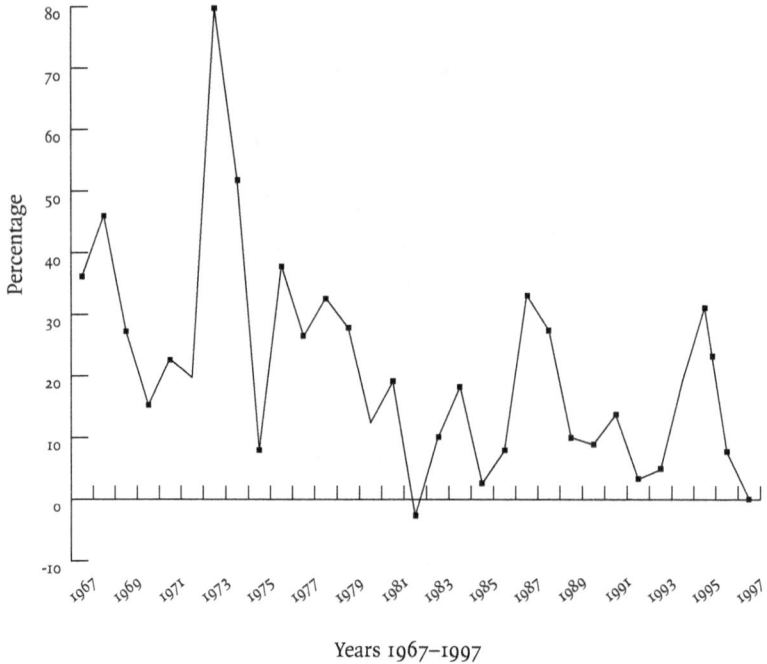

Years 1967–1997

War. South Korea was thus able to ratchet up through product cycles of increasing intensive capital investment and technological complexity as it moved from import substitution to export promotion.

These industrialization strategies expanded the volume of trade to an extent that exceeded high economic growth.

Figure 9.2 shows the increase in trade volume. The 1970s saw the average annual volume in trade grow by about 32 percent, whereas the 1980s saw a growth of about 14 percent and the 1990s about 11 percent. As a result, trade volume, which stood at $2.819 billion in 1970, jumped 100 fold to $280.778 billion.

The Chaebŏl-Centered Economic System: The Exclusion of Labor and Civil Society

As many researchers studying the development of the South Korean economy indicate, the state-driven, chaebŏl-centered drive pushed through the development process over a short period. An authoritative developmentalist state with critical roles played by policymakers and bureaucrats has driven South Korean development. The state-driven economy focused on large capital, excluding labor. In fact, the development process of the South Korean economy was one of condensed growth, achieved in a short period by giant chaebŏls. First, the number of subsidiaries of the five leading conglomerates increased more than three fold, from a total of sixty-two companies in 1972 to 197 in 1987, and to 258 in 1997.

The quantitative growth of large companies, however, meant not only an increase in the number of their subsidiaries; it also meant that these large companies controlled the daily lives of the people through the goods and services the company produced. In the past, the fostering of chaebŏl under state-mobilized development was focused on manufacturing. At the end of 1987, the number of manufacturing businesses among the subsidiaries of the five leading chaebŏl were even more numerous than that of the non-manufacturing sector. In terms of the sales volume of the manufacturing industry chaebŏl, total sales of the twelve largest companies accounted for 14.6 percent of total manufacturing sales in 1972 and 33.6 percent in 1987, respectively. In 1994, the shipments of thirty conglomerates made up 39.6 percent of shipments in the mining and manufacturing industries. The increasing proportion of chaebŏl in the manufacturing sector laid the foundation for chaebŏl control over the non-manufacturing sector and consequently extended the span of control to the whole of the South Korean economy.

According to the *White Paper on South Korea's Five Chaebŏl 1995–1997* published by the People's Solidarity for Participatory Democracy, five large companies accounted for 29.4 percent of total national assets and 30.0 percent of total liabilities in the nation's economy as of 1995–7, indicating that the chaebŏl had substantial control of the South Korean economy. But this kind of growth poses a problem in that it is limited to quantitative growth. The head of *Samsung*, Lee Kŏnhee (Yi Kŏnhŭi), unveiled the "Declaration of New Management from Quantity to Quality" in 1993. This example frankly revealed the reality of South Korea's economic growth. Except for some products, most export items produced by the chaebŏl did not match those of other countries in the world market in terms of quality. Moreover, the dependence upon imported machines, equipment, and intermediate goods was still high in producing export goods. According to the *Report on Competitiveness on*

National Industries, released by the Ministry of Commerce on July 14, 2000, D-RAM memory semiconductors and steel were dominant (in shares and technology) in the world market, while other export items were not competitive compared to items produced by advanced countries, including Japan.

Thus, state-mobilized development—a multiple industrialization process where import substitution and export promotion focused on fostering chaebŏl—brought a rapid increase in trade volume, the concentration on quantity rather than quality, and the incurrence of a chronic trade deficit. As a result, the increase in foreign liabilities became one of the major problems of the South Korean economy. Foreign liabilities slowed to some degree due to trade surpluses from 1986 to 1989, but showed a sharp rise later. In particular, as the capital market liberalized after the mid-1990s, the inflow of foreign funds, which focused on short-term capital, caused the imbalanced management of short- and long-term capital—the direct cause of the foreign currency crisis in 1997. To sum up, though led by chaebŏl, the high growth of the South Korean economy was unprecedented (except for Taiwan). But this growth came with a price to pay. Above all, the most serious problem was that workers were excluded from decision making. Long working hours and increasing industrial accident rates indicate who paid the price for high growth rates.

The working conditions of South Korean employees, including long working hours, were much worse than those of other developing, let alone advanced countries. In 1985, South Korea recorded an industrial accident rate of 1.8 accidents per 10,000 employees compared with 0.05 work-related accidents in Japan, 0.11 in the United States, 0.19 in Singapore, 0.57 in Hong Kong, and 0.80 in Mexico and Argentina. The rate of work-related accidents in South Korea was thirty-six times higher than those of Japan and at least twice as high as other countries.[2] The exclusion of workers from social integration prompted the emergence of a low-level civil society, which in turn became a dilemma for the developmentalist state and acted as a key factor in the formation of the financial crisis in 1997.

High economic growth accelerated urbanization. From 1960–95, South Korea's urban population increased by an average annual rate of 4.2 percent to 29 million in 1995, while the nation's entire population growth rate remained relatively stable at 1.7 percent. The urbanization rate climbed to 86.4 percent in 1995 from the 1960 rate of 35.8 percent.[3] Another characteristic of urbanization in South Korea is that it was concentrated in several major cities. The increase in population in capital regions as well as in Seoul was typical. In fact, South Korea's population increased dramatically from the 1960s to the 1970s. These decades also saw high economic growth, which then decreased substantially in the 1980s.

Moving back to suburban areas by increased housing prices, the urban population recorded negative growth figures in the 1990s. This back flow resulted in the rapid growth of satellite cities around Seoul. The population concentration in Seoul and regions around the capital is significant to understanding South Korea's character as a consumption society. The growth of the suburbs around Seoul does not simply relate to the concentration of population, but also the increased concentration of all sectors including the political, economic and cultural areas. The capital and the surrounding suburbs account for 65 percent of all bank savings, 58 percent of all industries, 82 percent of government and public sectors, 88 percent of major business headquarters and over 60 percent of insurance, real estate, and legal services.[4] Seoul and its satellites have a dominant role, which contributes to regional inequality in South Korean society. In addition to having divisions among the suburbs, the city of Seoul is divided further into local areas, creating regional inequality between the *Kangnam* (south of the Han River) and *Kangbuk* (north of the Han River) districts in Seoul.

As mentioned briefly, compressed modernization was initiated by the state and supported the chaebŏl. Employees and the general public did not have the opportunity to participate in the modernization process. In a similar way the chaebŏl led economic growth, the unprecedented case of urbanization, which focused on the capital and surrounding regions, caused inequality in land development. Over this relatively short period, compressed modernization severely influenced organizational culture and the operational rules of all social sectors. This study focuses on how compressed modernization influenced the operation and principles of social organizations and institutions and tried to set up the concept of a developmentalist *mentalitié*, not only as a result, but also as the driving force of compressed modernization. A developmentalist *mentalité* does not mean a personal sense of values or value orientation, but ways of practice and thinking that are set down in social organizations and institutions and shared by the members of these organizations and institutions. In the following section, I will examine how a developmentalist *mentalité* emerged in three fields: bureaucrats, enterprises, and identity formation.

THE DEVELOPMENTALIST MENTALITÉ IN BUREAUCRATIC ORGANIZATIONS

Yim Hyŏnjin (1998) understood the ruling structure of South Korea through the concept of "the organically unified state." According to him, an organically unified state is an independent concept that includes patriarchal, market, and bureaucratic authoritarianism, colonial totalitarianism, and a consul system. He also defines the developmentalist and entrepreneurial states as sub-concepts. In addition, Yim postulates that anti-communist ideologies and state-initiated capitalism brought about the concentration of state power, which consequently strengthened the government-centered bureaucracy and made bureaucratic decision making and administrative service part of major systematic principles.

"Loyalty to superiors" in Figure 9.3 was the only item agreed upon by both civil servants and the public. The figure clearly shows how civil servants and the public are familiar with centralized power and vertical order. On the part of the public, other items discussed including the motivation, political neutrality, responsibility, and sincerity of civil servants all remain at approximately 10–20 percent. These figures are more than half that of civil servants. More than 80 percent of civil servants gave themselves high marks concerning integrity, responsibility, and sincerity, while only 10–20 percent of the public agreed with them. The credibility gap between civil servants and the public is considerable. Meanwhile, civil servants think that they are deeply misunderstood or groundlessly mistrusted by the public.

South Korean bureaucracy has been reinforced in terms of systems since South Korea was liberated from Japanese colonial rule. Chŏng Yongdŏk (1999) and others point out the organizational characteristics that support hierarchical bureaucratic culture as follows. The first characteristic is a strengthened administrative organization. Amid the social disorder following liberation from Japanese colonial rule, the Korean War, and the extreme North-South confrontation under the cold war, South Korean bureaucracy grew into an oppressive organization, designed to exercise authorities, such as the army, police, intelligence, and prosecution departments. Many admin-

Figure 9.3 Differences in Attitude

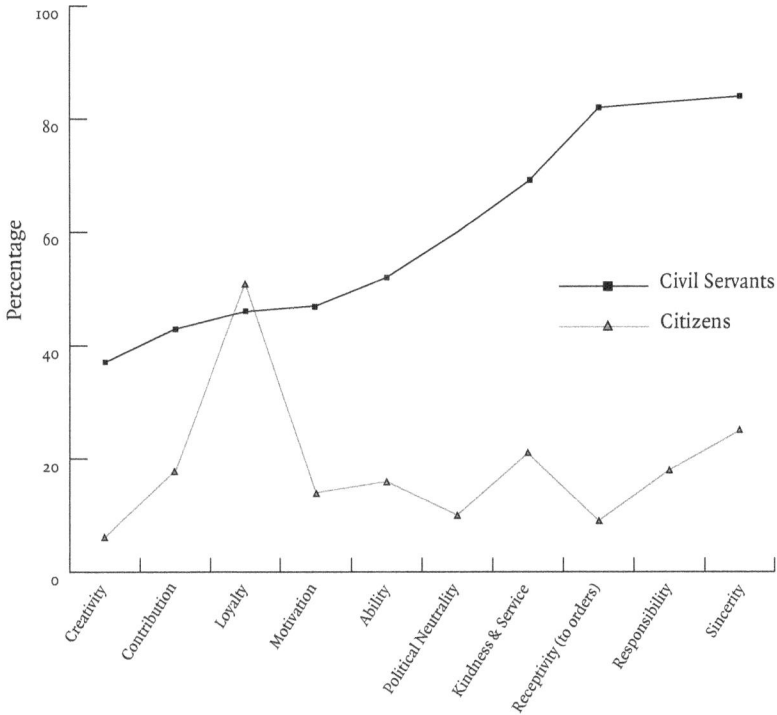

istrative organizations also regulate their customers, or the public, through the use of institutionalized excessive regulatory devices. Unlike Western countries, almost all of South Korea's organizations carry out regulatory functions related to social sectors without any clear distinction between compulsory directives and general administration.

The second characteristic of a hierarchal bureaucratic culture is the dominance of government initiative and the concentration of core administrative agencies. It is well known that the presidential office wields omnipotent power over the cabinet as well as the congress. The high-ranking officials and cabinet members tend to pay attention to the president and his advisors. The third characteristic is the underdevelopment of the representative system. Administration-led decision making and enforcement has weakened the power with which the congress controls the administration. In the end, the congress was dependent on the administration to provide the necessary information. Finally, the underdevelopment of civil participation in the government decision-making process was at issue. Many government committees, in which stakeholders and public interest groups express their opinions and interests, could barely exert their independence and autonomy.

In the name of administrative efficiency in the process of rapid economic development, state-initiated capitalism, where politics and economics are not separated from each other, became the basic origin of bureaucratic corruption. Corruption has been seriously discussed as a typical trait of compressed modernization in a bureaucratic society. Under the leadership of the Park regime and the export drive initiative, the unfair distribution of credit funds, financial favors, and incentives created a full-scale connection between political power and the chaebŏl. Consequently private corporations, including the chaebŏl compete with each other for special benefits from the government.

Moreover, irregularities and corruption led to moral hazards in the public sector. According to Pak Chunsik and Yu Sŏkch'un (1998), the "Confucian developmentalist state" had to utilize traditional human relations such as blood, regional, and school ties, rather than the autonomy of civil society, which made it difficult to accumulate capital through the expansion of trust needed for the long-term development of society. It was the vertical loyalty mobilized in the frame of Confucian favoritism, not voluntary participation.[5] Accordingly, instead of voluntary participation based on the trust and spontaneity of civil society, the top-down mobilization of the civic sectors became a common practice, which weakened the social trust. Owing to the diminishing of social trust, civil society paid little attention to the moral hazards of the public sector.

The bureaucratic system, as a core part of the organically unified state, developed a peculiar organizational culture. The developmentalist mentalité that is shared among bureaucratic systems breaks down to the following four points. First of all, an aristocratic military culture was necessary. This was the most striking way in which Park realized his policies. Many bureaucrats still seem to linger around this culture.

Second, a collective belief indicated that bureaucrats were the major subjects of economic growth and development. As pointed out in many studies, South Korean bureaucrats believed that they were the designated subjects of South Korean modernization and increased economic growth. Despite the positive aspects, in a sense this belief is related to the third characteristic of the *mentalité* that civil society and markets are to be regulated by bureaucrats. Bureaucrats share the belief that they control civil society and markets. Finally, bureaucrats share a strong belief that a democratic value orientation causes confusion and inefficiency. The institutionalization of anti-democratic decision making came from the idea that the information disclosure of the policymaking process, its enforcement, and discussion are the only causes of conflict and inefficiency. Thus, South Korea's bureaucratic culture affected not only bureaucratic society, but also the culture of commercial enterprises and, to a great extent, many social organizations.

THE FORMATION OF A DEVELOPMENTALIST MENTALITÉ IN BUSINESS ORGANIZATIONS

The above discussion shows that economic activities centered on business conglomerates dominated compressed modernization. In this organic system, corporate ownerships and administrations are combined on the basis of nepotism and familism, and management is diversified on this basis as well. In the process of economic growth, such business groups achieved remarkable growth by collaborating with political power and receiving favors. Using some businesses as a fulcrum for export policies and offering enormous incentives, the government left the chaebŏl to monopolize the fruits of economic success. Therefore, from the perspective of economic democratization, the problems found in conglomerates stem from democratization of distribution in addition to democratization of internal structure. Based on my review of the research, the developmentalist *mentalité* within the culture of corporate organizations, which formed in the process of rapid economic growth, can be described as follows.

The first feature is a strong, formal, and centralized power structure. Decisions are made mainly by the upper strata of the administration hierarchy, especially major decisions that require expenditure and those items that are supposed to go through settlement, which require formal approval by the upper levels of the administration. In South Korean businesses, approval procedures are regarded as a means of exercising authority and rule, rather than of discussion and participation. Such a decision-making system is attributed to nepotism, allegiance, and Confucian ethics that accompany respect for one's elders and superiors. The top-down, authoritative, decision-making system is also important. This system is organized on the basis of hierarchical structure, which is human-centered and in clear order. However, there are no definite descriptions of the relationship between authorities and responsibilities. Thus, passing down orders to subordinate officials has become a typical decision-making process in South Korean businesses. Bureaucratic organizations represent this top-down, decision-making system, many operational rules and procedures, and strict hierarchies of authority and control. Consequently, South Korean businesses are composed of complex characteristics combining mechanical, vertical, and horizontal structures.

Finally, the possession and the ruling structure of a unitary family are present. South Korean businesses are owned and managed by a unitary family because they have a short history, since their founders are alive. However, even the second and third generations of many conglomerates still rigidly maintain the hierarchy of a unitary family, which can be traced to Confucian cultural heritage. Song Min'gyŏng (1998) points out that the ruling structure of South Korean chaebŏl characterized by a unitary ruling system based on the preponderant ownership of the leader and his/her relatives. Therefore, the absence of both internal control systems, such as a board of directors or an audit and inspection department and external control systems is to blame for closed and arbitrary decision making by the conglomerate CEOs, many of whom lack specialized knowledge. This resulted in indiscreet expansions, which produced a drop in profits and efficiency and fragile financial structures due to excessive debt.[6]

On the other hand, financing has been rendered autonomous and this mode of financing has brought the financial market under the control of gigantic business groups. Such groups, after all, did not reform the unitary ruling system of conglomerates, but rather aggrandized and aggravated it. Accordingly, even the government, which held the only means to regulating the chaebŏl, lost control over them. The Park Chung Hee and Chun Doo Whan regimes repressed labor union movements and the development of civil society in order to advocate business groups to the extent that the government had no alternative social devices to regulate and restrain these business groups. This resulted in the government falling into the dilemma of a "developmentalist state."

The developmentalist state model thus accumulated a great number of negative underpinnings to the successful economic growth of the South

Korean economy, and this authoritative model became unsustainable on account of its internal contradictions as well as its success. However, while this model brought forth an unprecedented increase in conglomerate capital, it repressed not only the labor union sector but also the forces that could check and reform rapid growth. As a result, with the decline in state power and with checks and balances within the system still underdeveloped, the transition from a state-driven to a market economy led to the reinforcement of the conglomerate hegemony system. After all, since having stuck to the single purpose of joining the group of rich nations out of faith in national enrichment, the South Korean government averted its attention from the quality of life of its citizens and fixated on entering the arena of developed countries. In times of somewhat materialistic affluence, rather than considering how to manage a balanced national economy and how to maintain an individual's quality of life, they committed themselves only to expansion in a manner where appearances and formalities were regarded as more important than substantiality.

The discussion above deciphers the cultural codes of the so-called chaebŏl in South Korean society, which emerged during the process of compressed modernization. Economic growth mostly through governmental favors gave birth to cozy relations between politics and big business, which made it possible for decisions to be made and arbitrarily carried out by the CEOs. When obtained through a connection with an influential official in the government, preferences were not fundamentally grounded on the market system. Thus, nepotism allowed power to shift. This favoritism brought about an authoritative business culture which choked up reasonable intercommunication by insisting on top-down decision making. Second, instead of having developed conglomerates systematically, the government strongly suppressed other sectors that would have limited big business activities. As a result, at the same time as concentrated power of the government attenuated, giant businesses strengthened their influence on the entire society. Harsh control over civil society and labor campaigns resulted in weakening social activism. Many social activist groups have played significant roles in watching and debunking rent-seeking and corruption among bureaucrats and the chaebol. Therefore, despite the pluralistic political system in South Korea, paternalism and nepotism prevail in a South Korean business culture deficient in public ethics.[7]

The Individual and Collective Identity of South Korea

Institutional changes that compressed development also affected Koreans'
identity. Condensed growth and a developmentalist *mentalité* can be found in
South Koreans' identity changes as well. In this chapter, South Korea's identity changes are classified into the following four groups: authoritative hierarchy, materialism, abnormal individuals and groups, and closed nationalism.
First, a persuasive, strong, authoritative hierarchy insists that South Koreans
believe subordinates should obey their superiors. As a consequence, the democratic sphere and civic virtue remain underdeveloped. According to Yim
Hŭisŏp (1997), South Koreans have a strong class consciousness because they
understand and organize human relations and social ethics in order of rank—
sovereign and subject, father and son, husband and wife, and old and
young—and prescribe these relations as similar to the relationship between
ruler and subordinate.

Reigning political powers and bureaucrats, decision making by small
numbers of the powerful, an organizational culture of order and obedience,
and an unequal patriarchy were institutionalized when an internalized,
authoritative hierarchy appeared as a form of lifestyle or social culture. This
authoritative hierarchy is prevalent even in intellectual communities, where
rational discussions should be regarded as paramount. Personal networks
take priority over academic discussions, and the relationships between senior
and junior individuals supersede performance or competence in shaping
important human relations. Even in the intellectual world it is not the inter-
change between people with similar ideas, values, and visions, but the inter-
change between people with the same alma mater and hometown ties that is
paramount in South Korea. An intellectual, one not following authority and
rank, is either stigmatized as a unique person in the academic world or is
excluded from it.

Secondly, materialism serves as an important element in defining South
Korean identity. Materialism established its roots in the history of South
Korea for the past one-hundred years. The Korean society that went through
colonial rule and the Korean War had no chance to form into the middle
class. With the rapid collapse of the governing classes under Japanese colonization, only a few pro-Japanese bureaucrats and enterprises could survive.
The ruins of the Korean War prevented classes from disintegrating and left

everyone with no choice but to start their lives anew in poverty. In fact, during the first half of the twentieth century South Korea's modern society did not allow any upper classes or their cultures to develop because everyone was equally poor. In the latter half of the twentieth century, the upper class emerged through the accumulation of material wealth and the upper and middle classes increased in number after the 1980s. However, these classes did not have enough time to build their own cultural identities. These classes could not form their own cultural tastes by undergoing unique cultural experiences. Instead, they differentiated themselves from other classes through displaying material possessions and outward appearances such as the size of an apartment or car and avaricious expenditures for luxuries. Compared to other South Koreans, the upper and middle classes plunged themselves into the struggle to possess and spend money on material items because the mere accumulation of material wealth gave them a ticket to enter the upper strata of society.

The cultural identity of the upper class could be reached by anyone, merely through materialistic ostentation, without any cultural sophistication and commitment to civility. Paradoxically, this meant, Koreans believe, that whoever had material capital could become the upper class. The upper class was thus not held in awe. Respect and difference in status were not granted to them. Having degenerated into this morbid pursuit, materialism gave rise to anti-humanitarian criminal fortune and a large number of tragic deaths. The idea that materialistic success could not be achieved through normal and legitimate means was widespread in South Korean society. The general perception was that successful enterprises could not have piled up their wealth without succumbing to illegal measures. Finally, selfish individualism was singled out as a symbol of the change occurring in the identities of South Koreans. Rapid development of South Korea prevented desirable individual and group models from becoming prominent. Thus, as egoism prevailed over individualism, groups revealed themselves in the form of collective egoism. Likewise, a society composed of egoistic individuals and groups existed as a form of egoistic civil society and left as its legacy negative phenomena such as a network-related culture and an absence of public consciousness. Civil society, the driving force of democracy, came to hold conservative characteristics in line with the neo-liberalism pursued by national and private enterprises. The campaign to extend and democratize civil society began in 1987.

However, when the middle class suddenly turned back to conservatism early in the 1990s, democratization of many social sectors stagnated. Conservative characteristics led to this postponement.

South Korean individualism is characterized by a strong self-defensive propensity, and research shows that individualism in South Korea is either egoistic or expedient.[8] Instead of rational and self-reliant individuals, excessive, rugged indivualism prevails. The collective egoism of South Koreans can be viewed as a combination of traditional collectivism and rugged individualism, or as closed "pseudo-familism." In regard to the historical background of such egoistic individualism, Yim Hŭisŏp points to the absence of a civil community, self-defensive lifestyle (colonization, war), and a sense of individualism that had yet to be established as desirable values.[9]

Collective egoism as "pseudo-familism" can also be said to reveal itself as a mode of "South Korean immoral familism."[10] The evils of pseudo-familism include relationship problems, preference for group action (rather than rational discussion), weakened consciousness regarding public order and ethics, and the blockage of reasonable public opinions. These evils lead to an "egoistic" civil society. As a result, South Korean civil society formed an identity, one which overlapped with the traditions of a nation-centered history, the experiences of Japanese colonization, the division of the Korean peninsula, state-and-conglomerate-led development strategies, and social divisions brought on by regional differentiation.

Civil society came to bear the character of a grassroots organization, which established its inborn conservatism as a national trend. Hence, South Korean families could not develop a sense of "community" but rather "co-exist" with neighbors. Families settled down as alienated social organizations, and each family pursued its own material accumulation and composure exclusively. Finally, the identity change of South Koreans can be attributed to closed nationalism and internalized colonialism. South Koreans are not reasonably aware of others because they have an imbedded sense of national pride. Japanese colonization adopted an exclusive attitude towards foreigners as a matter of course, and South Korean nationalism has continued this legacy since the division of the Korean peninsula. The nation was accepted as a category of transcendental life. Nation-led modernization led to a misconception of recognizing state-centered nationalism and national sentiment as aspects of the same category, this in turn has been internalized by most South

Koreans. Good examples include war objectors and men refusing to join the army. People who object to the country going to war and those refusing to join the army are considered traitors, not pacifists.

At the same time, during the process of condensed modernization, the United States, by introducing Western systems and products into South Korea, became not only a blood ally who protected South Korea from communist revolutions, but also a model that South Korea should pursue in all sectors. The Americans were the people South Koreans were truly anxious to be, while Eastern Europeans merely represented the proverbial man who lets his failure be a lesson to all. South Korea sought to resemble America in all sectors, including politics, society, the economy, and culture. South Koreans were sensitive to discrimination against Koreans living in and visiting the U.S. and to Koreans living in Japan, while oblivious to discrimination against Southeast Asian people. However, South Koreans' hypocrisy was not seen as at all strange to them. South Koreans' longing and inclination for America were not imperialistic demands but rather the result of internalized colonialism, because this attitude had not been forced on them, but was voluntary. As we have seen briefly in the previous sections, the developmentalist *mentalité*, which emerges in bureaucratic, business, and family social systems is probably an aspect of the South Korean identity that has been Westernized. Also, this *mentalité* appears in similar forms in churches, educational institutions, the army, and local and regional communities.

BEYOND THE DEVELOPMENTALIST MENTALITÉ

In the previous sections, we discussed *mentalités* that emerged as South Korean society went through compressed modernization, including such areas as bureaucracies, enterprises, and individual and collective identities. Arranged are several common characteristics among these four spheres. First, when bureaucratic organizations, private corporations, and family systems are examined in detail, a culture of authoritative and centralized organization is conspicuously exhibited and can be identified by the degree of dispersed power and decision-making processes. Most researchers point out that school and hometown ties have a strong influence on the structure of human relations and networks inside these organizations. Many researchers indicate that the South Korean family, which has experienced condensed modernization, clearly shows how uncertain living conditions and excessive competition can distort the behavior and value inclination of a family system into one that exclusively chases its own interests.

Although western countries have introduced modern bureaucracy and market operating systems into South Korea, in reality South Korean bureaucracy and market competition are based on completely different principles and cultures. Many studies indicate that incorporating a fixed organization culture, rather than developing structures and operating principles unique to the South Korean environment, did not firmly establish inappropriately operated modern systems. In order to make its members agree to the use of power and to follow the rules, the bureaucratic or business organization needs members' trust. In turn, this confirmed that the organization is performing at a level of accountability that corresponds to the exercise of that power. Even though ruling classes exist, distrust and resistance to dominant order bring about political burdens and costs to the overall society.[11] Systematic change in such bureaucracies, businesses, and family structures display several characteristics in the individual and collective identity of who South Koreans are. Value inclinations such as materialism, an authoritative value system, and family collectivism are remarkable features, while the absence of civic moral virtues is regarded as especially important.

Why and how we should live well are not worthwhile questions to ask individuals and groups in South Korea. Park Chung Hee's slogan, "Let's live well," referred to western developed countries, our neighbor Japan, and the upper and middle classes. Koreans have internalized a competitive spirit, achievement-centered behavioral modes, and the desire for social upward mobility. However, there was no room for civic virtues like morality, civil consciousness, and accountability. The developmentalist mentalité regarded only the results as important and exclusively pursued self-centered understanding. With this mentality, rational individualism or association founded on morals and accountability could not develop. Rather, South Koreans have chosen to invest in strengthening their strategic networks and familial human relations to survive uncertain situations where all systems and rules are discredited.

In essence, a generalization of behavior occurred and South Koreans began to realize that they could manage themselves and survive within an organization by becoming good-natured people instead of improving their

competence. This resulted in the absence of localized neighborhood communities and simultaneously produced a myriad of organizations rooted in
regional and academic "alma mater" relationships as well as many pseudo-
family groups rooted in nepotism networks. The organizational culture,
based only on power with no accountability, alongside the absence of civic
moral virtues and a sense of community, extended into daily lives. As such,
South Korean metropolises, including Seoul, could not attain modern urban
development including neighborhood communities created through the voluntary participation of citizens, and rules and order. Instead, Seoul and other
cities like her tumbled down into objects of speculation finally resulting in a
jungle of heated competition.

In the early 1990s a real estate economy bubble started from speculation
of apartment prices and reduced the housing supply to less than 50 percent
of demand. The government responded by creating a speculation economy in
Pundang and Ilsan. Housing became "fashionable" and a "hot" commodity.
By the end of the 1990s housing supply rates soared up more than 80 percent.
However, for the past forty years real estate in Seoul and the suburban areas
could not provide sufficient space for human living or for the urban community. Apartment complexes become the objects of investment, not the spaces
for community. In 2006, real estate speculation, especially in the Kangnam
area, epitomized how polarized South Korean society had become.

South Korean spending produced by the developmentalist *mentalité* I have
discussed flourished on the hot wind of urbanization. Without a doubt, developmentalism led South Koreans to delight in avaricious consumerism beyond
ostentatious consumption. Going beyond general consumerism and confirm-
ing their identity through expenditure and satisfying their own desire, they
had acquired avaricious personalities and believed they should not only "keep
up with the Jones'" but possess and spend more than others. Coming into
existence around Seoul, avaricious consumerism combined with the developmentalist *mentalité*. Which behavioral mode, lifestyle, and identity should
South Koreans adopt in order to meet the new century? How do we set up this
culture? To respond to these questions, we should be able to draw a picture
of how South Koreans should live as citizens of the modern nation-state of
South Korea. Of course, one chapter is not enough to provide you with much
of an answer to these questions. In our society, on the whole, we can find
many critiques, reflections, and cause analyses on developmentalist *mentalités*.

However, it is hard to discover discussions on how to transcend a developmentalist *mentalité*. Many people criticize corrupt, scanty operational systems, the absence of civic moral virtues, the lack of a community sensibility, and the aggressive and competitive temperament for survival. Complaints are plentiful yet these critics do not disclose answers to how to overcome this, and their efforts toward a solution are not prominent either. This is similar to a situation where, while despairing about the failures of the South Korean political system and agreeing to reform, no one believes that the system can be renovated in a short period of time. The reason for being unable to predict the conquest of this *mentalité*, and the want of reflection on an alternative, is that the developmentalist *mentalité* is a deeply rooted and visceral part of the government, big business, public organizations, and family sectors. Since we are obsessed with the idea of how to live better than others and with how our families can live better than others, we do not dare assert the need to think of others in addition to ourselves.

NOTES

1. The Bank of Korea, *National Accounts*, 1990.
2. Kim Hyŏnsu, "Uri nara ŭi sanŏp chaehae wa chaehwal chiwŏn chŏngch'aek."
3. Republic of Korea National Statistical Office, *Republic of Korea Statistics Yearbook 1970–1995*.
4. Kim Yongung, *Chiyŏk kaeballon*.
5. Pak Chunsik and Yu Sŏkch'un, "Han'guk sahoe pujŏng pup'ae kijae wa yuhyŏng."
6. Song Min'gyŏng, "Kukka chudojŏk sŏngjang chaejae wa chaebŏl, kyŏngje wigi."
7. An T'aegwŏn, "Han'guk simin munhwa ŭi chaep'yŏn kwa munjae."
8. Yim Hŭisŏp, "Hyŏndae Han'guk in ŭi kach'igwan salm ŭi mokp'yo kach'i wa kyubŏm kach'i rŭl chungsim ŭro," 143–62.
9. Yim Hŭisŏp, *Han'guk sahoe pyŏndong kwa kach'igwan*.
10. Chang Kyŏngsŏp, "Han'guk kajok ŭi inyŏm kwa silche."
11. Chang Kyŏngsŏp, "Apch'uk kŭndaehwa wa pokhap wihŏm sahoe."

10

The Park Chung Hee Era and the Genesis of Trans-Border Civil Society in East Asia

GAVAN MCCORMACK

PEOPLE POWER AND THE MAKING OF HISTORY

The rapid maturing of South Korean civil society and democratic institutions following the "democratic revolution" of 1987 and the end of the cold war in 1989 has opened an intense debate on the nature and meaning of the Park Chung Hee (Pak Chŏnghŭi) era. Though the era survived in a modified form under the successor regimes to 1987, it now becomes almost an ancient, hotly contested past. As Zhou Enlai once reportedly observed of the French Revolution, 200 years is too short a time to reach a historical assessment. For the Park era, thirty is too short.

In the 1960s and 1970s, relationships between states in East Asia were primarily determined by their location within the global structures of the cold war, and military governments, giving priority to anti-communism and ruthlessly crushing democratic movements, were installed and maintained under Washington's sponsorship in Indonesia, the Philippines, and South Korea. It is sometimes said that the cold war ended in 1989 with the victory of the "free world" especially the United States. In East Asia it might better be seen to have ended with the defeat of "free world"-supported national security state regimes at the hands of the democratic resistance, or "people power," in the Philippines with the overthrow of the Marcos regime in 1986, in the Republic of Korea with the overthrow of the Chun Doo Hwan (Chŏn Tuhwan) regime in 1987, and in Indonesia with the overthrow of Suharto in 1998. These interventions, which today would run a high risk of being labeled "terrorist," forced drastic change in intra- and inter-state structures and put an end to regimes long sustained by Washington and Tokyo.

This chapter addresses the emergence during the Park era of "people power," not so much the domestic, intra-Korean movements as the transborder, cross-nation civil society, in other words, the genesis and early stages of global civil society. In the present context of spreading global terror, both state and private, the task of promoting or facilitating spontaneous citizen action to advance a democratic agenda has never been more urgent. The Park regime, especially under the Yusin Constitution of October 1972, combined to a highly unusual degree, economic growth and dynamism with political repression. It was an early model of what was to become known as the "national security state." While South Korea faced legitimate concerns over national security because of the continuing North-South confrontation, its national security state deployed its powers repeatedly and ruthlessly to maintain control and to crush any opposition, whether or not connected to North Korea.

The legal frame for repression was one inherited from pre-war Japanese fascism, the so-called peace preservation system that had originated in Japan in 1925. Under the National Security Law, adopted in South Korea in 1948 and revised several times thereafter, "anti-state" activities, including anything that might be interpreted as offering aid, praise or encouragement, or any effort to confer or correspond with, anti-state groups, defined as those whose intention was to "conduct or direct infiltration of government or to cause national disturbances" were punishable by penalties including death.[1] In practice, "anti-state" meant "North Korea," and in practice, as James B. Palais wrote, police authorities were "allowed to arrest people on trumped-up charges with little legal justification, force confessions through the use of torture, and prosecute them on the charge of treason."[2] The poet Kim Chiha explained the operation of the security system this way: "In South Korea, Lao Tzu, Confucius, Jesus, the Buddha, anybody and everybody concerned with fundamental truth or essential reality would be a communist."[3]

A key role in this state apparatus was played by the Korean Central Intelligence Agency (KCIA), which diplomat and Harvard scholar, Gregory Henderson, speaking to a congressional committee in 1976, described as "a state within the state." It was, he said, a "vast, shadowy world of an estimated 100,000 to 300,000 bureaucrats, intellectuals, agents, and thugs, often the real substance of South Korean rule for which the Korean government ministries and parties are frequently a slightly more respectable façade." The

KCIA played "a key role in virtually all government planning, North Korean affairs, international affairs, labor and its unions, the collection and shake-down of needed funds, many economic and tourist functions, military, aca-demic, and other infiltration, control over overseas Koreans and, above all, surveillance and direction of all Korean political activities."[4] In short, the KCIA under Park ran rampant, imposing widespread violence and terror, beyond and outside the service of legitimate state security. The confrontation with North Korea was no more a justification for this than is the contempo-rary U.S. confrontation with Al-Qaeda a justification for the atrocities of Guantanamo, Abu Ghraib, and Fallujah.

The international movement around Korea was stirred first by government abductions and the state terror tactics of the 1960s. It was a time when stu-dents, artists, and professionals were abducted from Europe (1967–9) and Kim Dae Jung (Kim Taejung) from Japan (1973). Some of them then being subjected to judicial execution (Francis Park also known as Pak Nosu, who had been studying at Oxford) and others, such as the musician (later distin-guished composer) Yun Yisang, barely escaped with their lives and never fully recovered from the torture they endured.[5] Attempts by Korean activists, whether from South Korea or Japan, to open links between the North and South were crushed and conspiracy trials resulted in severe sentences, occa-sionally death. The "Korean-in-Japan," Suh Sung (Sŏ Sŭng), returning after vacation at his Japanese home to take up a teaching assistantship at Seoul National University in March 1971, was arrested, indicted as part of a so-called campus spy ring of Korean residents of Japan and incarcerated for nineteen years.[6] The eight defendants in the People's Revolutionary Party case were executed in 1975.[7] Many others fled from the repression, to Germany, Canada, Australia, and the United States.

The case of Kim Dae Jung, opposition politician abducted from Tokyo in 1973 by South Korean security agents, imprisoned in 1976 over the "Declaration of National Salvation," sentenced to death in 1980 for "anti-state activities," in due course released, elected president in 1996, and awarded the Nobel Peace Prize in 2000, is well known and is the best example of the use of a national security apparatus for suppression of democratic dissent under Park and his successor regimes. Conventionally, Kim's survival is attributed to the intervention of governments, especially that of the U.S.,[8] but foreign pressure, whether from Tokyo or Washington, cannot be understood outside the broader context of international civil democracy. The attention of congressional committees slowly shifted in the 1970s toward the terror of South Korea's "state within a state," but the primary concern of official Washington was the maintenance of the anti-communist Seoul regime. Corruption and influence-peddling, the matters that collectively became known as "Koreagate," were of secondary importance.

The international movement had various objectives: to secure the release of prominent political prisoners such as Kim Dae Jung, Kim Chiha, the "Soh brothers," and others, but also, though more vague terms, to seek a resolution of the long-frozen Korean question and to try to prevent cold war, North-South hostility from breaking out into a renewed hot war. So, in this chapter, I want to address several strands of that movement: the London-based, British movement—not especially significant but one that I was directly involved in and can therefore easily speak about—the Tokyo-based, Japanese movement, and the German-based, European movement. I will call them, for simplicity's sake: London, Tokyo, and Berlin. There should, of course, also be a North America section, but there is not for the simple reason that I was not there and do not know it well enough. What follows is not an attempt to write a history of these movements, but to offer a rough sketch of processes neglected by most histories, a sort of prolegomena to the study that one day may be done.

Ultimately, the democratic revolution triumphed in South Korea in 1987. National division continues and the national security state, though mellowed, remains, but political prisoners were released, the truth about the repression practiced by the old regimes slowly began to emerge, and artistic freedom of expression and criticism flourished. The focus shifted from the struggle for democracy to the struggle to consolidate it and liquidate surviving components of the old regimes. The question now facing South Korea, and the international network around it, is how to develop, out of the complex events of this relatively recent past, a sense of history that somehow does justice to, while also transcending the passions and prejudices of the past. In recent years, the people who had struggled for these causes during the cold war, often at great personal cost, entered the mainstream of history. In 2001, the contributions to Korean democratization from people outside the country were formally acknowledged and a special body, the Korea Democracy Foundation, was established by President Kim Dae Jung to that end.

In October 2002, sixty-seven women and men who had contributed to the democratization struggle, thirty-three of them from Japan—including Wada Haruki (discussed in further detail below), novelist Oda Makoto, and others—were invited to Seoul, where they met and were publicly thanked by President Kim Dae Jung and former President Kim Youngsam (Kim Yŏngsam). In September 2003, a second group, which included members of the long-banned Japan-based Korean organization, Hanmindong, together with other Tokyo- and Europe-based activists (discussed below) was invited. In no other "Western" country has the process of democratization advanced, as in South Korea, to the point of national recognition, even celebration, of those who, a generation ago, were hunted, imprisoned, maligned, and exiled, and those who strove to help and express solidarity with them.[9]

PEOPLE AND PEOPLE POWER

London

The Park regime, especially as consolidated following the adoption of the Yusin Constitution, was in the mid-1970s at its peak: the rivalry between North and South Korea was intense, and the cold war hostility between the east and west blocs was acute. Many believed that with the ending of the war in Vietnam the cold war might next erupt as a hot war in Korea. In London, with a small group of colleagues and friends who had been active in opposition to the U.S. war in Vietnam, I was involved in setting up a group, which we called simply "The Korea Committee," designed to publicize and combat those dangers.[10] We conducted a conference in 1976, and in 1977 we produced a small book, published the following year in the United States as *Korea North and South: The Contemporary Crisis*. It was also translated into Japanese and Korean, although the Korean edition was completely unknown to us till many years afterwards.[11]

Thereafter, in one forum or another, as an NGO long before that word existed, we wrote papers, gave talks, participated in international conferences in Tokyo ("Emergency International Conference on Korea," 1976), Bonn, and elsewhere, met with various Korean representatives and activists, including North Korean diplomats, and visited North and South Korea.[12] We insisted on our autonomy and thus remained apart from the burgeoning "sponsored," solidarity movement. In one way or another, we continued our involvement in the emerging, international, civil society movement for support of what we described as "democracy and reunification" of Korea. In academic terms, our group was closely related to the London-based Association of Radical East Asian Studies (AREAS) and the U.S.-based Committee of Concerned Asian Scholars, which published the *Bulletin of Concerned Asian Scholars* from 1968 (*Critical Asian Studies* from 2000). We thought of ourselves as radical scholars, independent Marxists of a New Left affiliation.

Ours was a kind of "committed" scholarship, in the sense that we were avowedly critical of the U.S.-supported Park dictatorship and we studied Korean matters not so much for disinterested scholarly reasons, as in order to elucidate contradictions in the cold war system of U.S. domination and the domestic system of repression and militarism, to expose weaknesses, and to encourage and support those struggling for democratic rights and nationalist objectives. Most Korea scholars at the time avoided contemporary topics and tried hard to maintain close links with Seoul, which meant links with the regime. Our approach so offended "established" scholars that when the inaugural conference of the Association of Korean Studies in Europe was held in London in March 1977, we were explicitly refused admission.[13] The *Guardian* newspaper wrote of the central role played in the convening of that conference by Dr. Choe Suh Myon (Ch'oe Sŏmyŏn), secretary-general of the International Association of Organizations of Korean Studies, a man whose CV included the unusual distinction of a conviction for the murder of an opposition politician in December 1947.[14]

In general, I think this small, London-based group was right to resist co-option within either the Western fellowship of academic friends of Park or the alternative fellowship of friends of P'yŏngyang. But, while we correctly focused on the cold war rootedness of the Korean problem and the importance of the South Korean democratization struggle, called for solidarity with its victims, and looked to unification as the only viable, long-term solution to Korean problems, we suffered four forms of blindness.

First, we were insensitive to the dimension of the national security crisis that undoubtedly confronted the Seoul regime at this time. Second, influenced in general by the then current "dependency theory," and in particular by dependency theory-based studies of the South Korean economy in Japanese,[15] we could not see the potential for sustained, economic growth and wealth creation in the policies that the Park regime was pursuing, and we tended to exaggerate the role of corruption, concluding, wrongly, that the economic fruits of the export boom were being "appropriated by a tiny elite or remitted abroad."[16]

Third, while we maintained a distance from the blandishments of P'yŏngyang, we were nevertheless taken in by its economic "successes" (as indeed at the time so was the CIA); we were too kind to its nationalist pretensions, too inclined to interpret its discourse in theoretical Marxist terms and to think of the DPRK as "socialist," and too insensitive to its brutality and contempt for human rights. We thought we could perceive a "self-reliant" state, a newly emerging industrial country whose "remarkable" achievements would be remembered "long after the tottering neo-colony in South Korea has finally collapsed."[17] Fourth, we were, partly because of distance from the events but also partly because of our abstract intellectual orientation, remote from the actual movements for which we professed solidarity and did not understand their inner dynamic well. We knew then much less than we know now, and it is hard to think of anyone who got these matters right at the time, but that still does not excuse us for the particular ways in which we got them wrong.

Tokyo

Much more important than London was the Tokyo-based movement. Japanese progressive intellectuals first began to turn their attention seriously to Korea when the 1965 "normalization" treaty that restored relations between Japan and South Korea was signed despite huge demonstrations in Seoul protesting that it failed to address the deep issues of Japanese responsibility.[18] In 1973, however, the abduction of South Korean opposition leader Kim Dae Jung from downtown Tokyo in August 1973 galvanized the movement and the arrests and accelerated repression that followed under the Yusin constitution. A demonstration in protest against these events drew a mere seven people in Tokyo in December 1973, but following the death sentence of the poet Kim Chiha under the National Security Law in July 1974, hunger strikes involving prominent writers (including later Nobel Prize winner, Ōe Kenzaburō) in downtown (Sukiyabashi) Tokyo began to draw widespread attention and support.[19] One key organization was the Japan-Korea Liaison Council for

Solidarity with the Democracy Struggle in South Korea (Nikkan Renren, or Kankoku Minshuka Tōsō Ni Rentai Suru Nihon Renraku Kaigi). In the 1970s, Nikkan Renren mobilized Japan's most famous and respected authors (all of them "million sellers") to write to Prime Minister Tanaka calling for urgent intervention to save the life of Kim Dae Jung.[20] Until the relevant archives are opened, we will not know what precise impact these efforts had, but Nikkan Renren persisted in various activities in support of human rights and democracy and did not wind down till 1987.

Wada Haruki

The central role in this organization was played by Wada Haruki, a "civic scholar" par excellence. (Here, I use the individual principally to symbolize, in encapsulated form, the movement.) Wada, a University of Tokyo historian, born in Osaka in 1938, originally specializing in modern Russian and Soviet history, gradually widened his scope to include Korea through his engagement with Korean struggles. In the 1990s he was director of the Institute of Social Science at the University of Tokyo; he retired in 1998 and then became, in 2000, secretary-general of the National Association for Normalization of Relations between Japan and North Korea. Wada has authored major studies of the Korean War, North Korean state and society, the democracy struggle in South Korea and the relationship with Japan, and the Japan-North Korea relationship.[21]

In the course of his professional career Wada has espoused many unpopular causes. For his opposition to South Korean repression and Japanese collusion at a time when few cared or knew about it, and for his call for normalization of relations with North Korea when others insisted Japan should isolate and overthrow it, he faced and continues to face considerable hostility. Nowadays he is accused of active advocacy and praise for North Korea, denial of its abductions of Japanese citizens, and non-recognition of its responsibility for starting the Korean War in 1950.[22] Mostly these charges are bizarre. He was not a "supporter" of North Korea, rather his research played a key role in clarifying the North's responsibility for launching the Korean War in 1950 and he has been scrupulous in his analysis of the social and political realities of North Korea.

However, his interpretation focuses not on any intrinsic North Korean moral lapse or ideological obscurantism but on the division system imposed by the U.S. and the Soviet Union, frustrated Korean nationalism, and unresolved Japanese colonialism. His conception of North Korea as an embattled "partisan state" (that will not be liquidated until the long-fraught relationship with Japan is normalized) has been widely adopted internationally. Of the controversial issue of the abduction of Japanese citizens by North Korea between 1977 and 1982, Wada offended many by his insistence that evidence should be carefully, even forensically, analyzed before concluding that abduction had occurred, and by his adoption of the view that the problem was more likely to be resolved through normalization and subsequent consular and diplomatic channels following the opening of diplomatic relations than by policies designed to bring about the collapse of the North Korean regime. He pointed to the fact that the problem of the children of Japanese parents abandoned in China after 1945 was settled following Sino-Japanese normalization in 1972 and suggested this might be a model for resolving the abduction problem between North Korea and Japan. In the climate of early twenty-first-century Japan, principled moderation in this vein came to be viewed as pro-P'yŏngyang propaganda.

"TK" alias Chi Myŏnggwan

The regular dispatches from the mysterious "TK" published in the Japanese monthly journal Sekai between 1973 and 1988[23] and in occasional English translations, played a key role in developing a critical international awareness of the Park regime.[24] In 2003, the identity of TK was revealed as a collective of Christians and Christian missionaries, whose reports from Korea were coordinated in Tokyo by Chi Myŏnggwan. Chi, born in what is now North Korea in 1924, had been editor-in-chief of the influential Sasangye in the early 1960s. He came to Japan in 1972, was employed as a professor at Tokyo Women's University, returned to Korea in 1993, and became a professor at Hallym University near Seoul.

The same right-wing critics that lambast Wada Haruki also attack Chi. They refer to him as "possibly a North Korean agent," whose reports on political and social events in Korea "may have set back democratization by as much as a decade." They accuse him of focusing exclusively on South Korea when the human rights situation was worse in North Korea, of exaggerating the nature of the events at Kwangju in 1980,[25] and of misunderstanding the

U.S. "free world" cause.[26] They also attack Yasue Ryosuke, former editor at the Iwanami monthly journal *Sekai*, who commissioned the TK series, not only for launching and sustaining, but also for having conducted interviews with Kim Il Sung, for focusing attention on South Korean repression while turning a blind eye to the North, and in general for what critics see as the substitution of North Korean advocacy for journalism.[27]

Of *Sekai* it may indeed be said that attention to democracy and human rights in North Korea was long lacking. Yasue's editorial line attempted the almost impossible tasks of promotion of the democratic cause in South Korea, while seeking to constitute a bridge for communication with North Korea. His interviews with Kim Il Sung were early attempts to engage the North Korean ruler in dialogue when the rest of the world neither knew nor cared. Whether that strategy was the best, or the wisest, is another matter. Ironically, the only article in *Sekai* whose critical analysis of North Korea seemed to meet the standards of the right wing is one I wrote that was published in the special issue of 1993.[28] Chi Myŏnggwan notes in a recent book that his TK letters contained many positive references to North Korea and recognizes that the series was read and appreciated there. He argues that his group had deliberately adopted such a sympathetic tone with the intention to try to encourage dialogue with the North. In March 2003, however, when he made his first visit to North Korea since his childhood, he found that "though visiting 'the North' I could not meet with the people of 'the North,' and could not even venture outside the hotel. . . ."[29] His impressions were dark, and he came away apparently shocked, with a sense of impending crisis.

Chŏng Kyŏng Mo

Two other figures in the civil society movement outside Korea itself are Chŏng Kyŏng Mo (Chŏng Kyŏngmo) and Song Duyŏl (Song Tuyŏl), one in Japan and the other in Germany. Chŏng, born in Seoul in 1924, educated at Keio University (in Tokyo) and Emory College, had been an interpreter for the U.S. forces during the Korean War and a translator of the armistice agreement. After the war, he became a scientific bureaucrat in South Korea in the 1950s and 1960s, responsible inter alia for the early planning of the petrochemical industry, before fleeing as a dissident from Park Chung Hee's South Korea to Tokyo where he arrived in 1970, two years earlier than Chi. In Japan, he became well known as an independent publicist, author, critic, and thinker on Korean national questions and modern history, and an influential advocate of national reconciliation. In the 1970s, his writings were frequently published in major "progressive" media outlets such as *Sekai* and *Asahi shinbun*. In 1989, he accompanied the renowned Christian pastor, Moon Ikhwan (Mun Ikwhan) (who traveled from Seoul) on a mission to P'yŏngyang. They met with Kim Il Sung (Kim Ilsŏng) and, though obviously lacking any official status, signed a declaration on the principles to be followed in pursuing South-North reconciliation and eventual unification. Moon was later imprisoned in Korea for three years for this breach of the National Security Law, and he died in 1994. Chŏng came to regard their 1989 visit, illegal as it undoubtedly was at the time, as laying the ground for the 2000 South-North summit.

In 2003, Chŏng was included on the Korean government's list of overseas residents who had contributed to the democratic cause and invited to visit his homeland as a distinguished guest. By then seventy-nine years old, he declined, refusing to submit to pressure exerted by the "national security" bureaucrats to confess the criminality of his visit to North Korea and to promise to abide in the future to such a law; submit to that, he insisted, would be to betray his own conscience.[30] Chi and Chŏng are both Christians, who came to Japan from Park Chung Hee's Korea and sought ways to resist its oppression and support the struggle for democracy there. Both published in the same "progressive" Japanese media outlets and both became friends of *Sekai* editor Yasue, yet the two never met and there was no cooperation between them. Chŏng, the apparently lifelong exile without resources and with little backing, has written (and speaks) acerbically of Chi's respectability, his ability to travel freely while supposedly a political refugee in Japan, and the upwards trajectory of his career towards distinction, power, and acclaim following his return to Seoul in the 1990s.[31]

Berlin

The other case, well known in Korea, is that of Song Duyŏl. Song, born in Tokyo in 1944 of Korean (Cheju Island) parents and educated in Korea at Kwangju and later the philosophy department of Seoul National University, went to Germany in 1967 for graduate studies, first at Heidelberg University and then Frankfurt University studying under Jürgen Habermas.[32] After receiving his doctorate in 1972, Song taught first at Free University of Berlin and later at Muenster University, where to this day he is professor of philosophy. Song concentrated his research on the roots of the division system in Germany and Korea. Resisting cold war generalizations about totalitarianism, he gave priority to empirical, structural analysis and put primacy on first-hand observation. As in the German case of Peter Christian Ludz, who headed the German Democratic Republic (GDR) section at the Institute for Social Science Research at the Free University of Berlin and opened the way to the Ostpolitik of Willy Brandt, Song tried to perform a similar mission for Korea. His "immanent" approach, in Song's own words, meant that: "I try to understand them first by putting myself in their position, not from the head but from reality. [Even now] we know so little about North Korea that studying an obscure African tribe may be easier than doing research on North Korea."[33]

From 1973, intent on gathering first-hand information on the situation, he began a series, of visits, eighteen in all, to North Korea. In 1980, he was closely involved in the movement of overseas Koreans to protest against the massacre of students and citizens at Kwangju in May of that year, culminating in a protest march of 1,500 people, mostly Koreans, through the centre of Berlin. In 1991—like Chŏng Kyŏng Mo in 1989—he met with North Korean leader Kim Il Sung and a photograph of the event was widely publicized. Two years later Song received German citizenship and in 1994, as the solitary South Korean representative, attended Kim Il Sung's funeral in P'yŏngyang. From 1995 he was the key person responsible for organizing a series of "South-North scientific dialogues" held in Beijing (five times) and P'yŏngyang (once, in March–April 2004).

When invited to Seoul as a distinguished guest in September 2003, Song, a German citizen of considerable reputation in Europe,[34] accepted and eventually flew back to Seoul on September 22, 2003, after a thirty-seven-year absence. Although his visit, an official invitation of the Korea Democracy Foundation, carried the implicit backing of the president, with whom he was scheduled to meet, the national security bureaucrats—the "state within a state" that Henderson had described almost thirty years earlier—thought differently. He was detained, interrogated in intensive sessions of ten to fifteen hours daily, denied access to his legal advisers, and in due course indicted on charges inter alia, for playing a leading role in an "anti-state organization" as a high official of the (North) Korean Workers' party and as a proponent of

North Korean ideology. The mainstream national media denounced him as "the biggest North Korean spy in history."[35] The case exposed, as none other, the deep divisions in a society undergoing rapid change. One observer summed it up: "For the newspapers, Song is a criminal, for the television stations, a suspicious character, for the internet generation, a hero."[36] For both Chŏng and Chi, Song's breach of the National Security Law by unauthorized contact with North Korea was the crucial issue.

However, the close attention to the case by German government officials and international movement of support for Song could not be ignored. Amnesty International, prominent individuals including Günter Grass and Jürgen Habermas and a number of prominent Japanese protested at Song's detention and demanded his release. The prosecutors sought a fifteen-year sentence. In March 2004, a seven-year sentence was handed down, but it was reversed on appeal on July 21, a conviction on lesser charges carrying a suspended sentence was allowed to stand, but Song was released and eventually flew back to Berlin on August 5. Song's trial and imprisonment occurred at a time when South Korea was in turmoil over the indictment of the president. That issue was effectively resolved with the victory of the Uri Party in elections in April 2004. The conservatives who launched the attack on the president were also the keenest proponents of the National Security Law and the anti-communist national defense state and the most insistent on Song's punishment. In these April elections they suffered a humiliating defeat. In the wake of Song's departure, a full-scale debate erupted on the question of revision or abrogation of the National Security Law, and in September the majority Uri Party and two smaller parties jointly presented a bill for its abrogation.[37]

CONCLUSION

In South Korea, the final phases of liquidation of the Park national security state are fought out in the courts, the editorial columns, and the parliament. Even as the reality passes into history, the issue of national security remains unresolved. Apologists for the national security state now strive to achieve historical justification, arguing that the national security state, especially in its concentrated, Yusin version, with its oppressive apparatus of rampant police power, spying, torture, and breaches of human rights, was necessary and unavoidable at the time because of the North Korean threat. They likewise argue that the domestic opposition movement and the international forces that supported it were guilty at best of blindness to the reality of North Korean repression, at worst of submission to P'yŏngyang's orchestration and direction. Just as the Park state tended to daub its democratic opposition as covert supporters of Kim Il Sung, so its contemporary avatars consist of scholars, editors, and others who, then and now, criticize the repression of the Park regime.

They argue that progressive intellectuals from the 1970s one-sidedly attacked human rights abuses in South Korea while simultaneously being blind to, or positively covering up, much greater abuses in North Korea. In Japan, the movement on this front links up with the agenda of historical revisionism, revision of the constitution and of the Fundamental Law on Education, and hostility to North Korea, sharing some leaders, and forming part of the same neo-nationalist project. The *Historikerstreit* that gripped Germany over the question of degrees of cooperation with Nazism, or France over collaboration and colonialism, or the U.S. over the Vietnam War (where the Kerry campaign made it clear that the issue is still fiercely emotional: who are the traitors, who the patriots?) evolves in and around Korea over the division system, the cold war, and attitudes and approaches to North Korea.

Yet the anti-fascist and anti-dictatorship movement in South Korea in the 1970s and 1980s was in the end victorious, and the role of the international solidarity movement with it, vindicated by history as principled and worthy of commemoration. In retrospect, perhaps no single event was of greater importance in releasing this energy and starting the flow of change that resulted in momentous events than a simple poem. Kim Chiha's "Five Bandits" (O-jŏk) was published first in South Korea in 1970, translated into Japanese in 1972, and into English soon afterwards. Many of those who became active in the movements described above speak of the profound influence it exercised on their lives. The poet suffered much for it, but in the end he succeeded in changing history.

The movements described above were instrumental in saving the lives of Kim Dae Jung and Kim Chiha (among others), in communicating to the world the reality of life in South Korea, linking the South Korean democracy struggle with global movements in the same direction, and ultimately in helping to achieve the victory of the South Korean democratic revolution. These movements also exercised some, impossible to quantify, effects on the minds of those who served the Park regime as officials. One vivid testimony to this was the apology offered by Ch'oe Doksin (Ch'oe Tŏksin), former ambassador of South Korea to West Germany, at a 1978 conference to support the democratic opposition movement: "I would like to add one comment on my own involvement. I was ambassador of [South] Korea to Germany when the kidnapping of our countrymen took place. I stand before you now with my deepest apology, not for what I did but for what I did not do. I did not stop it."[38]

It is true, in retrospect, that the international civil society and democratic movements paid little attention to North Korea. Yet the focus of attention on South Korea had a necessary moral and historical logic. Lacking any connection with North Korea, and seriously deficient in information about it, Japan and the United States, and to a degree Britain and Europe, were intimately involved in supporting the repressive system in South Korea and bore a direct responsibility for it. Some intellectuals and some civil movements in Japan and the West were indeed inclined to believe the best of North Korea, according it a fundamental legitimacy as a state founded on resistance to Japanese colonialism. Swayed by sympathy for what they took to be the dilemmas of a small country seeking independence and justice in a lopsided world, some went beyond that to swallow uncritically crude propaganda about Juche (Chuch'e, self-reliance) and to adopt uncritical, supportive positions towards North Korea. Scholars and others were mobilized world-wide to celebrate North Korea's Juche credo that "man is the master of nature and . . . decides everything," ignoring the contradictory principle that such "mastery" was achieved only to the extent that one submitted absolutely to the will of the leader.[39]

Organizations that functioned more or less as fronts for P'yŏngyang convened conferences around the world on the problem of "the peaceful reunification of Korea" and offered occasional free trips to those who would put their names to platitudes or write poems or pledges of loyalty to Kim Il Sung or his son.[40] The process of grappling intellectually and politically with the reality of the North's dictatorship, and therefore the goal of Korean reunification, was more likely delayed, rather than advanced, by such activities. However, none of the organizations discussed in this chapter fall into this category. Many activists in the democratic opposition movement moved on after the victory of 1987 to extend their frame to North Korea, and to the underlying questions of the U.S. role and the taproot of all Korean problems, division. Those who denounce them are active still in attempting to shore up the national defense state, force the North Korean regime to collapse, and maximize South Korean cooperation, i.e., subordination to the United States. Overall, this chapter asks that the history of the Park Chung Hee era not neglect the dimension of international civil society links that evolved in and around the struggles of that time. Each generation must build anew the linkages of civil society to oppose war, oppression, and injustice, and in so doing always reflect upon, and learn from, past history.

NOTES

1. For an unofficial English translation of the National Security Law: http://www.kimsoft.com/korea/nsl-en.htm

2. James B. Palais, foreword to *Unbroken Spirits: Nineteen Years in South Korea's Gulag*, by So Sung, viii.

3. Quoted in TK, *Letters from South Korea*, 403.

4. Subcommittee on International Organizations of the Committee on International Relations of the House of Representatives, *Activities of the Korean Central Intelligence Agency in the United States*, part 1, March 17, 1976, 4. On these events in general: Don Oberdorfer, *The Two Koreas*, 91–92.

5. Gavan McCormack and Mark Selden, eds., *Korea North and South*, 190–191.

6. So Sung, *Unbroken Spirits: Nineteen Years in South Korea's Gulag*.

7. Thirty years later, in 2005, the National Intelligence Service concluded that the so-called party had been nothing but a pro-democratic student circle. All eight were cleared of any criminality in January 2007. McCormack, Kamiya, and Yonhap News, "Yokohama and Seoul."

8. Don Oberdorfer, *The Two Koreas*, 133–38.

9. Oda Makoto, Wada Haruki, and others representative of the Japanese peace movement during the Vietnam War period were also invited to Vietnam as guests.

10. Core members were Malcolm Caldwell, Nigel Disney, Peggy Duff, Walter Easey, John Gittings, Jon Halliday, Aidan Foster-Carter, and myself.

11. Gavan McCormack and Mark Selden, eds., *Korea: North and South*; Chang Ulbyong et al, trans., *Nambukhan ui pikyo yongu*.

12. Apart from conferences, Halliday and McCormack met for talks with North Korean diplomat Chu Chang-Joon in Switzerland in April 1997; Halliday and Caldwell visited P'yŏngyang in July 1977. Caldwell was later mysteriously murdered in Phnom Penh in January 1979. McCormack visited South and North Korea in March and May 1980 respectively.

13. Gavan McCormack, "The Politics of Korean Studies in Europe."

14. Martin Walker, "Korean Studies Starts a Row." For related comments on academia and connections with the Park regime see, Sugwon Kang, "President Park and His Learned Friends."

15. I quoted with approval the view of Sumiya Mikio, *Kankoku no keizai*, that South Korea's was "an overseas branch of the Japanese economy . . . its export boom no more than a 'subsidiary Japanese boom,'" Gavan McCormack and Mark Selden, eds., *Korea North and South*, 179. Other prominent Japanese commentators, such as Nishikawa Jun, took more or less the same view.

16. Gavan McCormack and Mark Selden, eds., *Korea North and South*, 92.

17. Ibid., 134.

18. For a recent study of this period, in the form of a documentary on (Korean) television, KBS "Beru no naka no Kan-Nichi kyōtei bunsho–Kan-Nichi ryokoku wa naze 40-nenkan mo chinmoku suru no ka?" Sunday Special, August 15, 2004. I am grateful to Mr. Yi Yan-su for supplying a copy of this film and his Japanese translation of the script.

19. Wada Haruki, "70–80 nendai ni okeru Nikkan rentai undō no shisō to kōdō," manuscript of talk given by Wada at commemorative meeting in Seoul, December 12, 2000, on the occasion of the tenth anniversary of the death of the democratic activist and lawyer, Cho Yŏng-Ne. My thanks to Professor Wada for providing a copy of this unpublished paper.

20. Authors included Shiba Ryōtarō, Matsumoto Seichō, and Itsuki Hiroyuki. The message was in Shiba's handwriting.

21. Wada's many works are easily accessible and are therefore not listed here.

22. For one, especially vitriolic attack: Shigemura Toshimitsu, *Saishin Kita Chōsen detabukku*. See also Wada Haruki's home page where this material and Wada's response, is reproduced: http://www.wadaharuki.com.

23. Brought together as three volumes, *Kankoku kara no tsūshin* and in a one volume compilation in English, *Letters from South Korea*. The Japanese first volume was reissued by Iwanami, without explanation or revision, in 2003.

24. I myself used to read TK [Chi Myonggwan] religiously, quoting from it in lectures, broadcasts, and articles.

25. The TK reports, widely circulated at the time, gave the figure of about 2,000 people killed at Kwangju. Now the figure of 200 seems accepted. In 2003, the then *Sekai* editor put this figure to Chi, who accepted it without demur. Chi Myonggwan and Okamoto Atsushi, "Kokusai purojekuto to shite no 'Kankoku kara no tsūshin,'" 66.

26. Nishioka Tsutomu, "Fukumen o totta 'TK-sei' hajishirazu no ryōshin," 177–91.

27. Inagaki Takeshi, "Sore de mo Kita Chōsen o bengo suru 'korinai menmen,'" 128–39. See also Tanizawa Eiichi, *Akuma no shisō*, 155–70; Nishioka Tsutomu, "Fukumen

o totta," 177, also criticizes Iwanami Publishing Company for re-publishing TK's writings in 2003 without making clear that up to 40 percent of the content might be false, as editor Yasue apparently conceded to the monthly Korean journal *Wŏlgan Chungang* in April 1988. That criticism seems just.

28. "Kita Chōsen wa dō kaisuru ka," 278–86, abridged translation of "Kim Country: Hard Times in North Korea," 21–48. Inagaki Takeshi, "Sore de mo Kita Chōsen," 134. Describing this as an "outstanding essay" (*sugureta ronbunok*) is quite out of keeping with the Korea-related material published by *Sekai* before or since and concludes, wrongly, that someone other than Yasue must have been responsible for editing this issue of *Sekai*.

29. Chi Myŏnggwan, *TK-sei no jidai to ima*, 59–60.

30. "Hongoku dōhō e no kōkaibun," September 29, 2003. http://www.online-ryu.com; also author's conversation with Chŏng Yokohama, November 7, 2004.

31. See various issues of the journal *Ryu*, published privately by Chung.

32. For an outline of Song's career and of the "Song affair," see Kajimura Tai'ichiro, "Song Tuyŏl kyoju jiken,"

33. Soo-min Seo, "'Border Rider.'"

34. A documentary on Song's life was screened at the fifty-third Berlin Film festival in February 2004. He is said to be currently working on a three-part study of the light and darkness of modernity, titled "Return of Modernity." Soo-min Seo, "'Border Rider.'"

35. Quoted in Kajimura Tai'ichiro, "Song Tuyŏl kyoju jiken."

36. A KBS television director, quoted in Kajimura Tai'ichiro, "Song Tuyŏl kyoju jiken."

37. In 2004, the furor over the National Security Law deepened as it was revealed that the country's third largest political party, the Democratic Labor Party, was under investigation for possible breaches because of its opposition to the war in Iraq. "A Suspicious 'Public Security Institute,'" *Hankyoreh*, October 18, 2004.

38. Ch'oe Dŏksin, Emergency International Congress on Korea, Bonn, June 5–6, 1978. (My thanks to Sam Noumoff of McGill University for reminding me of this statement.) Ch'oe defected to North Korea in 1986.

39. See discussion in Gavan McCormack, *Target North Korea*, 72–74.

40. Ibid., 72–73.

Bibliography

Amsden, Alice. *Asia's Next Giant: South Korea and Late Industrialization*. New York: Oxford University Press, 1989.

An Pyŏngjik. *Kŭndae Chosŏn ŭi kyŏngje kuju* [The economic structure of modern Chosŏn]. Sŏul: Pibong Ch'ulp'ansa, 1989.

An T'aegwŏn. "Han'guk simin munhwa ŭi chaep'yŏn kwa munjae" [Rearrangement and problems of South Korean civil culture]. In *Han'guk chŏngch'i sahoe kaehyŏk ŭi iron kwa silche* [Theory and practice of reform in South Korean politics and society] edited by Chŏngsin Munhwa Yŏn'guwŏn [Academy of Korean Studies] 41–78. Sŏul: Chŏngsin Munhwa Yŏn'guwŏn, 1999.

Baku Konkō [Pak Kŭnho]. *Kankoku no keizai hatten to Betonamu Sensō* [South Korean economic development and the Vietnam War]. Tōkyō: Ochanomizu Shobō, 1993.

Balassa, Bella. *The New Industrializing Countries in the World Economy*. New York: Pergamon Press, 1981.

Baldwin, Frank, Diane Jones, and Michael Jones. *America's Rented Troops: South Koreans in Vietnam*. Philadelphia: American Friends Service Committee, n.d.

Bank of Korea, *National Accounts*. CD. 1990.

Berlin, Isaiah. *Two Concepts of Liberty*. London: Oxford University Press, 1958.

Blackburn, Robert M. *Mercenaries and Lyndon Johnson's "More Flags": The Hiring of Korean, Filipino, and Thai Soldiers in the Vietnam War*. Jefferson, NC: McFarland & Company Publishers, 1994.

Boettcher, Robert, and Gordon L. Freedman. *Gifts of Deceit: Sunmyung Moon, Tongsun Park, and the Korean Scandal*. New York: Holt, Rinehart, and Winston, 1980.

Boyer, William W., and Byong Man Ahn. *Rural Development in South Korea: A Sociopolitical Analysis*. Newark: University of Delaware Press, 1991.

Brandt, Vincent S. R. "Urban Poverty in Korea: Two Theoretical Perspectives."

Unpublished paper delivered at University of Washington Korea Seminar, 1974.

Brandt, Vincent S. R., and Man-gap Lee. "Community Development in the Republic of Korea." In *Community Development: Comparative Case Studies in India, the Republic of Korea, Mexico, and Tanzania*, edited by Robert Dore, 47–136. Paris: UNESCO, 1981.

Burmeister, Larry. "The South Korean Green Revolution: Induced or Directed Innovation?" *Economic Development and Cultural Change* 35, no.4 (July 1987): 767–90.

Chang, Hajun, Hongjae Park, and Gyue-Yoo Chul. "Interpreting the Korean Crisis: Financial Liberalization, Industrial Policy, and Corporate Governance." *Cambridge Journal of Economics* 22, no.6 (1998): 735–46.

Chang Kyŏngsŏp. "Apch'uk kŭndaehwa wa pokhap wihŏm sahoe" [Compressed modernity and the society of complex dangers]. In *Tongasia ŭi sŏnggong kwa chwajŏl* [Success and frustration of East Asia], edited by Pigyo Sahoe Yŏn'guhoe [Comparative Social Research Association] 371–414. Ilsan: Chŏnt'ong kwa Hyŏndae, 1998.

———. "Han'guk kajok ŭi inyŏm kwa silche" [Theory and reality of the South Korean family]. *Chŏrhak kwa Hyŏnsil* [Philosophy and reality] no. 22 (1994): 55–66.

Chang,Yu-tzung, Chu Yun-han, and Huang Min-hwa. "The Uneven Growth of Democratic Legitimacy in East Asia." *International Journal of Public Opinion Research* 18, no. 2 (2006): 246–55.

Chang, Yu-tzung, Chu Yun-han, and Park Chong-min. "Authoritarian Nostalgia in Asia," *Journal of Democracy* (March 18, 2007): 66–80.

Chi Myŏnggwan [TK]. *TK-sei no jidai to ima*. Tōkyō: Ichiyosha, 2004.

Chi Myŏnggwan, and Okamoto Atsushi. "Kokusai purojekuto to shite no 'Kankoku kara no tsushin." *Sekai* (September 2003): 49–67.

Cho Hŭiyŏn. *Pak Chŏnghŭi wa kaebal tokchae sidae* [Park Chung Hee and developmental dictatorship], Sŏul: Yŏksa Pip'yŏng, 2007.

Cho Yongjung. "Tak'yument'ari: Kukka Chaegŏn Ch'oego Hoeŭi" [Documentary: The Supreme Council of the National Reconstruction]." *Sin tonga* (May 1983): 114–79.

Ch'oe, Dŏksin. Emergency International Congress on Korea, Bonn, June 5–6, 1978.

Choi, Jangjip. *Labor and the Authoritarian State: Labor Unions in South Korean Manufacturing Industries, 1961–1980*. Seoul: Korea University Press, 1989.

Ch'ŏn Pyŏnggyu. *Ch'ŏnma ch'owŏn e nolda: Tongbaek Ch'ŏn Pyŏnggyu kohŭi chajŏn* [A heavenly horse plays in the grass field: Autobiography of Tongbaek Ch'ŏn Pyŏnggyu former minister of finance in commemoration of his seventieth birthday]. Sŏul: Ch'ŏn Pyŏnggyu Kohŭi Chasŏjŏn Kanhaeng Wiwŏnhoe, 1988.

Chŏng Chaegyŏng. *Pak Chŏnghŭi sasang sŏsŏl: Hwiho rŭl chungsim ŭro* [Introduction to Park Chung Hee's ideology: Focused on Park's calligraphy]. Sŏul: Chimmundang, 1994.

Chŏng Kyŏngmo. "Hongoku doho e no kokaibun." *Ryu* (September 29, 2003). Limited circulation. Gavan McCormack private collection.

Chong Yongdŏk. "Han'guk haengjŏng kaehyŏk ŭi Chaengjŏm kwa kwajae [Issues and questions of South Korean administration reform]. In *Han'guk chŏngch'i sahoe kaehyŏk ŭi iron kwa silche* [Theory and practice of reform in South Korean politics and society], edited by Chŏngsin Munhwa Yŏn'guwŏn [Academy of Korean Studies] 83–131. Sŏul: Chŏngsin Munhwa Yŏn'guwŏn, 1999.

Chun, Soonok. *They Are Not Machines: Korean Women Workers and Their Fight for Democratic Trade Unionism in the 1970s.* Aldershot, England and Burlington, VT: Ashgate, 2003.

Chunghwahak Kongŏp Ch'ujin Wiwŏnhoe Kihoektan. *Han'guk kongŏp palchŏn e kwanhan chosa yŏn'gu 3: chŏngch'aek kyŏlchŏng imyŏnsa* [The report of the Korean industrial development 3: The behind the scenes story of policymaking]. Sŏul: Chunghwahak Kongŏp Ch'ujin Wiwonhoe Kihoektan, 1979.

CIA World Fact Book. https://www.cia.gov/library/publications/the-world-factbook/geos/ks.html.

Clifford, Mark L. *Troubled Tiger: Businessmen, Bureaucrats, and Generals in South Korea.* New York: M. E. Sharpe, 1994.

Correspondence. Under Secretary of State for Security Assistance to James T. Lynn from Carlyle E. Maw. 30 December 1975, File 13, Box 9, Gerald Ford Library.

Critchfield, Richard. *Villages.* Garden City, NY: Anchor Press, 1981.

Crotty, Jim, and Gary Dymski. "Can the Global Neoliberal Regime Survive Victory in Asia? The Political Economy of the Asian Crisis." Published Studies ps5, Political Economy Research Institute, University of Massachusetts at Amherst, 2000, http://www.peri.umass.edu/fileadmin/pdf/published_study/PS5.pdf.

Crotty, James, and Gary Dymski. "The Korean Struggle: Can the East Asian Model Survive?" Z, (July–August 1998): 1–43.

Cumings, Bruce. "Anti-Americanism in the Republic of Korea." In *Joint U.S–Korea Academic Studies: The United States and South Korea: Reinvigorating the Partnership* Vol. 14. Washington, DC: Korea Economic Institute of America, 2004.

———. *Korea's Place in the Sun.* New York: W. W. Norton, 1997.

———. "The Origins and Development of the Northeast Asian Political Economy: Industrial Sectors, Product Cycles, and Political Consequences." *International Organization* 38, no. 1 (1984): 1–40.

Eckert, Carter J. *Offspring of Empire: The Koch'ang Kims and the Colonial Origins of Korean Capitalism 1876–1945.* Seattle: University of Washington Press, 1991.

Embassy Telegram to Secstate (Secretary of State). "Subject: Meeting with President

Park: Missile Strategy," 1 May 1975, Box 11, File: State Department Telegrams to
SECSTATE-ESDIS (2), Gerald Ford Library.

———. "Subject: ROK Views of U.S. Security Commitment," 18 April 1975, Box 11, File:
Korea, Gerald Ford Library.

Evans, Peter. *Embedded Autonomy: States and Industrial Transformation*. Princeton, New
Jersey: Princeton University Press, 1995.

The Freedom House Website. http://www.freedomhouse.org.

Gleysteen, William H. Jr. *Massive Entanglement, Marginal Influence: Carter and Korea in Crisis*.
Washington, DC: Brookings Institute Press, 1999.

Gordon, Andrew. *The Evolution of Labor Relations in Japan: Heavy Industry, 1853–1955*.
Cambridge: Council on East Asian Studies, Harvard University, 1985.

Grajdanzev, Andrew. *Modern Korea*. New York: Institute of Pacific Relations, 1944.

Halm, Chaibong. *South Korea's Miraculous Democracy*. Santa Monica, CA: Rand
Corporation, 2008.

Ham Sŏkhŏn. "Sae nara rŭl ŏttŏkk'e seulkka?" [How do we establish a new nation?
(part two)]. *Sasanggye*, June 1961.

Han Honggu [Han Hongkoo]. "Kihoejuŭi ch'ŏngnyŏn Pak Chŏnghŭi: Namja ŭi
pyŏnsin mujoe?" [Opportunist youth, Park Chung-Hee: Is a man's transformation
innocent?], 2003. http://h21.hai.co.kr/arti/culture/culture_general/6403.html (site
now discontinued).

———. "Tongnae posŭ, wang posŭ e t'udŏldaeda: Pak Chŏnghŭi wa Han-Mi
kwan'gye" [The village boss complains to the kingpin: Park Chung-Hee and the
Korea-U.S. relationship]. In *Taehan Min'guksa* [History of the Republic of Korea]. Vol.
2, 63–87. Sŏul: Han'gyŏre Sinmunsa, 2006.

Han Hongkoo. *See* Han Honggu.

Han Tohyŏn. "1930-yŏndae nongch'on chinhŭng undong ŭi sŏnggyŏk" [The character
of the Rural Revitalization movement in the 1930s]. In *Han'guk kŭndae nongch'on sahoe
wa Ilbon chegukchuŭi*, 233–77. Sŏul: Munhak kwa Chisŏngsa, 1986.

Han Wansang. *Minjung sahoehak* [People's sociology]. Chongno Sŏjŏk, 1989.

Han'guk Ŭnhaeng Chosabu [Research department, The Bank of Korea]. *Kyŏngje
t'onggye yŏnbo* [Economic statistics yearbook]. Sŏul: Han'guk Ŭnhaeng, 1994.

Henderson, Gregory. "Constitutional Changes from the First to the Sixth Republics:
1948–1987." In *Political Change in South Korea*, edited by Ilpyong J. Kim and Whan Kihl
Young, 22–43. New York: Paragon House, 1988.

———. *Korea: The Politics of the Vortex*. Cambridge, MA: Harvard University Press, 1968.

Hwang Kapson. *Nongch'on sahoe kaebal non*. [Theory of rural development]. Sŏul:

Pagyŏngsa, 1973.

Inagaki Takeshi. "Sore de mo Kita Chōsen o bengo suru 'korinai menmen.'" *Shokun* (October 2003): 128–39.

Johnson, Chalmers. *Japan: Who Governs? The Rise of the Developmental State*. New York: W. W. Norton, 1995.

———. *MITI and the Japanese Miracle: The Growth of Industrial Policy, 1925–1975*. Stanford, CA: Stanford University Press, 1982.

Kajimura Tai'ichiro. "Song Tuyŏl kyoju jiken." *Sekai* (November 2004). Translated by Gavan McCormack in "Democracy and National Security in South Korea: The Song Duyŏl Affair." *Japan Focus* (December 10, 2004). http://japanfocus.org/-Kajimura-Tai_ichiro/1585.

Kang, David C. *Crony Capitalism: Corruption and Development in South Korea and the Philippines*. New York: Cambridge University Press, 2002.

———. "Regional Politics and Democratic Consolidation." In *Korea's Democratization*, edited by Samuel S. Kim. Cambridge, NY: Cambridge University Press, 2003.

Kang Man'gil. *Koch'ossŭn Han'guk hyŏndaesa* [Modern Korean history rewritten]. Sŏul: Ch'angjak kwa Pip'yŏngsa, 1994.

Kang, Sugwon. "President Park and His Learned Friends: Some Observations on Contemporary Korean Statecraft." *Bulletin of Concerned Asian Scholars* 7, no. 4 (October–December 1975): 28–32.

Kang Wŏnt'aek. "Sedae, inyŏm kwa No Muhyŏn hyŏnsang" [Generation, ideology, and the Roh Moo-hyon phenomenon] *Kyegan sasang* [Quarterly thought], (Fall 2002).

Kim, Byung Kook. "The Leviathan: Economic Bureaucracy under Park Chung Hee." Paper delivered at the annual meeting of the American Political Science Association, Boston, MA, August 29–September 1, 2002.

Kim Chŏnggi. "Kŭregori Hendŏsŭn ŭi hoego: K'enedi 5.16 chinap chakchŏn ŭl moksal," [The memoir of Gregory Henderson: The Kennedy administration did not choose to suppress 5.16 military coup]. *Sin tonga* (May 1987): 220–35.

Kim Chŏngnyŏm. *A, Pak Chŏnghŭi* [Ah, Park Chung Hee]. Sŏul: Chungang M&B, 1997.

———. *Ch'oebin'guk esŏ sŏnjin'guk munt'ŏk kkaji: Hang'guk kyŏngje chŏngch'aek 30-nyŏnsa* [From the poorest to the threshold of an advanced nation: A thirty-year history of Korea's economic policy]. Sŏul: Randŏm Hausŭ Chungang, 2006.

———. *Hoegorok: Han'guk kyŏngje chŏngch'aek 30-nyŏnsa* [A thirty-year history of Korea's economic policy]. Sŏul: Chungang Ilbo and Chungang Kyŏngje Sinmun, 1990.

Kim Chun. "5.16 ihu nodong chohap ŭi chaepyŏn kwa 'Han'guk noch'ong ch'eje' ŭi sŏngnip" [Reorganization of labor unions and the establishment of the Korean

Federation of Trade Unions since 5.16]. *Sahoe wa yŏksa* [Society and history] 55 (1999): 103–44.

Kim, Chung-Yum. *Policymaking on the Front Lines, Memoirs of a Korean Practitioner 1945–1979.* Washington, DC: The World Bank, 1994.

Kim, Hong Nack, and Sunki Choe. "Urbanization and Changing Voting Patterns in South Korean Parliamentary Elections." In *Political Change in South Korea,* edited by Ilpyong J. Kim and Whan Kihl Young, 139–68. New York: Paragon House, 1988.

Kim Hyŏnga [Kim, Hyung-A]. *Pak Chŏnghŭi ŭi yangnal ŭi sŏnt'aek: Yusin kwa chunghwahak kongŏp.* Translated by Sin Myŏnju. Sŏul: Ilchogak, 2005.

Kim Hyŏnsu. "Uri nara ŭi sanŏp chaehae wa sanjae posang chedo." [Korean industrial accidents and compensation system]. *Chinbo P'yŏngnon* 2 (1999): 122–49.

Kim, Hyung-A [Kim Hyŏnga]. "Behind the Carter-Park Standoff: South Korea's Nuclear Weapons and Missile Capability Program, 1974–1979." A paper delivered on February 26, 2004 at the Korea Colloquium, Institute of Korean Studies, Harvard University and on March 3, 2004 at the University of Washington, Seattle.

———. "The Eve of Park's Military Rule: The Intellectual Debate on National Reconstruction, 1960–1961," *East Asian History,* no. 25–26 (June/December 2003): 113–40.

———. *Korea's Development under Park Chung-Hee: Rapid Industrialization 1961–1979.* New York: RoutledgeCurzon, 2004.

———. "State Building: The Military Junta's Path to Modernity through Administrative Reforms, 1961–1963." In *The Park Chung Hee Era: The Transformation of South Korea,* edited by Ezra Vogel and Byung-Kook Kim. Cambridge, MA: Harvard University Press, 2011.

Kim Ilsŏng. "Modŭn him ŭl yŏsŏkkae koji ŭi chŏmnyŏng ŭl wihayŏ" [All efforts for occupying the six highlands]. In *Kim Ilsŏng Chŏjakchip* [Kim Il-sŏng's collected writings], Vol. 15: 354–428. P'yŏngyang: Chosŏn Nodongdang Ch'ulp'ansa, 1981.

Kim, Kwan S. "The Korean Miracle (1962–1980) Revisited: Myth and Realities in Strategy and Development." http://kellogg.nd.edu/publications/working papers/WPS/166.pdf (accessed September 20, 2007; site now discontinued).

"Kim pujang kwa Ilbon kowich'ŭng kwa ŭi hoedam" [The meeting of Kim Jong Pil, the director of the Korean central intelligence, with high-ranking Japanese politicians]. Taehan Min'guk Oemubu, oegyo munsŏ, tŭngnok pŏnho 796 [ROK Ministry of Foreign Affairs, diplomatic documents, registration no. 796], Kim Chongp'il t'ŭksa Ilbon pangmun, 1962, 10–11, [Special envoy Kim Jong Pil's visit to Japan, October–November, 1962].

Kim Samsu. "Pak Chŏnghŭi sidae ŭi nodong chŏngch'aek kwa nosa kwan'gye," [Labor policies and labor relations during the Park Chung Hee era]. In *Kaebal tokchae wa Pak Chŏnghŭi sidae* [Developmental dictatorship and Park Chung Hee era], edited by Yi Pyŏngch'ŏn, 183–212. Sŏul: Ch'angbi, 2000.

Kim, Samuel S. "Korea's Democratization in the Global-Local Nexus." In *Korea's Democratization*, edited by Samuel S. Kim. Cambridge, NY: Cambridge University Press, 2003.

Kim, Seung-Kyung. *Class Struggle or Family Struggle?: The Lives of Women Factory Workers in South Korea*. Cambridge and New York: Cambridge University Press, 1997.

Kim Sŏngjin. *Pak Chŏnghŭi rŭl malhada: kŭ ŭi kaehyŏk chŏngch'i, kŭrigo kwaing ch'ungsŏng* [Talking about Park Chung Hee: His reform politics and the excessive loyalty]. Sŏul: Sam kwa Kkum, 2006.

Kim, Sunhyuk. "Civil Society in Democratizing Korea." In *Korea's Democratization*, edited by Samuel S. Kim. Cambridge, NY: Cambridge University Press, 2003.

Kim Yonghwan. *Kaebal nyŏndae wa IMF wigisi ŭi chaejŏng: Kŭmyung chŏngch'aek pisa* [Finance during the developmental era and the IMF crisis: A secret history monetary policy]. Sŏul: Maeil Kyŏngje Sinmunsa, 2006.

Kim Yongung. *Chiyŏk kaeballon* [Regional development]. Sŏul: Pommunsa, 1999.

Kimiya Tadashi. "Betonamu sensō to Betonamu tokuju," [The Vietnam War and its economic implications for South Korea and Taiwan] 243–67. In *Kankoku Taiwan no hatten mekanizumu* [Development mechanism of South Korea and Taiwan], edited by Hattori Tamio and Satō Yukihiko. Tōkyō: Azia Keizai Kenkyūjo, 1996.

———. "1960-nendai Kankoku ni okeru reisen gaiko no 3 ruikei: Nikkan kokkō seijōka, Betonamu hahei, ASPAC" [Three types of South Korean cold war diplomacy in 1960s: Korea-Japan normalization, military involvement in the Vietnam War, and ASPAC] 91–145. In *Shijō kokka kokusai taisei* [Market, state, international regime], edited by Okonogi Masao and Chung In Moon. Tōkyō: Keiō Daigaku Shuppannkai, 2001.

———. *Pak Chŏnghŭi chŏngbu ŭi sŏnt'aek: 1960 nyŏndae such'ul chihyang hyŏng kongŏphwa wa naengjŏn ch'eje* [The policy choice of Park Chung Hee administration: Its export-oriented industrialization and the cold war regime]. Sŏul: Humanit'asŭ, 2008.

"Kin Gokuretsu Kankoku daihyō danchō ni kiku" [Question to Republic of Korea Delegation Chief Kim Hangyŏl], *Mainichi shimbun*, August 28, 1969.

Koo, Hagen. *Korean Workers: The Culture and Politics of Class Formation*. Ithaca, NY: Cornell University Press, 2001.

Korea-State Department Telegrams to Secstate-Nodis, No. 14, April 1976 (Declassified 8 June 2001), NSF, Box 9, Gerald Ford Library.

Korean Broadcasting System (KBS). "Beru no naka no Kan-Nichi kyotei bunsho—Kan-

Nichi ryokoku wa naze 40-nenkan mo chinmoku suru no ka?" [The Japan-South Korea agreement—Why have Japan and South Korea both been silent for forty years?]. Sunday Special, August 15, 2004.

Kukka Chaegŏn Ch'oego Hoeŭi Chonghap Kyŏngje Chaegŏn Wiwŏnhoe [The Supreme Council of National Reconstruction Subcommittee of the Comprehensive Economic Reconstruction]. *Chonghap kyŏngje chaegŏn kyehoek* [The comprehensive plan of national reconstruction]. July 31, 1961.

Lankov, Andrei N. *From Stalin to Kim Il Sung: The Formation of North Korea, 1945–1960*. New Brunswick, NJ: Rutgers University Press, 2002.

Lee, Hoon K. *Land Utilization and Rural Economy in Korea*. University of Chicago Press, 1936.

MacFarquhar, Roderick. "The Post-Confucian Challenge." *The Economist*, February 9, 1980.

Maekk'omaek, Kŏbŏn [Gavan McCormack], and Mak'ŭ Seldŏn [Mark Seldon]. *Nam-Pukhan ŭi pigyo yŏn'gu*. Translated by Chang Ŭlbyŏng, et al. Sŏul: Irwŏl Sŏgak, 1988.

Makōmakku, Gavan [Gavan McCormack]. "Kita Chōsen wa do kaisuru ka," [What goes on in North Korea]. *Sekai*, no. 587 (October 1993): 278–86. Abridged translation of McCormack, Gavan. "Kim Country: Hard Times in North Korea." *New Left Review*, no. 198 (March–April 1993): 21–48.

Makōmakku, Gavan [Gavan McCormack], and Maku Seruden [Mark Selden], eds. *Chōsen wa dō natte iru ka*. Translated by Itō Kazuhiko et al. Tōkyō: Sanichi Shobō, 1981.

McCormack, Gavan. "The Politics of Korean Studies in Europe." *Journal of Contemporary Asia 7*, no. 3 (1977): 387–92.

———. *Target North Korea: Pushing North Korea to the Brink of Nuclear Catastrophe*. New York: Nation Books, 2004.

McCormack, Gavan, and Mark Selden eds. *Korea, North and South: The Deepening Crisis*. New York: Monthly Review Press, 1978.

McCormack, Gavan, Kamiya Setsuko, and Yonhap News. "Yokohama and Seoul: Dealing with Crimes of State in Japan and South Korea." *Japan Focus*, January 29, 2007, http://japanfocus.org/products/details/2339.

Memo. Rostow to Lyndon B. Johnson, 7 December 1967, NSF, Country, Box 91, Lyndon B. Johnson Library.

Memorandum. George Springsteen, Executive secretary of the Department of State, to Lieutenant General Brent Scowcroft. 4 February 1975. Country File: Korea (3), National Security Adviser: Presidential Country Files for East Asia and the Pacific, Box 9, Gerald Ford Library.

Memorandum to the assistant to the president for national security affairs, written by
Robert S. Ingersoll, acting secretary of state. 2 July 1975, Box 2, file no. 9, Gerald Ford
Library.

Memorandum to Carl Albert, Speaker of the House of Representatives, Office of the
Deputy Assistant Secretary (security assistance), OASD/ISA, n.d. "Comments on
Secretary Schlesinger's Discussions in Seoul" on the issue entitled: "U.S. Reaction in
Event of North Korean Aggression." Documents concern relations between the USA
and the ROK between the fall of Saigon (April 1975) and the Tree Incident in the DMZ,
18 August 1976. Washington, DC, Gerald Ford Library.

Memorandum of conversation between Brent Scowcroft, Ambassador Richard Sneider,
and William Gleysteen. "Subject: August 18 Incident at Panmunjŏm: U.S.—Korean
Relations." Box 10. File: Korea no. 20. Gerald Ford Library.

Memorandum of conversation, Kennedy and ROK Ambassador Kim, 17 June 1963, NSF,
Country. Box 127. John F. Kennedy Library.

Memorandum for General Scowcroft from Thomas J. Barnes, "Subject: Secretary
Schlesinger's Discussions in Seoul," 29 September 1975, NSF, Country. Box 9. Gerald
Ford Library.

National Security Decision Memorandum (NSCM) 282 and 309, National Security Study
Memoranda and Decision Memoranda, 1974–1977. Box 2. Gerald Ford Library.

Niinobe Akira. "Jōyaku teiketsu ni itaru katei" [The process of Korea-Japan basic
treaty]. Kikan seikyū no.16 (1993): 36–43.

Nishioka Tsutomu. "Fukumen o totta 'TK-sei' hajishirazu no ryoshin." Shokun (October
2003): 177–91.

No Chaehyŏn. Chŏngwadae pisŏsil [The Blue House secretariat]. Sŏul: Chungang Ilbosa,
1992.

No Chang-sŏp, et al. A Study of Rural Society under Development: A Socio- Economic and
Educational Analysis and Evaluation of Three Rural Areas. Seoul: Ehwa University Press,
1965.

O Wŏnch'ŏl. Han'gukhyŏng kyŏngje kŏnsŏl [Korean model economic construction:
Engineering approach]. Vol. 5, 7. Sŏul: Kia Kyŏngje Yŏn'guso, 1996, 1997, respectively.

———. "Kungmin ton, han p'un do pujŏng ŭn andwae," [Not even a single cent of
corruption of the national fund is acceptable], Sin tonga April, 1995, 410–25.

———. "Nuclear Development in Korea in the 1970s." Pacific Research, Australian
National University. November 1994.

———. Pak Chŏnghŭi nŭn ŏttŏk'e kyŏngje kangguk mandŭrŏnna [How did Park Chung-Hee
make an economically strong country?] Sŏul: Tongsŏ Munhwasa, 2006.

———. "Sanŏp chŏllyak kundansa" [A history of the industrial strategy corps]. Han'guk kyŏngje sinmun [Korean economic daily], May 31, 1993.

———. "Taet'ongnyŏng ŭi pimyŏng: 20-gae sandan ŭl mujang sik'yŏra" [The president's secret order: Arm twenty divisions]. Wŏlgan chosŏn (June 1994): 470–82.

———. "Yudot'an kaebal, Chŏn Tuhwan kwa Miguk i magatta" [Development of guided missiles and the obstruction of Chun Doo Hwan and the United States]. Sin tonga. (January 1996): 388–411.

Oberdorfer, Don. The Two Koreas: A Contemporary History. Reading, MA: Addison-Wesley, 1997.

Ogle, George E. South Korea: Dissent within the Economic Miracle. London: Zed Books, 1990.

Okamoto Atsushi. "Kokusai purojekuto to shite no 'Kankoku kara no tsushin.'" Sekai (September 2003): 49–67.

Ōta Osamu. Nikkan kōshō: Seikyūken mondai no kenkyū [Korea-Japan normalization negotiations: A study of the problem of property claims]. Tōkyō: Kurein, 2003.

Pae Ŭihwan. Porikkogae nŭn nŏmŏtchiman [Though South Korea survived the starvation: The memoir of Pae Ŭihwan, the principal representative of Korea-Japan negotiation]. Sŏul: K'oria Herŏldŭ and Naeoe Kyŏngje Sinmun, 1992.

Paek Nakch'ŏng. Hŭndŭllinŭn pundan ch'eje [The shaky division system]. Sŏul: Ch'angjak kwa Pip'yŏngsa, 1998.

Pak Chŏnghŭi. See Park Chung Hee.

Pak Chihyang, et al. Haebang chŏnhusa ŭi chae insik. 2 vols. [Rethinking history around the time of liberation]. Sŏul: Ch'aek Sesang, 2006.

Pak Ch'unghun. Idang hoegorok [Memoir of Idang, Pak Ch'unghun, the former minister of commerce and industry]. Sŏul: Pagyŏngsa, 1988.

Pak Chunsik, and Yu Sŏkch'un. "Han'guk sahoe pujŏng pup'ae kijae wa yuhyŏng" [On the causes and modes of corruption in Korean society]. Sahoe palchŏn yŏn'gu [Journal of social development studies] 4 (1998): 59–88.

Pak Hŭibŏm. Han'guk kyŏngje sŏngjang ron [The arguments of South Korean economic growth]. Sŏul: Koryŏ Taehakkyo Asia Munje Yŏn'guso, 1968.

Pak Hyŏnch'ae. Minjok kyŏngje wa minjung undong [The national economy and the minjung movement]. Sŏul: Ch'angbisa, 1988.

Pak Hyŏnch'ae, and Cho Hŭiyŏn. Han'guk sahoe kusŏngch'e nonjaeng [The Korean social formation debate], 1–2. Sŏul: Hanul, 1989.

Pak Kŭnho. See Baku Konkō.

Pak Myung Lim. "Chaeya: Social Movement and Democracy during the Park Era, 1961–1979." In The Park Era: The Transformation of South Korea, edited by Byung-Kook Kim and

Ezra Vogel. Cambridge: Harvard Press, 2011.

Pak Seil. *Taehan Min'guk: Sŏnjinhwa chŏllyak* [Republic of Korea: An advancing strategy]. Sŏul: 21-segi Puksŭ, 2006.

Park, Chung Hee [*Pak Chŏnghŭi*]. *Minjok ŭi chŏryŏk* [Nation's staying power]. Sŏul: Kwangmyŏng Ch'ulp'ansa, 1971.

——. *Pak Chŏng-hŭi Taet'ongnyŏng yŏnsŏlmun chip* [The collected speeches of President Park Chung Hee, 15 vols]. Sŏul: Taet'ongnyŏng Kongbo Pisŏgwansil, 1965-

——. *Our Nation's Path: Ideology of Social Reconstruction.* 2nd edition. Seoul: Hollym Corporation, 1970. First edition published in 1962.

——. *Saemaul: Korea's New Community Movement.* (Collected Speeches on the New Community Movement). Seoul: Korea Textbook Company, 1979.

——. *Saemaŭl undong: Pak Chŏnghŭi Taet'ongnyŏng yŏnsŏl sŏnjip* [The New Village movement: President Park Chung Hee's selected speeches]. Taet'ongnyŏng pisŏsil, 1978.

——. Taet'ongnyŏng Pisŏsil [Presidential secretariat]. *Pak Chŏnghŭi taet'ongnyŏng yŏnsŏl munjip* [President Park Chung Hee's speeches]. Taet'ongnyŏng Pisŏsil, 1963–1979.

——. *Uri to hal su ittai: Pak Chŏnghŭi Taet'ongnyŏng ŏrok.* [We, too, can do it: President Park Chung Hee's sayings.] Sŏul: Ŭnhaengnamu Tonguhoe, 1999.

Park, Y. K. *Labor and Industrial Relations in Korea: System and Practice.* Seoul: Sogang University Press, 1979.

People's Solidarity for Participatory Democracy. *Han'guk ŭi 5 dae chaebŏl baeksŏ 1995–1997* [White paper on five conglomerates of South Korea 1995–1997]. Unpublished report, 1999.

P'ohang Chech'ŏl Hongbosil. [POSCO information office] *Yŏngilman esŏ Kwangyangman kkaji: P'ohang chech'ŏl 25-nyŏnsa* [From Yŏngil Bay to Kwangyang Bay: A twenty-five-year history of POSCO]. P'ohang: P'ohang Chech'ŏl Hongbosil, 1993.

Prebisch, Raul. *Change and Development, Latin America's Great Task: Report Submitted to the Inter-American Development Bank.* New York: Praeger, 1971.

"Proclamation by the Committee, May 16, 1961." In *Han'guk minju hyŏngmyŏng ch'ŏngsa* [A history of South Korea's democratic revolution]. Sŏul: Han'guk Minju Hyŏngmyŏng Ch'ŏngsa P'yŏnch'an Wiwŏnhoe, 1962.

Redfield, Robert. *Peasant Society and Culture.* Chicago: University of Chicago Press, 1956.

Reports and Recommendations of Jan M. Lodal and Dave Elliott, NSC, to Secretary [Henry] Kissinger. July 11, 1975 (Declassified on 27 May 1997). Country. Box 2, file no. 9.

Republic of Korea. Kyŏngje Kihoegwŏn. *Han'guk t'onggye yŏn'gam* [Korea Statistical Yearbook]. 2000.

———. National Statistics Office. *South Korea Statistics Yearbook*. http:\\kostat.go.kr.

———. Nongŏp chidoso [Agricultural guidance office]. *1976-77 Tonggye maul ŭl yŏngnong kyobon* [1976–77 Textbook of village winter season agricultural management]. 110 pages. Hongch'ŏn Kun Nongch'on Chidoso, 1977.

Ri Shōgen [Yi Chŏngwŏn]. *Higashi Ajia reisen to Kan-Bei-Nichi kankei* [East Asia's cold war and the triangle relations among the United States, South Korea, and Japan]. Tōkyō: Tōkyō Daigaku Shuppankai, 1996.

"The Road to National Survival," *Maeil kyŏngje sinmun*, 1977, 112.

Satterwhite, David H. "The Politics of Economic Development: Coup, State, and the Republic of Korea's First Five-Year Development Plan (1962–1966)." Ph.D. Dissertation, University of Washington, 1994.

Schmitter, Philippe C. "Still the Century of Corporatism." In *Trends Toward Corporatist Intermediation*, edited by Philippe Schmitter and Gerhard Lehmbruch, 7–53. Beverly Hills, CA: Sage, 1979.

Sen, Amartya. *Development as Freedom*. Oxford University Press, 1999.

Seo, K. K. *The Steel King: The Story of T. J. Park*. New York: Simon & Schuster 1997. Translated by Yun Tongjin as *Ch'oego kijun ŭl kojiphara* [Insist on the highest standard!]. Sŏul: Hanŏn Ch'ulp'ansa, 1997.

Seo, Soo-min. "'Border Rider': Song Dreams of Finally Coming Home." *Korea Times*, April 15, 2003.

Seoul Embassy Telegram to Secretary of State, Washington D.C., American Embassy, Ottawa July 1975. NSF. Country. Box 9. Gerald Ford Library [Declassified January 29, 1998].

Shigemura Toshimitsu. *Saishin Kita Chōsen detabukku*. Tōkyō: Kodansha, 2002.

Shin, Gi-wook, and To-hyon Han. "Colonial Corporatism: The Rural Revitalization Campaign, 1932–1940." In *Colonial Modernity in Korea*, edited by Michael Robinson and Gi-wook Shin. Cambridge: Harvard University Press, 1999.

Song Hogŭn. "Han'guk, musŭn il i irŏnago inna: Sedae, kŭ kaltŭng kwa chohwa ŭi miha" [Korea, what is happening now? Generation, the aesthetics of its conflict and harmony]. Sŏul: Samsŏng Kyŏngje Yŏn'guso, 2003.

———. "Pak Chŏnghŭi chŏngkkwŏn ŭi kukka wa nodong: Nodong chŏngch'i ŭi han'gye" [State and labor of the Park Chung Hee regime: The limits of labor politics]. *Sahoe wa yŏksa* [Society and history] 58 (2000): 199–224.

Song Min'gyŏng. "Kukka chudojŏk sŏngjang chaejae wa chaebŏl, kyŏngje wigi" [Nation-led development system, conglomerates, and economic crisis]. Sŏul: Tangdae Pip'yŏng, 1998.

State Department Telegram 3104 (Seoul), December 23, 1967, NSF, Country. Box 91, Lyndon B. Johnson Library.

Suh, Sang-Chul. *Growth and Structural Changes in the Korean Economy, 1910–1940.* Cambridge, MA: Harvard University Press, 1978.

Sumiya Mikio. *Kankoku no keizai.* Tōkyō: Iwanami, 1976.

Sung, Suh. *Unbroken Spirits: Nineteen Years in South Korea's Gulag.* Lanham, MD: Rowman and Littlefield, 2001.

"A Suspicious 'Public Security Institute,'" *Hankyoreh*, October 18, 2004.

Taehan Min'guk Chŏngbu, Kyŏngje Kihoegwŏn [Republic of Korea, Economic Planning Board]. *Che-il ch'a kyŏngje kaebal o kaenyŏn kyehoek powan kyehoek* [The first economic development five-year plan, the revised plan]. Sŏul: Kyŏngje Kihoegwŏn, 1964.

Taniura Yoshio. "Kankoku no kōgyōka to kaihatsu taisei" [Korean industrialization and development system]. *Ajia keizai kaihatsu kenkyū.* Tōkyō: Ajia Keizai Kaihatsu Kenkyūjo, 1990.

Tanizawa Eiichi. *Akuma no shiso, Kuresutosha.* 1996.

TK [Chi Myŏnggwan]. *Kankoku kara no tsushin.* Tōkyō: Iwanami, 1972–1977.

———. *Letters from South Korea.* Tōkyō: Iwanami, 1976. Reprinted by Iwanami. Tōkyō: Iwanami, 2003.

Tongil Pangjik Pokchik T'ujaeng Wiwŏnhoe. *Tongil Pangchik Nodong Chohap undongsa* [History of the Tongil Textiles Union Movement]. Sŏul: Tolbege, 1985.

U.S. Congress. U.S. House of Representatives. *Investigation of Korean-American Relations: Report of the Subcommittee on International Organizations of the Committee on International Relations.* Washington, DC: U.S. Government Printing Office, 1978.

U.S. Congress. House of Representatives. Subcommittee on International Organizations. Committee on International Relations. *Activities of the Korean Central Intelligence Agency in the United States, Part 1,* March 17, 1976.

U.S. Library of Congress. Selected Internet Resources. National Security: South Korea. http://www.loc.gov/rr/international/asian/korea/resources/korea-security.html.

Vogel, Ezra F. *The Four Little Dragons: The Spread of Industrialization in East Asia.* Cambridge, MA: Harvard University Press, 1991.

Wada Haruki Homepage. http://www.wadaharuki.com.

Wada Haruki. "70–80 nendai ni okeru Nikkan rentai undō no shiso to kodo" [Address, commemorative meeting for the tenth anniversary of the death of the democratic activist and lawyer, Cho Yŏngnae]. Sŏul. December 12, 2000.

Wade, Robert. *Governing the Market: Economic Theory and the Role of Government in East Asian Industrialization.* Princeton, NJ: Princeton University Press, 1990.

Walker, Martin. "Korean Studies Starts a Row." *Guardian*, March 30, 1977.

Wells, Kenneth M. *South Korea's Minjung Movement: The Culture and Politics of Dissidence.* Honolulu: University of Hawai'i Press, 1995.

Widaehan saengae: Pak Chŏnghŭi taet'ongnyŏng hwiho rŭl chungsim ŭro [A mighty life: centering on the calligraphy of President Park Chung Hee]. Sŏul: Minjok Chunghŭnghoe, 1989.

Wŏnp'ung Mobang Haego Nodongja Pokchik T'ujaeng Wiwŏnhoe. *Minju nojo 10 nyŏn: Wŏnp'ung Mobang Nodong Chohap hwalttong kwa t'ujaeng* [Ten years of the democratic union movement: The activities and the struggles of the Wonpoong Textile Labor Union]. Sŏul: P'ulbit, 1988.

Woo, Jung-en. *Race to the Swift: State and Finance in Korean Industrialization.* New York: Columbia University Press, 1991.

World Bank. *The East Asian Miracle: Economic Growth and Public Policy.* Oxford: Oxford University Press, 1993.

Yi Chŏngwŏn. *See* Ri Shōgen.

Yi Kihong. *Kyŏngje kŭndaehwa ŭi sumŭn iyagi: Kukka changgi kyŏngje kaebal ibanja ŭi hoegorok* [A hidden story of economic modernization: A memoir of the planner of national long-term economic development]. Poisŭsa, 1999.

Yi Kwangsu. "Nongch'on kyebal" [Rural development]. *Maeil sinbo*, November 26, 1916–February 18, 1917.

Yi Naeyŏng. "Sedae chŏngch'i ŭi tŭngjang kwa chiyŏkchuŭi." [Regionalism and the appearance of generational politics]. *Asea yŏn'gu* 46, no. 4 (2003): 283–309.

Yi Pyŏngch'ŏl. *Hoam chajŏn* [Hoam autobiography]. Sŏul: Chungang Ilbosa, 1986.

Yi Pyŏngch'ŏn. *Kaebal tokchae wa Pak Chŏnghŭi sidae: Uri sidae ŭi chŏngch'i kyŏngjejŏk kiwŏn* [Developmental dictatorship and the Park Chung Hee era: The political economic origin of our era]. Sŏul: Ch'angbisa, 2003.

Yi Sangu. "Pak Chŏnghŭi nŭn yongin ŭi chŏnjae yŏnna?" [Was Park a genius in people management?]. *Sin tonga.* July 1984, 348–68.

Yi Tongbok. "Bessi saryŏnggwan, K'at'ŏ e hangmyŏng hago Pak Chŏnghui rŭl towa chuhan Miguk ch'ŏlsu kyehoek ŭl chwajŏl sik'ida" [Commander Vessy thwarted U.S. plans to withdraw its troops from Korea by disobeying Carter and by supporting Park Chung Hee]. *Wŏlgan chosŏn*, July 2001.

Yi Wŏndŏk. *Han-Il kwagŏsa chŏri ŭi wŏnchŏm* [The origins of the Korea-Japan deals concerning their historical relations]. Sŏul: Sŏul Taehakkyo Ch'ulpanbu, 1996.

Yim Huisŏp. *Han'guk sahoe pyŏndong kwa kach'igwan* [Social changes and values of South Korea]. Sŏul: Nanam, 1994.

————. "Hyŏndae Han'gugin ŭi kach'igwan salm ŭi mokp'yo kach'i wa kyubŏm kach'i rŭl chungsim ŭro" [Values of modern South Koreans—Focusing on the aim, value, and normative value of life]. *Minjok munhwa yŏn'gu* [Study of national culture], no. 30 (1997): 143–62

Yim Hyŏnjin. *Chigu sidae segye ŭi pyŏnhwa wa Han'guk ŭi palchŏn* [World change and the development of South Korea in the global age]. Sŏul: Sŏul Taehakkyo Ch'ulp'anbu, 1998.

Yoon Seok-man. *See* Yun Sŏngman.

Yu Sangyŏng. "Han'guk sanŏphwa esŏ ŭi kukka wa kiŏp ŭi kwan'gye: P'ohang Chech'ŏl kwa kukka chabonjuŭi" [State-Business relations in the course of South Korea's industrialization: POSCO and state capitalism], Ph.D. Diss. Department of Political Science, Graduate School, Yonsei University, 1995.

Yu Wŏnsik. *5.16 pirok hyŏngmyŏng ŭn ŏdiro kanna* [5.16 Secret record, Where did the revolution go?] Sŏul: Inmul Yŏn'guso, 1987.

Yugyŏng Chaedan. *Pak Kŭnhye int'ŏbyujip* [Pak Kŭnhye interview collection]. Sŏul: Yugyŏng Chaedan, 1990.

Yun Sŏngman [Yoon Seok-man]. "P'ohang chech'ŏl ŭi kigwan hyŏngsŏng chŏllyak e kwanhan yŏn'gu" [A study of the institution building strategy of Pohang Iron and Steel] Ph.D. Diss., Chungang Taehakkyo Taehagwŏn, Haengjŏng Hakkwa, 2000.

Contributors

MYUNGKOO KANG is a professor of media studies at Seoul National University. His publications include books and articles on discourse politics of modernization and politics of journalism in various referred journals. Currently he is working on a book on the cultural history of consumption in South Korea, focusing on the material and cultural conditions of modern life since the Korean War in the early 1950s.

HYUNG-A KIM is associate professor of Korean politics at the College of Asia and the Pacific in the Australian National University. She is the author of *Korea's Development under Park Chung Hee: Rapid Industrialization, 1961–1979* (RoutledgeCurzon, 2004); "From Anti-Communist Industrialization to Civic Democracy in South Korea." In *Nation Building, State Building, and Economic Development: Case Studies and Comparisons*, edited by S.C.M. Paine (New York: M.E. Sharpe, 2009); and the senior editor of *Reassessing the Park Chung Hee Era: Development, Political Thought, Democracy, and Cultural Influence*.

YOUNG JAK KIM is a professor of Koongmin University, Seoul, Republic of Korea.

TADASHI KIMIYA is a professor of the Graduate School of Arts and Sciences at the University of Tokyo. He is currently studying the impacts of the U.S.-China rapprochement on the Korean peninsula in 1970s. He is the author of *Kankoku: minshuka to keizai hatten no mekanizumu* (ROK—Its Dynamism of Democratization and Economic Development) and *Pak Chŏnghŭi chŏngbu ŭi sŏnt'aek: 1960 nyŏndae such'ul chihyang hyŏng kongŏphwa wa naengjŏn ch'eje* (The

Policy Choice of Park Chung Hee Administration: Its Export-Oriented Industrialization and the Cold War Regime).

HAGEN KOO is a professor of sociology at the University of Hawai'i at Manoa. His major publications include an award-winning book, *Korean Workers: The Culture and Politics of Class Formation* (Ithaca, NY: Cornell University, 2001) and *State and Society in Contemporary Korea*, edited (Ithaca, NY: Cornell University, 1993). He is currently completing a new book, *The Fractured Middle: The Impact of Globalization on Class Order in South Korea.*

GAVAN MCCORMACK is an emeritus professor in the College of Asia and the Pacific, Australian National University. A graduate of the universities of Melbourne and London (Ph.D. from London in 1974), he taught at the Universities of Leeds (UK), La Trobe (Melbourne), and Adelaide before joining the ANU in 1990. He was elected Fellow of the Academy of Humanities of Australia in 1992.

NAK-CHONG PAIK is an emeritus professor of Seoul National University and editor of the quarterly journal, *Ch'angbi* in Seoul, Republic of Korea.

JAMES B. PALAIS, the late Korean historian passed way in 2006 after serving as a professor of Korean history from 1970 until 2005 at the University of Washington, Seattle, United States of America. He is known for publishing many articles and most notably *Confucian Statecraft and Korean Institutions: Yu Hyŏngwŏn and the Late Chosŏn Dynasty* (Seattle: University of Washington Press, 1996).

CLARK W. SORENSEN is the director of the Korean Studies Program at the University of Washington and co-editor of *Reassessing the Park Chung Hee Era: Development, Political Thought, Democracy, and Cultural Influence.*

SEOK-MAN YOON served as CEO of POSCO Engineering & Construction (2009–10) and as President of POSCO (2006–9). He holds a doctorate from Chung Ang University, South Korea and was Vice Chairman of the Korean Association for Public Administration (2004–6).

Index

119; transition time, 120

Congress, U.S., 32, 35, 36

congressional power, in bureaucratic culture, 175–76

constitutions: post-Park era, 116; Third Republic regime, 110, 162n1; Yusin system, 6, 15n10, 90, 127, 162n2

corruption, 107, 112–13, 176, 193

Councils for Rural Revitalization, 155–56

Critchfield, Richard, 148–49

cross-border civil society. See democracy values, international solidarity movements

cultural/social identity, compressed modernization impact, 180–83

Cumings, Bruce, 89

currency conversion plan, 69–70

Decree on Korean Agricultural Associations, 155

defense industry, expansion: overview, 19–21, 37–38, 51; mobilization strategies, 27–29, 39n20; modernization program, 29–31; nuclear/missile programs, 31–34, 40n36; planning and preparation, 21–24, 39n14; triumvirate member roles, 24–26

Demag Cranes & Components, 46–47

demobilization strategies, labor. See labor policies and relations

democracy values: Freedom House survey, 4–5, 15nn6–7; post-Park administrations, 111, 116, 190–91, 198–99; Rhee administration, 109; time factor, 120–21. See also developmentalist mentalité

democracy values, international solidarity movements: overview, 14, 190–91, 199–202; Berlin-based activity, 197–99; London-based activity, 191–93; national security context, 187–90;

Tokyo-based activity, 193–97

democracy values, Park era: overview, 12–13, 19–21; barrier arguments, 107–8, 112–19; in hierarchy of national goals, 97–99, 103; and nationalism ideology, 97–102; suppression tactics, 110–11. See also labor policies and relations

Democratic Justice Party, 146

Democratic Labor Party, 204n37

Democratic Republican Party, 60, 71

demonstrations. See protests/demonstrations

Deng Xiao Ping, 3

Department of Reconstruction, 152

Development as Freedom (Sen), 12

developmentalist mentalité: overview, 13–14, 166–67, 183–86; in bureaucratic organizations, 174–77; in business organizations, 177–83; compressed modernization context, 168–74; social identity impact, 180–83

DFL (American Development Loan Funds), 70

Disney, Nigel, 202n10

DKG Group, steel investment, 45–46, 63n3

Duff, Peggy, 202n10

Dynamic Village Development Committee, 147

Easey, Walter, 202n10

economic failure, in democracy barrier argument, 108, 117

Economic Planning Board (EPB), 5, 23, 52–53, 71

economic policy: overview, 4–6, 168–72; in civil democracy movement, 192–93; dependency theory, 192, 203n15; in hierarchy of national goals, 5–6,

www.ingramcontent.com/pod-product-compliance
Lightning Source LLC
Chambersburg PA
CBHW021814270326
41932CB00007B/182